Entrepreneurial Marketing for SMEs

Entrepreneurial Marketing for SMEs

Luca Cacciolatti
University of Westminster, UK

and

Soo Hee Lee
University of Kent, UK

© Luca Cacciolatti and Soo Hee Lee 2016

All rights reserved. No reproduction, copy or transmission of this publication may be made without written permission.

No portion of this publication may be reproduced, copied or transmitted save with written permission or in accordance with the provisions of the Copyright, Designs and Patents Act 1988, or under the terms of any licence permitting limited copying issued by the Copyright Licensing Agency, Saffron House, 6–10 Kirby Street, London EC1N 8TS.

Any person who does any unauthorized act in relation to this publication may be liable to criminal prosecution and civil claims for damages.

The authors have asserted their rights to be identified as the authors of this work in accordance with the Copyright, Designs and Patents Act 1988.

First published 2016 by
PALGRAVE MACMILLAN

Palgrave Macmillan in the UK is an imprint of Macmillan Publishers Limited, registered in England, company number 785998, of Houndmills, Basingstoke, Hampshire RG21 6XS.

Palgrave Macmillan in the US is a division of St Martin's Press LLC, 175 Fifth Avenue, New York, NY 10010.

Palgrave Macmillan is the global academic imprint of the above companies and has companies and representatives throughout the world.

Palgrave® and Macmillan® are registered trademarks in the United States, the United Kingdom, Europe and other countries.

ISBN: 978–1–137–53256–5

This book is printed on paper suitable for recycling and made from fully managed and sustained forest sources. Logging, pulping and manufacturing processes are expected to conform to the environmental regulations of the country of origin.

A catalogue record for this book is available from the British Library.

Library of Congress Cataloging-in-Publication Data

Cacciolatti, Luca, author.
    Entrepreneurial marketing for SMEs / Luca Cacciolatti, Soo Hee Lee.
   pages cm
    ISBN 978–1–137–53256–5 (hardback)
    1. Small business marketing. 2. Small business – Management. 3. Marketing – Management. I. Title.
HF5415.13.C23 2015
658.8—dc23   2015023258

Contents

List of Figures	viii
List of Tables	ix
Preface	x

1 Introduction   1
    1.1 What is entrepreneurial marketing?   2
    1.2 Reading guidelines   4

2 The Nature of the Small and Medium-Sized Enterprise   6
    2.1 What is a SME? A taxonomy of small businesses   6
    2.2 Factors affecting marketing in SMEs   11
        2.2.1 The effect of size   11
        2.2.2 Availability of resources   14
        2.2.3 Market orientation and marketing intelligence   17
        2.2.4 Marketing orientation and business life cycles   20

3 Small Business Owners and Their Environment   28
    3.1 Two typologies of small business owners   29
        3.1.1 Entrepreneurs and owner-managers   29
        3.1.2 Entrepreneurial culture and personal characteristics   32
    3.2 Entrepreneurial orientation   35
    3.3 Environment and opportunities   37
        3.3.1 The external environment: institutional factors affecting SMEs   38
        3.3.2 Competitors, suppliers, intermediaries and consumers   40

4 Entrepreneurial Cognition and Learning   46
    4.1 Entrepreneurial cognition and Kolb's experiential learning   46
    4.2 Institutions and entrepreneurial behaviour   47
    4.3 Entrepreneurs' adaptation to the environment   49

5 Growth Strategies within an SME Context   57
    5.1 Factors affecting SMEs' business growth   58
        5.1.1 Owner-manager's culture   58

	5.1.2	Available resources	60
	5.1.3	Business-owner personal characteristics	61
	5.1.4	Company size and life stage	62
	5.1.5	Competition and other marketing constraints	63
5.2		The diversity of the drivers to growth	64
5.3		Differentiation versus 'me-too' strategies	65
5.4		Marketing decision-making and performance: measures available to SMEs	67
	5.4.1	Marketing decision-making influencing factors	67
	5.4.2	Measures to inform marketing decision-making and to monitor performance	71

6 The Role of Structured Marketing Information in SMEs' Decision-Making — 89

6.1 The relationship between business growth and information use — 91
6.2 Types, source and frequency of information use — 92
6.3 Marketing intelligence: SMEs' and owner-managers' characteristics — 94

7 Internationalisation Strategies — 104

7.1 Internationalisation: enablers, motives and models — 104
  7.1.1 Enablers of internationalisation — 104
  7.1.2 Motives of internationalisation — 105
  7.1.3 Models of internationalisation — 107
7.2 Internationalisation strategies — 110

8 Value Propositions: How to Build SMEs' Offering — 116

8.1 Understanding the concept of 'value' — 118
8.2 Segmenting the market — 120
8.3 Socio-geo-demographic segmentation — 122
8.4 Demographic and geo-demographic segmentation methodology — 123
  8.4.1 Classification features — 125
  8.4.2 Socio-geo-demographic segmentation strengths and weaknesses — 129
8.5 Psychographic segmentation — 131
  8.5.1 Psychographic segmentation strengths and weaknesses — 132
  8.5.2 Behavioural segmentation — 133
  8.5.3 Considerations on variables selection and on segmentation use — 134

	8.6	Targeting and positioning	138
	8.6.1	Targeting	138
	8.7	Product concept design	142
	8.7.1	Levels of product manipulation	143
	8.7.2	Types of products	144
9	**Pricing and Distribution Decisions in a Context of Low Distribution Capacity**		**150**
	9.1	Pricing strategies	151
	9.2	Distribution strategies	154
10	**Building Brands in SMEs**		**157**
	10.1	Brands functionality and the branding activity	157
	10.1.1	Differentiating function	158
	10.1.2	Communication function	158
	10.1.3	Relational function	159
	10.1.4	The 'value' element of branding	161
	10.2	Mission statements and consumers' experience	162
	10.3	The importance of branding and branding success factors	162
	10.3.1	Why branding is important	162
	10.3.2	Success factors in branding	164
11	**Supply Chain Relationships Management: SMEs' Partners**		**173**
	11.1	Different partners... different audiences	174
	11.2	Supply chain flows	176
	11.3	Creating value through relationships	178

Notes   185

Bibliography   187

Index   213

List of Figures

5.1	SME growth phases, adapted from Chaston	63
5.2	Frequency of purchase affecting marketing decision-making and performance within an SME context	68
5.3	Perceptual map	80
9.1	White bread shoppers' profiles	152
9.2	Value continuum	153
11.1	Simple structure of a supply chain	174
11.2	Diagram of supply chain flows, adapted from Mentzer	177

List of Tables

2.1	EU criteria to define SMEs	8
5.1	Factors affecting marketing decision-making and performance within an SME context	74
5.2	Sales per customer	75
5.3	Repeat purchase	76
5.4	Example of rating scale	77
5.5	Example of a rating dataset	78
5.6	Comparison of customers' preferences to our average score	78

Preface

This book is aimed at explaining key topics and challenges of entrepreneurial marketing in a coherent and logically presented sequence. The topics, represented in the constitutive chapters of the book, are linked to each other according to a specific rationale that satisfies the necessary condition for contextualising the practice of marketing amongst SMEs. The book considers the nature of the SME and the relative institutional effects of the environment in which the SME operates. Therefore, the book truly integrates both entrepreneurial and marketing perspectives of the subject within the same book.

Furthermore, all chapters, although linked with each other through a light narrative, critically discuss major issues of entrepreneurial marketing with relevant and up-to-date academic knowledge. All chapters present a set of introductory questions reflecting entrepreneurial marketing-related problems that the reader is called to reflect upon before reading the chapter. The presence of these questions sets up the base for a critical and engaged approach to reading the chapter. This approach is the foundation of a problem-based learning philosophy which encourages the reader to engage more critically with the subject dealt with. The primary audience of this book are undergraduate and postgraduate students who want to approach the subject of entrepreneurial marketing in a coherent and summative, yet comprehensive, way. Most importantly, this is a book that maintains academic rigour while being reader-friendly.

This book was designed to encourage lecturers and students to adopt a problem-based learning (PBL) approach by making use of the information of this book (according to their expertise and creativity) in their classes along with case studies, simulations and critical discussions. PBL is about learning from the solution to specific problems, which also means learning to raise questions, identify problems, structure and deconstruct problems, and finally, solve problems. The PBL approach in marketing sprung up as a reaction to the criticism that marketing graduates were trained in non-integrated curricula whose modules did not reflect the need for training oriented towards problem-solving, was quite static rather than dynamic, and lacked integration with the industry's reality. Hopefully, the book will assist readers in improving their holistic thinking and problem-solving skills.

1
Introduction

In your everyday life, you might have encountered products or services that were not provided by large corporations. While you might have purchased a well-known brand of soft drink from a small coffee shop, the shop might have been run by a family or by an entrepreneur. Likewise, you might have gone to a small bakery and have purchased some stone-baked bread. Again, this business was not run by a multinational, but by an entrepreneur or a family.

Also, the car or motorbike you drive, although produced and sold under a big brand name, is, in fact, produced by assembling lots of small mechanical parts that are often produced by small businesses. These small businesses often supply larger organisations.

In everyday life, the chances of interacting with small businesses are very high. Small businesses are generated by the inventiveness of people (the entrepreneurs) who have a particular ability to identify opportunities. These people are also particularly brave, in the sense that, although they are aware of the risks they might incur in starting and running a business, they are not afraid of taking risks.

Although the motivations that push entrepreneurs (and often their families) to embark on a business adventure there are many entrepreneurs that – with their brave actions – contribute to the wealth of local economies by providing chances for local employment. They also contribute to local life with the provision of important products and services, be it a mini-market, a corner shop, or a cleaning company. Some of these small businesses start as very tiny businesses and then expand and grow over the years to the size of large organisations. Many multinationals that operate on international markets nowadays started as small businesses 100 or 150 years ago.

Entrepreneurs not only contribute to the wealth of local economies, but from a sociological point of view, in some emerging economies (e.g., Brazil, Russia, India and China, or in the case – of other communist countries, like Cuba and Vietnam), entrepreneurs also play an important role determining social change, slowly contributing to the emergence of market economies as opposed to planned economies. They generate a shift in the image of entrepreneurship: repositioning small business owners by moving them from negative associations towards idols of success.

However, over 30 years of globalisation caused markets to become increasingly competitive – by increasing the difficulty of doing business successfully – but also opened markets to opportunities due to their increased fragmentation – allowing firms to specialise their offer in order to appeal to more and more different and demanding customers. Small businesses face the big challenge imposed by their limited size: a limitation in available resources..

In order to address the challenges of this new world, entrepreneurs and small business owners need a better understanding of their markets and of which customers purchase what product, where and at what price. Small businesses face an increasingly desperate need to engage with marketing, which can help them support their operations in the market in an efficient and effective way. Marketing is essential to small businesses in order to provide their customers and consumers with what they need and want. However, conducting marketing in small businesses is different than in larger organisations because multinationals do not have the constraints in terms of resources that small businesses have. Nevertheless, small businesses can capitalise on having the flexibility to adapt to changing market conditions and on their typical decision-making speed, which larger organisations, with more rigid hierarchical organisational structures, lack.

1.1 What is entrepreneurial marketing?

Small and Medium Sized Enterprises (SMEs) are more sensitive to changes in the environment than larger businesses. They have fewer resources to face economic downturns, but they also have a special flexibility in the way they operate, allowing them to take swift decisions when these are needed. They also have inner characteristics, such as management style, affecting how their operations are run, which is significantly different from how larger companies run their businesses.

A particularly interesting strand of academic literature on SMEs has been developing in the interface between marketing and entrepreneurship. While taking the unique nature of SMEs into consideration, researchers have been actively trying to understand how these characteristics relate to SME marketing practices. Entrepreneurial marketing is therefore a subject of increasing academic interest, particularly as opposed to marketing practices in larger businesses.

SMEs have a peculiar perception of the value of marketing, and this affects their strategic thinking in marketing, which is therefore affected by their unique nature. This makes their attitude towards marketing very different from larger organisations. Most SMEs do not have a formal marketing department; some SMEs do not even admit they do marketing. For some of them, marketing is a taboo subject, and they do not like the idea of being associated with the mass production coming from multinationals. SMEs are often proud that their products are homemade or manufactured in a small business.

After stating this, it should be noted it is also true that SMEs perception of the effectiveness of marketing, either consciously or unconsciously, will determine a more or less formalised development of their marketing strategy, and this will ultimately affect their marketing practices.

Carson et al.[2] suggest that the small scale of SMEs determines their little impact on their environment, and they have very little power to modify environmental forces to their advantage. In economic terms, SMEs have to accept the industry's imposed price, and they must accept the fact they have no real impact on the overall market. Furthermore, Hill [5] maintains SMEs are usually the weaker partner in a marketing channel relationship. This pushes them towards a type of marketing that will determine how SMEs perceive the value of marketing and how they should approach it.

Because of their small or medium size, along with the lack of formal hierarchical structures and the generalist small business owner's know-how, some SMEs are not aware they are marketing practitioners. Their marketing is therefore unconsciously incorporated into their way of doing business [3]. And because of that, SMEs also have the tendency to focus on short-term goals rather than long-term objectives because of their limited time to dedicate to planning, their limited marketing and strategy expertise, and their lack of resources, due to resource constraints. Therefore, small business owners tend not to be 'planners' but 'men of action'[8].

An important characteristic of entrepreneurial marketing is the figure of the 'entrepreneur'. S/he has a great ability to identify and exploit opportunities. Due to their unique cognitive abilities [10, 11], entrepreneurs show idiosyncratic abilities and pursue patterns of opportunity identification [6]. Some authors [1] indicate that entrepreneurial opportunity recognition and business development are influenced by (1) entrepreneurial alertness, (2) information asymmetry and prior knowledge, (3) social networks, (4) personality traits, and (5) opportunity type.

The integration of the two disciplines of marketing and entrepreneurship is therefore critical to the marketing-entrepreneurship interface and to the development of entrepreneurial marketing as a subject area. Entrepreneurial marketing therefore represents an alternative marketing management approach under the specific conditions that characterise SMEs [4, 7, 12, 13]. As indicated by some researchers, 'entrepreneurial marketing entails the proactive identification and exploitation of opportunities for acquiring and retaining profitable customers through innovative approaches to risk management, resource leveraging and value creation'. [9]

1.2 Reading guidelines

Before heading forward with the next chapters in the book, we decided to include a very short section giving some reading guidelines. This book is thought and designed for university researchers and doctoral students.

We are all different, and we all have different learning styles. Some of us tend to learn by imagery and visual stimulation; others are more inclined to learn better when the stimulation is auditory or sensorial. Some people are more analytical and need a certain level of abstraction, while other students need a very practical approach.

Although it is not possible to cover all learning styles in a book as such, it is nonetheless possible to give some suggestions on how to read this specific book.

The very first thing to do with the book is to look at the table of contents to familiarise yourself with the chapters of the book. This gives you an idea of how the book is structured, how many chapters it is made of, and what main topics are dealt with..

Once you are familiar with the book's structure, we recommend looking at the topics dealt with in each chapter. You can find this in the table of contents (as subsections of each chapter).

We would recommend reading all the chapter sections in a chapter as if you were reading a post on a blog. The brevity of all sections should help you digest the content of the book better while speeding up your learning.

Although most of the chapters are written in a brief and accessible way, you will find that they mainly focus on theory.

References

[1] Ardichvili A, Cardozo R, Ray S. A theory of entrepreneurial opportunity identification and development. Journal of Business Venturing. 2003; Vol.18 (No. 1): pp. 105–23.
[2] Carson, Cromie S, McGowan P, Hill J. Marketing and Entrepreneurship in SME's: An Innovative Approach. Englewood Cliffs, NJ: Prentice Hall; 1995.
[3] Carson D, Gilmore A. Marketing at the interface: not 'what' but 'how'. Journal of Marketing Theory and Practice. 2000; Vol.8 (No. 2): pp. 1–7.
[4] Collinson E, Shaw E. Entrepreneurial marketing – a historical perspective on development and practice. Management Decision. 2001; Vol.39 (No. 9): pp. 761–6.
[5] Hill J. A multidimensional study of the key determinants of effective SME marketing activity: part 1. International Journal of Entrepreneurial Behaviours & Research. 2001; Vol. 7(No. 5): pp. 171–204.
[6] Holmen M, Magnusson M, McKelvey M. What are innovative opportunities? Industry and Innovation. 2007; Vol.14 (No. 1): pp. 27–46.
[7] Miles MP, Darroch J. Large firms, entrepreneurial marketing processes, and the cycle of competitive advantage. European Journal of Marketing. 2006; Vol.40 (No. 5/6): pp. 485–501.
[8] Moriarty J, Jones R, Rowley J, Kupiec-Teahan B. Marketing in small hotels: a qualitative study. Marketing Intelligence & Planning. 2008; Vol.26 (No. 3): pp. 293–315.
[9] Morris MH, Schindehutte M, LaForge RW. Entrepreneurial marketing: a construct for integrating emerging entrepreneurship and marketing perspectives. Journal of Marketing Theory and Practice. 2002: pp. 1–19.
[10] Shane S. A general theory of entrepreneurship: the individual-opportunity nexus. Northampton, MA: Edward Elgar; 2003.
[11] Shane S, Venkataraman S. The promise of entrepreneurship as a field of research. Academy of Management Review. 2000; Vol. 25 (No. 1): pp. 217–26.
[12] Shaw E. Marketing in the social enterprise context: is it entrepreneurial? Qualitative Market Research: An International Journal. 2004; Vol. 7 (No. 3): pp. 194–205.
[13] Stokes D. Entrepreneurial marketing: a conceptualisation from qualitative research. Qualitative Market Research: An International Journal. 2000; Vol. 3 (No. 1): pp. 47–54.

2
The Nature of the Small and Medium-Sized Enterprise

When we study small businesses we often wonder: how do we define small businesses? How small or big is a small business? And what size is a medium or large business? These are all legitimate questions that students reading about entrepreneurship may encounter.

SMEs (small and medium-sized enterprises) present differences with larger organisations. Although the most obvious distinction is size, this variable is not the only discriminant used to define what a small business is.

This chapter describes the main characteristics which governmental organisations use to define what SMEs are. Section 2.1 defines SMEs while presenting a taxonomy – i.e., a classification based on selective criteria – of small businesses.

As often happens in the biological world, small organisms or animals struggle for survival as fragile prey of bigger, stronger competitors. Nevertheless, over time, small animals have developed different strategies to grant the survival to their species. Likewise, SMEs often lack resources (e.g., financial and human capital), as well as marketing know-how, so they are obliged to focus mainly on production and sales rather than marketing. Marketing in SMEs is affected by many factors, such as firm size, availability of resources, the ability to manage market knowledge, and the firm's stage of business development). These factors affecting marketing in SMEs are described in section 2.2.

2.1 What is a SME? A taxonomy of small businesses

Different definitions of SMEs exist; in fact, it is a somewhat sophisticated exercise to try to define what a small or medium-sized enterprise is.

The Nature of the Small and Medium-Sized Enterprise 7

Due to the importance of SMEs in world economies, both academics and governmental bodies have defined them. Some of these definitions reflect the national context, so that different countries in the world define in a different way what they mean with the word SME. These definitions are wide ranging. For instance, an SME is defined as an organisation that considers itself small or medium in size [21, 71]. Although this definition might appear to be a little bit generic and somewhat inaccurate, it bears some important insight on the SME world: small businesses are peculiar entities that differ one from the other.

In spite of the proposed definitions of various organisations and individuals, it is generally accepted in both academia and among governmental bodies that SMEs are difficult to define comprehensively. Therefore, different accurate criteria to classify SMEs are needed in order to avoid misclassifications.

The category we classify under the adjective 'small' might well include 'micro' firms, which are extremely small.

Similarly, the adjective 'medium' might well indicate a category that includes both small and large companies that are on average smaller than the large ones and bigger than the small ones. Yes, we understand: it is becoming confusing! Another case could be the misuse of the adjective 'large' for not-so-large, or even some medium-sized, organisations. You can now see why it was absolutely necessary to try to shed light on how to classify small businesses according to accurate criteria. So, what size business should be defined as 'small'? And how does a small firm differ from a micro firm? And what is meant by the adjectives 'medium' and 'large' when considering businesses?

The Bolton report [9] was the first formal attempt to define small and medium-sized businesses according to their size on a statistical basis. At the time, there was no formal definition for an SME; in fact, businesses were classified simply as small, medium or large. Bolton used several dimensions, split by industry, to define the boundaries between small, medium and large. These definitions were based on common characteristics of SMEs – 'centralisation of decision making, a low level of formal managerial training and skills, close personal relations and informality, (and) limited resources and market power, thus making them [the firms] vulnerable to external market shocks' [8].

However, a system of definitions based on different criteria for different industries caused problems in comparisons. How could we compare a small business operating in the food and drink sector with a small business operating in mechanical engineering? The definition of SMEs' size was further complicated by the different financial criteria in different industries. In fact, these would have been affected by changing economic trends (e.g., inflation), and change would not have been consistent across all industries and all countries.

The solution came after the Bolton report, when the UK Companies Act [1] provided a clearer definition by introducing some thresholds based on firms' financial and economic conditions. The financial indicator introduced was the annual turnover – the total sales value a firm generates in one year of activity. The economic indicators introduced were the annual balance sheet total – i.e., a measure of the firm's assets or its wealth – and the number of employees – a measure of its capacity in terms of human capital.

The act set the annual turnover for a small business at approximately £2.8m and £11.2m for medium-sized businesses. The maximum annual balance sheet total was approximately £1.4m for small businesses and £5.6m for medium-sized businesses. Likewise, it established the maximum number of employees as 50 for small businesses and 250 for medium-sized firms.

Use of 'SME' began in 1996, when the European Commission created the acronym and established the rule of thumb that an SME has up to 250 employees. However, in order to be considered an SME, a company has to fit the following size criteria based on number of employees, annual turnover, total assets value and ownership share as given in the Table 2.1 [29-32]:

Although research in entrepreneurship has progressed a lot since the 1970s, the Bolton report included some important elements that were brought to the attention of the institutions (e.g. Governmental bodies), so that they could define better what small businesses are. Despite Bolton's concerns about the measures to be adopted to better classify firms, some small businesses are not totally reflected into EU and UK size criteria, mainly due to their ambiguous nature.

Table 2.1 EU criteria to define SMEs (EURO figures are the official reference figures)

Criteria	Employees Up to	Turnover Up to	Balance Sheet Total Up to
Micro business	9	£ 1.7m / € 2m	£ 1.7m / € 2m
Small business	49	£ 8.2m / € 10m	£ 8.2m / € 10m
Medium business	249	£ 41m / € 50m	£ 35.2m / € 43m

Source: Author's own.

Some examples are small firms operating under well-known brand names, often with franchising contracts. They are run as small businesses, but they have great influence on local markets. Another example are small firms that are subsidiaries of a mother company or part of a holding. These firms operate independently by an accounting point of view; however, they do not always have independence on strategic or operational issues, which might be influenced (when not decided) by other firms (e.g., the mother company in a small group or the brand holder in a holding, which are controlling the group).

In order to better classify these small businesses that exist with a particular status (for example, under franchising agreements or in the form of subsidiary) the Bolton report suggests potential indicators:

(1) the influence the company has on the market,
(2) the company's independence from controlling organisational structures in decision-making issues, and
(3) the personal influence of the business owner/entrepreneur.

We can see that these criteria might help us classify those firms that are at the moment reflected in an inaccurate way and perhaps in some cases even misclassified. Use of these criteria is limited by the current difficulty of finding precise measures for these cases.

Readers might argue with the first point, which is the influence the company has on the market; since the market share of small firms is very little, SMEs do not have a big influence on the market. To support this statement, we could note that SMEs' market share is generally so small that there is no way they can affect the price and quantities of their products on the market.

This might sound sensible in macroeconomic terms. However, thinking SMEs do not have influence on the markets in which they operate is incorrect because many small businesses, in aggregate, might have a big impact on their market. Furthermore, some SMEs operate in such small markets (or try to sell their products to such small niches) that, in fact, they dominate them, in local terms.

Bolton[9] showed an overall understanding of the phenomenon of entrepreneurship as a macroeconomic process. This point of view is today considered a little too far from real practice because SMEs have their major weight in local economies; however, the belief that SMEs are low impact is often inappropriate, with several authors arguing in favour of the importance SMEs have on Western economies in terms of both regional and national growth.

When looking at Bolton's second point, SMEs' independence from controlling structures – external (e.g., other firms that own shares in the enterprise) or internal (e.g., rigid vertical hierarchy) – it is true that the SME presents certain independence in the decision- making processes.This flexibility allows business owners to make decisions without the pressures deriving from any form of control practised by rigid bureaucratic structures, such as those found in many larger organisations or MNEs (multinational enterprises). However, at the moment, the level of flexibility is not a criterion for defining and classifying companies.

With respect to Bolton's last point, the influence of the owner-manager refers to the personal influence of the business owner on the overall managerial activities. Small businesses are characterised by an owner who is involved with all aspects of the business and who operates outside of a formal managerial structure. Very often, the managerial powers are centralised, so there is very little delegation in the management or daily business running.

Current research proves that SMEs in general, especially micro firms, are often unstructured, and the owner-manager deals more or less formally with all the aspects of the business. This general role of the business owner is often characterised by a focus on operational activities (e.g., production) and often ignores the commercial side (e.g. marketing and sales). Some authors [3] support that small businesses tend toward a more formalised structure when the number of their employees reaches 10 to 20 people. It is sometimes indicated [13] that this point

> is the key to a definition of the real small firm – the one with potential; the one that economists cannot understand; the one that is so different from the large firm. Essentially, the real small firm can be described as having two arms, two legs and a giant ego – in other words, it is an extension of a person, be s/he the owner-manager or entrepreneur [omitted]. The personality of the manager is imprinted on the way it operates, and the personal risks they and their family face if the firm fails influences how business decisions are made.

However, SMEs are not defined just according to their size; the way they do business is an important aspect in defining whether the company can be classified as an SME. The management style adopted, the orientation to entrepreneurship of the business-owner, the roles played by uncertainty, innovation and risk, as well as the scope of operations [20, 77] are all important factors that help to define SMEs.

Small firms face greater uncertainty than larger organisations due to their scarce resources; therefore, the business owner's inclination to entrepreneurship (also known as entrepreneurial orientation) is an important asset to balance the owner-manager's behaviour between risk and opportunity. Entrepreneurial orientation has a direct link with innovation; although the perception of the importance of innovating is often felt strongly in the small business, there are huge limitations to its actual implementation. Innovation in small firms could be quickly implementable due to the SMEs' flexible nature, but they face huge constraints in terms of budget and know-how. Nevertheless, the entrepreneurial orientation of the small business owners is essential if the firm has to operate in business environments characterised by scarce resources, like during economic crises.

SMEs operate in small markets, their access to financial and human capital is limited, as well as it is limited their customer base. They often provide limited quantities of products that cannot influence the price of quantity of products at the macroeconomic level. However, SMEs are better able to adapt to change and better able to survive uncertainty [13]. SMEs pass through different life stages, and those that survive the natural selection process (from a business evolution point of view) can grow stronger – sometimes jumping, over time, from the status of small company to large company and eventually MNE. Large companies, corporatations and multinationals, are the consequence of small firms set up by entrepreneurs that have grown over time [13].

2.2 Factors affecting marketing in SMEs

SMEs face many challenges due to the limited resources they have to operate with. According to current authors in the SME marketing literature [17-18, 39, 54, 59, 73, 76], the marketing activity in SMEs is influenced mainly by three factors: internal resources, external resources and attitudes towards marketing and business.

It should be noted that the aforementioned factors are all affected by the size of the SME, and this is reflected in their marketing, in the scale of operations, and so on. In what follows we will see how size, available resources, marketing intelligence, attitude towards business and marketing as well as business life cycles affect marketing in SMEs.

2.2.1 The effect of size

Size affects the way SMEs do business. Very large firms need a rigid, predetermined structure, in which all the people inside the firm know what their roles are. SMEs are small and often unstructured. It is very common for the small business owner to be versatile and to engage with any aspect of the business, from production to commercialisation.

From the literature, it appears evident that small firms present a 'distinctive marketing style' [18] that observes no conformity to the formal structures and frameworks used by bigger companies. The cause is found in their limited marketing activity. This lack of resources is reflected in SMEs' marketing activity, which becomes 'simplistic, haphazard, often responsive and reactive to competitor activity' [18].

Firm size affects the decision-making process, as most of the decisions in SMEs are made by the owner on the basis of intuitive ideas and common sense. This might present the advantage of flexibility in adaptation to market changes or the competitive environment granting a higher speed in the response to marketing stimuli. The disadvantage can be found in the lack of support of a well-established and tested structure that supports all activities. No traditional marketing theoretical framework applies to SMEs, but every marketing effort is reinvented by the small company.

The absence of a traditional marketing theoretical framework does not necessarily mean that SMEs are totally incompatible with marketing. The nature of SMEs is compatible with marketing philosophies [76]. However, SMEs present integration between strategic management and marketing, whereas in larger companies these functions are split [17, 44]. The fusion between the strategic and marketing function in SMEs is observed by Frank and Krake [35], who explain that, in SMEs, the influence of the entrepreneur is stronger and more direct than in larger companies.

Therefore, firm size has an impact on the organisation of the SME, on its management, and possibly on its culture as well. However, by itself, size may not be a critical factor in determining financial performance. For example, it is possible that a larger company achieves higher turnovers than an SME, but the business growth in terms of volume and value might be lower, or even negative, if compared to the growth of the smaller business. Although financial performance is not necessarily related to firm size directly, in this regard, the main difference between large and small companies is the latter's lack of financial resources and 'share of voice' [76], meaning the right access to information.

SMEs show unique features that appear to be different from traditional marketing in large companies [18]. Carson and Cromie support the idea that the most significant differences between small and big firms are business objectives, management style and marketing practice, rather than the relative size. According to Carson and Cromie [18], small and big companies should not only be classified by their relative size – an idea supported by the Committee for Economic Development[1] – but also by their qualitative characteristics. Also, they feel, 'the scope and the scale of operations, the independence and the nature of their ownership arrangements, and their management style' should be taken into consideration [18].

When looking at how firm size affects SMEs' marketing, when we take into consideration the scope and scale of operations, the management style typical of a specific SME, and the nature of the type of ownership, it is clear that there are too many dimensions taken into consideration when classifying SMEs and MNEs on quantitative size-related parameters. A qualitative approach to comparison appears to be more appropriate to obtain a less biased judgement. Several authors [12, 18, 72] suggest that one of the distinguishing features of SMEs is the management style, as it is an important factor to the success of the small organisation, and an inappropriate style can be a barrier threatening the existence of SMEs.

Tyebjee et al. [73] are of the opinion that many companies present a chaotic organisation because they already struggle with operative issues (e.g., cash flow monitoring and production schedules settings) that end up losing sight of the outside world, their market, their customers' needs and wants, and where they should direct their marketing efforts.

Size influences the management style of the organisation and consequently the business culture. The allocation of resources is not a straightforward operation for SMEs and, because of the lack of expertise and the need to focus on operations, most of the marketing problems appear difficult to deal with.

Another main factor associated with the sizes of SMEs and larger companies is the different stages of the business life cycle [18]. This idea is based on the work of Justis [53], who argues that small firms work through different stages in their business lives, and this affects their existence. Most SMEs are not aware of the stage in which they are operating, and, therefore, it might be difficult for them to change their position from a 'task-oriented' company to a 'coordination and strategic planning' company [65], and higher attention is given to the changing role of top management as the company grows [18].

As Tyebjee, Bruno and McIntyre [73] propose,

> Each company passes through a four-stage marketing development process that affects firm size. In the initial stage, entrepreneurs sell customised products to friends and contacts. They must then exploit

a larger marketplace through the stages of opportunities marketing, responsive marketing and finally diversified marketing [73].

SMEs are more likely to be in the lower stages of the business life cycle, whereas bigger or corporate companies tend to be at the higher stages. This has a strong impact on the importance given to marketing activity, since firms start engaging with some initial marketing activity in order to progress to reactive selling. The more the company advances in the stages, the closer it gets to what the authors call a 'DIY (do it yourself) marketing' approach, then move on towards an 'integrated proactive marketing' approach.

Therefore, size is related to the stage of development or business cycle, so small companies tend to be in a more primitive stage of marketing development than bigger companies. This affects management and consequently, the acquisition and allocation of resources.

This does not mean, though, that SMEs cannot formulate and implement marketing strategies, add value and grow. As soon as the company grows, the attitude of the role of the management changes, and marketing orientation increases, along with marketing expertise. Resources become more accessible by virtue of the achieving strategy of growth, and consequently, they should be better allocated within the company, and size is inevitably related to the amount of resources a firm can access.

2.2.2 Availability of resources

So far, we mentioned that SMEs, because of their small size, often find accessing resources difficult. They have to work with limited resources. In this section, we will see the types of resources small firms generally struggle with, such as financial capital, i.e., money (and, to an extent, forms of economic capital, such as the firm's physical assets, like premises and machineries), human capital, i.e., labour, and intellectual capital, i.e., marketing know-how, as well as time.

Marketing and entrepreneurship literature suggests that SMEs are often negatively affected by the scarcity of resources. Entrepreneurs are generalists, and they often have limited access to capital; this situation does not allow investments that might improve the firms' marketing decision making, such as investing in the creation of a marketing department or the access to outsourced marketing expertise in the form of consulting. Sometimes the small business owner suffers a degree of marketing ignorance, as s/he might be unaware of the benefits of marketing. This further limits the potentiality of the SME, whose focus is – on many occasions – concentrated on generating sales through push strategies while keeping costs under control, rather than on the creation of value for consumers and customers.

In both academic and industry literature, a plethora of case studies and empirical evidence illustrates the difficulties SMEs encounter due to the lack of resources.[2] Most of these case studies recognise that the lack of financial support is a major constraint for SMEs.

From an entrepreneurial marketing perspective, Carson and Cromie[18] identified three broad barriers to the marketing activity of SMEs: (1) limited resources, (2) a lack of specialised expertise and (3) the limited impact of the company on the marketplace.

Limited resources, as we mentioned, include money (under the form of financial capital), but are not limited to money only. In fact, marketing knowledge and time are two other important resources that are often lacking in SMEs. The lack of personnel dedicated to marketing hampers firms' marketing decision-making. The small business owner is sometimes working alone, or with a very limited staff, and their total focus is on production, sales and everyday business administration. With regard to 'specialist expertise', Gilmore et al. [37] state that managers in SMEs tend to be generalists, as traditionally the owner or director of an SME is a craft expert who is unlikely to be trained in business disciplines.

Many SME owners have a strong technical background related to their business, but lack business or marketing knowledge [36]. However, higher quality marketing activity by an SME often leads to better performance. This is something we can find in many other studies. Therefore, an SME that has expertise in marketing can better support their decision-making and is more likely to outperform other firms in the market.

However, the level of expertise in a firm is influenced by the stage of development of the company [73]. Marketing is, generally, one of the least disciplines being adopted systematically by a small business. This is particularly true for those businesses that are in their first stages of development, as these will tend to develop skills in finance and production first, unlike those SMEs that are in an expansion phase (or growth phase), and start focusing on rudimental tools of marketing, (e.g., outsourced marketing communication through advertising) to improve their efficacy. The acquisition of marketing expertise is a further step that might be taken at a later stage.

The last of the three limitations proposed by Carson and Cromie[18] is the limited impact on the marketplace. Smaller companies have fewer orders and customers and, therefore, fewer employees. As a logical consequence, the impact of an SME on the geographical area or in the industry should be very small. This is especially true for micro firms.

However, SMEs create a consistent body of firms that indeed have an impact on the wealth and livelihood of local economies. If we take the example of a small country, we can see that the Scottish Government [51] reported that large firms account for just 1% of the Scottish economy, while SMEs contribute up to 40% of the Scottish food wholesaling Gross Value Add (GVA). But this appears to be true for larger countries, too, as a recent report from the European Commission [27] indicates that SMEs in the Eurozone account for more than 98% of all enterprises, offering 67% of total employment and contributing to 58% of the European GVA. These were only two examples, but this appears to be reflected in all Western economies.

The scarcity of resources SMEs have to deal with creates pressure in meeting opportunity costs related to business activities, and this often reflects on the financial, economic and marketing choices made by small firms. There are some strategic factors that have to be developed by a small firm if they want to keep the competitive edge on the market[5]; in fact, the use of resources is often associated with strategic factors that can enable or hamper success [64].

For instance, in the case of a growth strategy, a large market share [43] is a strategic factor. Hence, firms that aim at expansion and growth should also keep in mind that growth is associated with an increase in market share (in terms of value, and not only volume). So, there is a dangerous spiral for small businesses to take into account: as the competitiveness of a strategy is affected by the cost of the resources to implement it, limiting the firm strategic options.

There is imperfect competition in free markets [5], and the main reasons why some firms are worse off than others are to be found in four main weaknesses: barriers to market entry, wrong profit maximisation, weak financial position and lack of market understanding.

When looking at the barriers to market entry, some firms lack the capital (both financial and intellectual) to enter a market where other players are already established. This is strongly related to weak financial position, which does not allow firms to produce at competitive prices (sometimes because of inefficient production processes and low contractual power in the procurement of supplies). Sometimes only a strong marketing orientation might help a small firm enter a market and compete with established firms. However, SMEs often lack marketing know-how, as shown in one study [22], which highlighted that most small business owners declared they had problems with marketing.

However, marketing is not the only cause of SMEs' lack of competitiveness. Sometimes SMEs are unable to maximise profits because they have little purchasing power (when dealing with procurement) and little distributive power (when selling goods). In some SMEs, production could exceed demand, creating inefficiencies in the management of the inventory and stock. This is often due to the lack of planning or forecasting that is more typical of larger organisations.

Also, the lack of understanding of the needs of the market, as well as bad managerial practices that do not allow a company to create value for consumers (or final customers), create a mismatch between organisational actions and returns. As maintained by Barney:

> A firm enjoys a competitive advantage when it is implementing a value-creating strategy not simultaneously implemented by large numbers of other firms. If a particular valuable firm resource is possessed by large numbers of firms, then each of these firms has the capability of exploiting that resource in the same way [6].

This lack of value creation can occur with too much focus on the utilisation of financial and monetary resources and on short-term financial objectives. This reflects SMEs problems dealing with marketing, affected by the focus of their business knowledge, their management style and attitudes towards marketing [35]. Kraft and Goodell [59] and Huang and Brown [45] agree that most small companies have problems dealing with marketing. The focus of SMEs on product and price, instead of on customer value, is often too strong [17], and the small firms' vigorous sales orientation – as opposed to customer orientation – largely determines the character of their marketing [44].

2.2.3 Market orientation and marketing intelligence

Business size and availability of resources are not the only factors affecting marketing in SMEs. However, very small firms with very few resources find it difficult to engage with market research and often lack relevant information from the market that might enable them to make better marketing decisions. Marketing information therefore plays a strategic role in small firms' decisions: it allows new entrants to the market to find specific niches in which to position their products [39], and it allows existing actors to offer value to consumers and customers in competitive markets.

According to Kotler [58], all good planning must start with market research, as this reveals customers' needs, perceptions and preferences and, therefore, the information can be used to cluster customers into segments.Marketing information is important because it allows companies to adapt better to their competitive environment [73]. The theory of evolution, according to Charles Darwin, suggests that an organism can survive if it adapts to changes in its environment. This is true for businesses, too, as they have to adapt continuously to changing external conditions, so they need to acquire information to better prepare and respond to changes in the environment they operate within.

Market orientation is defined as 'the organization-wide generation of market intelligence, dissemination of the intelligence across departments and organization-wide responsiveness to it' [57].

Information that gives insight on the market conditions – consumers' preferences, competition, threats and opportunities related to the political, economic, sociocultural, technological and legal environments – all provide the firm that engages with marketing intelligence with knowledge that can be used to achieve competitive advantage. This is true independent of the strategic position the firm adopts, be it cost leadership or quality leadership.

From the point of view of a cost-driven strategy (also known as cost leadership), for instance, consumer insight is helpful to understand the needs and wants of the, 'where frills can be eliminated and how to develop an attractively-priced position' [24]. Insight on competitors' offers might enable the small firm to adapt their offer to match their competitors', or even to exceed it with better value-for-money offers, in case the small firm is adopting a cost leadership strategy.

Consumer insight is essential to successful marketing as 'proper insight ensures you are not moving into completely uncharted territory' [26].

From a perspective of competitiveness, Hayward [42] uses the example of unsuccessful customer relationship management (CRM) to highlight the importance of gathering information about the market the firm operates in. A lack of understanding of the market might cause major failure in identifying and understanding key groups of consumers. Being able to integrate different sources of consumer data and insight and put it into action [42] is essential if a firm wants to increase its likelihood of being competitive in the market.

Information allows a firm to better understand the market and adapt to changing conditions. Hayward also emphasises the reasons why businesses fail to respond to obvious signals of change (losing competitive advantage).

In larger firms, the main constraint to the management of the knowledge acquired with marketing intelligence is often the company's hierarchical structure, as there might not be ways for the signals – or relevant information – to reach the people who are higher in the hierarchy and can act on them, or the company may not be not flexible enough. Organisations mine data frequently and in growing volumes, and they need to extract the key information to understand the future, which is not easy [42]. However, small businesses do not have this problem. Their organisational structures are flexible enough to keep direct control over information flows.

From the point of view of a product differentiation strategy (also known as quality leadership), even more than when pursuing cost leadership, consumer insight is helpful to understand the needs and wants of the customers so as to create a mix that offers value through differentiation. In this regard, Dunn [26] highlights the importance of getting firsthand experience of the customer base:

> Most organizations make some effort to get to know their customers. They might dabble with profiling, do some demographic segmentation, perhaps commission attitudinal research. But building up a figure of non-existent composite customers is not the same as getting to know real people. You need to look at real behaviour, real motivation – and you need to be able to link all that knowledge.... The key to being able to do that is having a sound data strategy.

Successful businesses rely largely on marketing research and on the insight derived from their field sales forces for intelligence on customers[73]. Marketing goals in successful businesses are driven by the customer needs. Customers, in fact, evaluate brands on different attributes and not just on price; consequently, price is often not the most important variable entering the purchase decision [24].

Customers are heterogeneous, and it is therefore important to know them: their demographics, lifestyles and preferences. As Humby [46] notes,

> Quite clearly, in the real world, the "average customer" doesn't actually exist – or at best forms only the same tiny fraction of the customer base as any other handful of individuals whose profit contribution and feelings about the brand are identical. Individual customers are just that – individuals. Each one is a brand asset – but each has a different value.

Some customers might spend a lot of money, but they might be inclined to switch loyalties often. Other customers might not pay much for a specific product, but might be very loyal and 'champion the brand at every opportunity' [46].

A good marketing mix becomes a vital element to the survival of a company. Knowing the customer is one of the core aspects of good practice aiming for the creation of an appropriate marketing mix to satisfy different consumers' demand for value. As a consequence, practitioners need a deeper understanding of consumer behaviour [54], as consumers' knowledge is the most valuable asset for improving a firm's marketing.

2.2.4 Marketing orientation and business life cycles

Marketing in SMEs is affected by the business life cycle of the firm, which has an effect on the development of the firm's orientation to marketing (also known as marketing orientation). In what follows, we will describe how a small firm's marketing orientation generally changes along with the different stages of its development.

Marketing orientation is defined in many ways in current literature. For instance, it is sometimes seen as 'a way of thinking in doing business that is based on the integration and co-ordination of all marketing activities' [34]. The cultural and philosophical grounds on which marketing orientation is built involve putting the customers' interest first [61]. Although some academics [10-11] view marketing orientation as a strategic and behavioural characteristic of the firm, rather than an underlying philosophy, the most common accepted priorities for a marketing-oriented firm are the following [4]:

- a priority in customers when evaluating the company and its products and the extent to which both the company and its products satisfy specific customers' needs;
- a priority in elevating marketing as the prevailing culture of the company so the entire organisation will mobilise towards satisfying customers' needs; and
- a priority in adjusting products according to the market needs and wants, rather than according to the company's perceptions and beliefs, so that customer satisfaction can be delivered.

Although the term 'marketing orientation' is sometimes used interchangeably with the term 'market orientation', these are very different concepts [33]: the former is related to the inclination to engage with marketing, and the latter to the inclination to search for information from the market to support marketing decision-making.

SMEs are generally not characterised by strong marketing orientation. In fact, many small business owners differ from larger firms' managers in their attitude towards marketing. SMEs tend to approach marketing with a negative attitude, perceiving marketing as a potential cost, and the management of distribution channels and sales as problematic areas requiring lots of effort – as 'uncontrollable problems' [18].

Marketing orientation changes over time in firms; therefore, an SME's marketing orientation is likely to differ at the four main stages of the business life cycle, which are defined as [73]: the start-up phase, business growth, maturity and decline.

Marketing orientation and business life cycles are analysed jointly because of their complementarity, on the ground that SMEs in different life stages, (e.g., start-up, growth, maturity, and decline) present different orientations to marketing.

The attitude towards marketing also affects brand orientation, defined by Urde [74] as 'an approach in which the processes of the organisation revolve around the creation, development, and protection of brand identity in an ongoing interaction with target customers with the aim of achieving lasting competitive advantages in the form of brands' [74].

From a strategic point of view, marketing orientation, according to Urde [74] is the 'link between the resources and competences of the firm and the development of lasting competitive advantages'. This idea is supported by Barney [6–7], Grant [38], Hamel and Prahalad [39], Dierickx and Cool [25].

Marketing orientation shifts the importance from the production to the customer; therefore, customer orientation is a component of marketing orientation. There are four practices [63] driving customer orientation: relationships, interactivity, valuing customers over time and customisation. These practices can contribute to the development of successful value chains benefiting potential growth.

Although big companies are already aware of the importance of marketing for their different departments, the same cannot be said of SMEs. Since marketing orientation is strictly related to the level of development of the firm and its business cycles, it is important to note that SME development is more likely to affect the firms' marketing orientation, with bad effects on all of its marketing [2, 19, 23, 28, 40, 68, 73, 75].

Truly, every company is different, and different firms can be at different stages of business development. For instance, within the same competitive environment, it is possible to find some companies with more business experience than others, some with more employees and resources than others, and some with different managerial approaches than others and so on, yet they are all SMEs.

But, what marketing orientation is generally associated with each stage of business development in SMEs?

Tyebjee et al.[73] maintain that all organisations pass through four stages of marketing orientation. The first stage is defined as 'DIY marketing', where a company presents little or marketing experience, but its entrepreneurs are rich in terms of ideas and technical expertise. They seem to rely on a network of personal relationships deriving from contacts gained during previous working experiences or in different environments.

Moneywise, the company cannot afford a formal marketing activity through the organisation of a marketing department, as the production volumes are too low to support that. Strategically, the company tries to 'get its foot in the door of the market' and 'tries to identify customers whose needs are not being met by established competitors – "the elephants"' [73].

The enabler to marketing at this point seems to consist of a personalised relationship with the stakeholders, so that buyers have the attention of the top management. Know-how and personal trust in the owner is the driver of the business growth.

The second stage is called 'opportunistic marketing', where the company, moneywise, rapidly approaches (if it has not already reached) economies of scale that increase efficiency and grant more financial independence through a higher product credibility. This happens thanks to greater standardisation of the product lines, so more buyers find the products more appealing.

At this stage, strategically, the company starts competing directly with more experienced or long-established companies in the quest for more and more customers. The aim is to expand the customer base and generate turnover through new channels of distribution. To do that, there is a greater focus on marketing, and an infant marketing department comes to life, and it is often staffed exclusively by sales people'.At this stage, a rough but incremental acquisition of information from the market begins to be considered important for the successful growth of the company. At the end of stage two, most companies should be ready for explosive growth. However, in real practice, many fail to organise adequately for the third stage.

Stage three is 'responsive marketing', in which the company expands quickly. This implies, moneywise, that income is higher, and more money means the possibility of hiring more people with different competencies, higher budgets for promotion and customer service, and, most importantly, market research. This gives birth to the marketing function. The risk is that some confusion may arise as management starts facing problems with poor organisation and the division of responsibility, which requires the ability to plan and delegate. This increasing dynamicity has the advantage of pushing creativity, which contributes to the creation of a sophisticated marketing department.

Tactically, at this stage, informal relationships and monitoring become hard to pursue because the number of customers is too high for the business owner to deal with them personally, and successful businesses start showing the need for marketing information and the development of marketing intelligence. Strategically, the company should pursue product-market positioning to sustain growth as 'market saturation may slow growth, or competitive forces may make additional gains in market share economically infeasible, or the prospect of antitrust action may make further dominance in a single business unattractive'[73].

In the final stage, 'diversified marketing', a company has a constant flow of income and is able to fund all of its different functions. The business pursues diversification as a main aim, and different divisions manage the objectives, operating each one on different product lines; therefore, the company has a wider portfolio. A general supervising marketing function at the corporate level takes place, which contributes to the maintenance of the company's image through communication with the general public and identifies potential growth opportunities.

The marketing orientation of the SME is affected by its stage of business development. Firms at their initial developmental stages generally show low marketing orientation, and therefore place less importance on customers' segments, targeting and positioning and the brand development process, preferring to focus on, for example, production or financial control. Marketing orientation is strictly related to the business life cycle of the firm, i.e., the more a company develops and grows, the higher its tendency to be marketing oriented. Marketing orientation, therefore, plays an important role on an SME's business growth.

References

[1] UK Parliament. UK Companies Act1985.
[2] Alsbury A. Quick Answers to Small Business Questions. Jay R, Alsbury A., eds. London: Prentice Hall; 2001.
[3] Atkinson J, Meager N. Running to Stand Still: The Small Business in the Labour Market. In: Atkinson J, Storey DJ, editors. Employment, The Small Firm and the Labour Market. London: Routledge; 1994.
[4] Avlonitis GJ, Gournaris SP. Marketing orientation and its determinants: an empirical analysis. European Journal of Marketing. 1999; Vol. 33(No. 11/12): 1003–37.

[5] Barney J. Strategic Factor Markets: Expectations, Luck and Business Strategy. Management Science. 1986; Vol. 32 (No. 10): pp. 1231–41.
[6] Barney J. Firm Resources and Sustained Competitive Advantage. Journal of Management. 1991; Vol. 17 (No.1): p. 99.
[7] Barney J. Gaining and Sustaining Competitive Advantage. Reading: Addison-Wesley; 1997.
[8] Blackburn R. Segmenting the SME market and implications for service provision: a literature review. In: ACAS (Advisory, Conciliation and Arbitration Service), editor. Research Paper ref 09/12. London: ACAS; 2012.
[9] Bolton JE. Small Firms. Report of the Committee of Inquiry on Small Firms. London: HMSO; 1971.
[10] Bonoma T. The Marketing Edge: Marking Strategies Work. New York, NY: Free Press; 1985.
[11] Bonoma T, Clark B. Marketing Performance Assessment. Boston, MA: HBS Press; 1992.
[12] Broom HN, Longenecker J, Moore CW. Small Business Management. Cincinnati, Ohio: South Western Publishing Co.; 1983.
[13] Burns P. Entrepreneurship and Small Business. 2nd ed. China: Palgrave MacMillan; 2007.
[14] Business Link. Here's how I've changed my business for the better – Case studies from businesslink.gov.uk: Department of Trade and Industry; 2005.
[15] Business Link. Here's how I've started my business – Case studies from businesslink.gov.uk: Department of Trade and Industry; 2005.
[16] Business Link. Here's how I run my business – Case studies from businesslink.gov.uk: Department of Trade and Industry; 2005.
[17] Carson, Cromie S, McGowan P, Hill J. Marketing and Entrepreneurship in SME's: An Innovative Approach. Englewood Cliffs, NJ: Prentice Hall; 1995.
[18] Carson D, Cromie S. Marketing planning in small enterprises: a model and some empirical evidence. Journal of Consumer Marketing. 1990; Vol. 7(No. 3): 5–18.
[19] Carson DJ. The evolution of marketing in small firms. European Journal of Marketing. 1985; Vol. 19 (No. 5): pp. 7–16.
[20] Casson M. The Entrepreneur: An Economic Theory. Oxford: Martin Robertson; 1982.
[21] Choueke RWE. Management education in higher education institutions related to the needs of small business management. Preston: Thesis from University of Central Lancashire; 1992.
[22] Cohen WA, Stretch SM, editors. Problems in small business marketing as perceived by owners. Proceedings of Research Symposium on the Marketing/Entrepreneurship Interface; Chicago, IL; 1989..
[23] Cooper AC. (1982) The entrepreneurship – small business research. In: Kent S, D. Sexton and K. Vesper (eds.) *Encyclopaedia of Entrepreneurship*, Englewood Cliffs, NJ: Prentice-Hall.
[24] de Chernatony L, McDonald M. Creating Powerful Brands in Consumer, Service and Industrial Markets. 2nd ed. Oxford: Butterworth-Heinemann; 2001.
[25] Dierickx I, Cool K. Asset stock accumulation and sustainability of competitive advantage. Management Science. 1989; Vol. 35 (No. 12): pp. 1504–11.
[26] Dunn E. It's marketing Jim, but not as we know it. London: dunnhumby; 2006.

[27] Ecorys . EU SMEs in 2012: at the crossroads: annual report on small and medium-szed enterprises in the EU, 2011/12. Rotterdam: Ecorys; 2012.
[28] Ennis S. Growth and the small firm: using causal mapping to assess the decision-making process – a case study. Qualitative Market Research: An International Journal. 1999; Vol. 2 (No. 2): pp. 147–60.
[29] European Commission. (2005a) 2003/361/EC. In: Union E (ed.) *L 124. Official Journal of the European* European Commission. (2003) Observatory of European SMEs: Highlights from the 2003 Observatory. In: SMEs Highlights from the 2003 Observatory 2003: Observatory of European SMEs. 2003. No. 8 Jacqueline Snijders, Micha van Lin, Rob van der Horst eds *Union:* 36–41.
[30] Commission Recommendation, 2003/361/EC, (2005).
[31] European Commission. The New SME Definition: User Guide and Model Declaration. Brussels: Enterprise and Industry Publications; 2005.
[32] European Commission. The New SME Definition. Brussels: Enterprise and Industry Publications; 2008.
[33] Evans A. Market orientation versus marketing orientation: the case for a new terminological set. Discussion Paper Series in Economics, No. 93401993.
[34] Felton A. Making the marketing concept work. Harvard Business Review. 1959; Vol. 37(No. 4): 55–65.
[35] Frank BG, Krake JM. Successful brand management in SMEs: a new theory and practical hints. Journal of Product & Brand Management. 2005; Vol. 14(No. 4): pp. 228–38.
[36] Fuller PB. Assessing marketing in small and medium-sized enterprises. European Journal of Marketing. 1994; Vol. 28(No. 12): pp. 34–49.
[37] Gilmore A, Carson D, Grant K. SME marketing in practice. Marketing Intelligence & Planning. 2001(MCB University Press): pp. 6–11.
[38] Grant RM. Contemporary Strategy Analysis: Concepts, Techniques, Applications. 2nd ed. Cambridge: Blackwell; 1995.
[39] Hamel G, Prahalad CK. Strategic intent. Harvard Business Review. 1989; Vol. 67 (No. 3): pp. 63–78.
[40] Hanks SH, Watson CJ, Jansen E, Chandler GN. Tightening the life-cycle construct: a taxonomic study of growth stage configurations in high-technology organizations. Entrepreneurship: Theory & Practice. 1993; Vol. 18 (No. 2): pp. 5–30.
[41] Hauge E, Havnes P-A. The Dynamics of SME Development – Two Case Studies of the Internationalisation Process. RENT XV Conference; Turku – Finland: Adger Research Foundation, Norway; 2001. p. 14.
[42] Hayward M. Customers Are for Life, Not Just Your Next Bonus. London: dunnhumby; 2005.
[43] Henderson BD. Henderson on Corporate Strategy. New York: Mentor; 1979.
[44] Hill J. A multidimensional study of the key determinants of effective SME marketing activity: part 1. International Journal of Entrepreneurial Behaviours & Research. 2001; Vol. 7(No. 5): pp. 171–204.
[45] Huang X, Brown A. An analhysis and classification of problems in small business. International Small Business Journal. 1999; Vol. 18(No. 1): pp. 73–85.
[46] Humby C. Brand is Dead, Long Live the Customer. London: Dunnhumby; 2005.
[47] IFC. Enabling SMEs to Enter the International Supply Chain: The United Nations Trade Faciliation Network; 2005.

[48] IFC. Access to Finance for Small and Medium Enterprises (SMEs). Monitor. June 2006; No. 3.
[49] IFC. Creating Opportunities for Small Business: World Bank Group; 2007.
[50] IFC. Linkage Programs to Develop Small and Medium Enterprises. Monitor; 2008.
[51] Johnston K, Gregory C. Food and Drink Industry Evidence Base Paper rev. HAJ1. Scottish Government – Rural and Environment Research and Analysis Directorate; 2007.
[52] Joquico JP. SMEs face constraints in adopting CSR. Business Weekly. 22 June 2008.
[53] Justis RT. Marketing Your Small Business. Englewood Cliffs, NJ: Prentice-Hall; 1981.
[54] Keller KL. Conceptualizing, measuring, managing customer-based brand equity. Journal of Marketing. 1993; Vol. 57 (No. 1): pp. 1–22.
[55] Kinross. Meadowhead: Soil Association; 2006.
[56] Kleindl B. Competitive dynamics and new business models for SMEs in the virtual marketplace. Journal of Developmental Entrepreneurship. 2000; Vol. 5 (No. 1): pp. 73–86.
[57] Kohli AK, Jaworski BJ. Marketing orientation: the construct, research propositions, and managerial implications. Journal of Marketing. 1990; Vol. 54 (April): pp. 1–18.
[58] Kotler PH. Marketing Management: Analysis, Planning, and Control. 7th ed. Englewood Cliffs, NJ: Prentice-Hall; 1991.
[59] Kraft FB, Goodell PW. Identifying the Health Conscious Consumer. Newbury Park, CA: Sage; 1989.
[60] Lamprinopoulou C, Tregear A, Ness M. Agrifood SMEs in Greece: the role of collective action. British Food Journal. 2006; Vol. 108 (No. 8): pp. 663–76.
[61] Moorman C, Zaltman G, Deshpande R. Relationships between providers and users of market research: the dynamics of trust within and between organizations. Journal of Marketing Research. 1992; Vol. 29 (3 August): pp. 314–29.
[62] O'Rourke MPA. SME's Biggest Barriers and Risks Identified in 'Think Big'. Sidney: RSM Bird Cameron; 2008; Available at: www.eyeswideopen.com.au.
[63] Pitta DA, Franzak FJ, Little MW. Maintaining positive returns in the value and supply chain: applying tomorrow's marketing skills. Journal of Consumer Marketing. 2004; Vol. 21(July No. 7): pp. 510–19.
[64] Rumelt RP, Wensley R. In search of the market share effect. Proccedings of the Academy of Management. 1981: pp. 2–6.
[65] Scholhammer H, Kuriloff A. Entrepreneurship and Small Business Management. New York: John Wiley; 1979.
[66] SCOTENT. Farm Administration Courses – SE/1769/Apr06: Scottish Enterprise; 2006.
[67] SCOTENT. Food Chain Industry Exchange – SE/1770/Apr06: Scottish Enterprise; 2006.
[68] Simpson M, Padmore J, Taylor N, Frecknall-Hughes J. Marketing in small and medium sized enterprises. International Journal of Entrepreneurial Behaviour & Research. 2006; Vol. 12 (No. 6): pp. 361–87.

[69] Sparkes A, Brychan T. The use of the Internet as a critical success factor for the marketing of Welsh agri-food SMEs in the twenty-first century. British Food Journal. 2001; Vol. 103 (No. 5): pp. 331–47.
[70] Steinhoff D. Small Business Management Fundamentals. Maidenhead: McGraw-Hill; 1978.
[71] Storey DJ. Understanding the Small Business Sector. New York, NY: Routledge; 1994.
[72] Tate CE, Megginson LC, Scott CR, Trueblood LR. Successful Small Business Management. Dallas: Business Publications; 1975.
[73] Tyebjee TT, Bruno AV, McIntyre SH. Growing ventures can anticipate marketing stages. Harvard Business Review. 1983; Vol. 61 / Jan–Feb (No. 1): pp. 62–6.
[74] Urde M. Brand Orientation: A Mindset for Building Brands into Strategic Resources. Journal of Marketing Management. 1999; Vol. 15 (No. 1–3): pp. 117–33.
[75] Wai-sum S, Kirby DA. Approaches to small firm marketing. European Journal of Marketing. 1998; Vol. 32 (No. 1/2): pp. 40–60.
[76] Wong HY, Merrilees B. A brand orientation typology for SMEs: a case research approach. Journal of Product & Brand Management. 2005; Vol. 14(No. 3): pp. 155–62.
[77] Wynarczyk P, Watson R, Storey DJ, Short H, Keasey K. The Managerial Labour Market in Small and Medium Sized Enterprises. London: Routledge; 1993.

3
Small Business Owners and Their Environment

In your life, you must have come across different small businesses. Sometimes you might have found that in some, you encounter very proactive people running the business. Sometimes, these proactive people tend to be very good communicators; they make you smile, and they might also joke with their customers. Among these people, you might find some who are easily taken by passion: they might get really excited about their customers' experience, become very talkative, push customers to try new products, or simply engage in exciting conversations. You can see their passion for what they do.

Other times, you might have encountered quieter people. They might have been running the shop, but they appeared less talkative and communicative. Sometimes, they might have given you the impression they were not so passionate about their jobs, although they might have been conducting themselves professionally. These people might also be less 'bubbly' personalities, and you might have seen them quite engaged with their administrative issues, rather than spending much time talking to customers.

Well, these two examples are some of the stereotypical behaviours you might find in different business owners. Academic literature on entrepreneurship created some very interesting classifications of business owners, and as a matter of fact, most researchers agree on the existence of at least two main profiles: entrepreneurs and owner-managers. The sections to follow will give you more insight on the typologies of small business owners and will mark the difference between entrepreneurs and owner-managers, providing insight on cultural differences between the two (Section 3.1). In what follows, you will also come across the concept of entrepreneurial orientation, i.e. the level of entrepreneurship displayed by different business owners (Section 3.2). This concept is important, as it is strictly related to their perceptions of risk and of what opportunities can be pursued for a reward.

3.1 Two typologies of small business owners

As already mentioned, academics all over the world have researched the typologies of small business owners and have so far come to the conclusion that there are two main categories: entrepreneurs and owner-managers. These typologies of small business owners have their own specific cultures and their owner specific personal characteristics. All the differences in their profiles affect the way they perceive reality and the way they learn from personal experience. In what follows, you will have the chance to see in more detail what the main differences are and what characterises these two profiles of small business owners.

3.1.1 Entrepreneurs and owner-managers

In existing academic literature on entrepreneurship, there is no total agreement on the definition of the word 'entrepreneur', as there is often some confusion between this word and the terms 'small business owner' or 'owner-manager'. Nevertheless, entrepreneurs are identified in people who have the ability to identify opportunities and to turn their exploitation into a profitable activity.

A couple of centuries ago, Jean Baptiste Say [49] – a French economist – defined, in his opinion, the characteristics of the entrepreneur:

> Judgment, perseverance, and a knowledge of the world, as well as of business. He is called upon to estimate, with tolerable accuracy, the importance of the specific product, the probable amount of the demand, and the means of its production: at one time he must employ a great of number of hands; at another, buy or order the raw material, collect labourers, find consumers, and give at all times a rigid attention to order and economy; in a word, he must possess the art of superintendence and administration. He must have a ready knack of calculation, to compare the charges of production with the probable value of the product when completed and brought to market.

> In the course of such complex operations, there is an abundance of obstacles to be surmounted, of anxieties to be repressed, of misfortunes to be repaired, and of expedients to be devised. Those who are not possessed of a combination of these necessary qualities, are unsuccessful in their undertakings; their concerns soon fall to the ground,

and their labour is quickly withdrawn from the stock in circulation; leaving such only, as is successfully, that is to say, skilfully directed.

Thus, the requisite capacity and talent limit the number of competitors for the business of adventurers. Nor is this all: there is always a degree of risk attending such undertakings; however well they may be conducted, there is a chance of failure; the adventurer may, without any fault of his own, sink his fortune, and, in some measure his character; which is another check to the number of competitors, that also tends to make their agency so much the dearer.

Say's description of the entrepreneur invokes intelligence, wit, analytical ability, self-control, leadership, willingness to take on challenges, and an overall sense for adventure. Nowadays, cutting edge research on entrepreneurs confirms Say's initial observations, pushing them forward towards a deeper understanding of the typologies of small business owners.

It really looks like entrepreneurs need to have skills in different knowledge areas, coupled with specific personal characteristics, in order to be successful entrepreneurs. Among the characteristics identified as being typical of entrepreneurs, there is the ability to take charge of operations or a business [10], as the entrepreneur often has a managing style that pushes him/her to concentrate all the decisions him/herself, rather than delegate. Often, entrepreneurs follow their gut feelings, and although they take the risk for their decisions, they generally do make decisions on their own.

Entrepreneurs combine and coordinate the utilisation of resources [22] and creatively use innovative combinations [50-51]. In fact most entrepreneurs tend to be quite innovative, if not necessarily always creative per se. They are unconventional people who spot opportunities for resource allocations in order to achieve a specific competitive advantage. Entrepreneurs also apply efficiency in the use of economic factors and have the ability to increase value. They modify existing resources around them, and by combining available resources, they manage to add value to their activities for a profit. They truly understand the opportunity-risk-award equation [39], as they have the ability to balance existing risks with existing opportunities, and they do this with the clear intent of obtaining a reward (that does not have always necessarily to be monetary in nature, as we will see in other chapters, in the description of the motivations for entrepreneurship).

Entrepreneurs discover hidden information and act, taking advantage of information asymmetry [30-32] as they tend to be outgoing and communicative people, able to obtain information from their social 'circles' and networks. To this ability, they also match the skill to foresee market trends and respond promptly to changes in the market[21] by using a sense of 'alertness' that enables the identification of opportunities to exploit[35-38].

A more recent and concise definition of entrepreneur – that includes the concepts expressed by Say – is offered by Burns[8], who states that 'entrepreneurs use innovation to exploit or create change and opportunity for the purpose of making profit. They do this by shifting economic resources from an area of lower productivity into an area of higher productivity and greater yield, accepting a high degree of risk and uncertainty in doing so'.

The entrepreneur's ability to identify and exploit opportunities in the different ventures they engage with is highlighted in all the definitions. The entrepreneur is often perceived as the new and contemporary 'cultural' hero [9]. Furthermore, as pointed out by Anderson[21], 'if you look around you, most of the largest companies have their foundations in one or two individuals who have the determination to turn a vision into reality'. In the past two centuries, we have lots of examples: Mercedes-Benz, Ferrari and Lamborghini in the automotive industry; Läkerol, Coca Cola, Glenfiddich, McDonald's, Dean of Huntly in the food and beverage industry; Virgin Atlantic and British Airways for airliners; Microsoft, AMD, Apple, Dell for the computing industry, and so on.

A crucial characteristic in entrepreneurs is the cognitive style[1], i.e., 'the way of thinking about, and processing, vital information upon which decisions are made' [1]. This is connected to their personality but with their personal experience, too [24]. 'The style of the successful entrepreneur will of necessity be intuitive because of the characteristics of the environment in which they are operating. These characteristics are incomplete information, time pressure, ambiguity, and uncertainty'[1].

Entrepreneurs can therefore be stereotyped as intuitive creatures who have the ability to spot opportunities to gain an advantage where other people cannot spot opportunities. Nevertheless, the stereotype of the entrepreneur also involves little aversion to risk – entrepreneurs are brave men and women – coupled with intelligence, i.e. the ability to understand situations and learn from them.

So far, we described what is meant by the word 'entrepreneur', and what characteristics are commonly accepted as being typical of entrepreneurs. We now introduce the concept of owner-manager.

Burns[8] sustains the idea that entrepreneurs and business owner-managers are not always and necessarily the same entity. While entrepreneurs identify opportunities in the market through intuition (often a new product that may generate an appeal or a trend) owner-managers might not identify the same opportunity because of an intuition. Entrepreneurs spot opportunities, to innovate – sometimes taking risks – to pursue their vision, to exploit the opportunity. This may be lacking in business owner-managers who would not act on 'gut feeling' but would follow a much more structured, methodical and rational behaviour in making decisions. Intuition distinguishes entrepreneurs from owner-managers; thus, not all the business-owners or managers are entrepreneurs.

Owner-managers are small business owners who lack the personal characteristics and attitudes described as being typically associated with entrepreneurs. Previous studies [5, 15, 19, 25, 34, 41, 44, 55, 57] showed that the population of small business owners is heterogeneous with a split between entrepreneurs and business owners. Therefore, not all business owners are entrepreneurs, and the main distinction between the two consists of the use of intuition [1].

In this regard, there difference difference between business owners who do business to achieve a series of personal goals – such as higher income, a certain lifestyle, and autonomy – and those business owners doing business with the purpose of growing a profitable business that allows them to accumulate wealth [15, 52, 58]. These types of business owners are defined either as 'caretakers' – who are characterised by little strategic focus, little desire to grow or innovate, like owner-managers – or as typical 'entrepreneurs' – thriving on change, able to come up with ideas, and pushed by their adventurous spirit and proactivity to pursue opportunities. These entrepreneurs tend to present restless behaviour, always active and pushed by curiosity, whereas owner-managers tend to show more structured administrative skills.

3.1.2 Entrepreneurial culture and personal characteristics

The typology of small business owner is determined by the owner's personal characteristics as well as by the existing entrepreneurial culture. The culture of the entrepreneur is affected by his/her own personal characteristics and personal experience. Culture is 'the way we do things around here' [20]. On the other hand, sometimes culture within an organisational context is used as a metaphor to explain complex behavioural processes within an organisation [45].

It is suggested that several types of organisational culture can exist, and perhaps co-exist, such as the propensity of entrepreneurs to demonstrate an effective response to change [7], customer-focused [54], marketing-orientated

[12], the propensity to implement policies and procedures [26] – also known as enterprise culture – and the propensity to learn [16].

The entrepreneur and his/her culture have a strong impact on the business s/he runs; Chapman [14] maintains that 'it is the personality, the beliefs, the values and the behaviour of this single individual that exerts a powerful impact on the past, present and future of the business. Their destinies are inextricably linked'.

Culture, vision and values play an important role in the way the company perceives business reality, the ideals behind aims and objectives, positioning in the market, and the company's identity, along with the identity of its brands.

In SMEs, the culture is strongly affected by the business owner. The mindset of the owner of the company seems to play an important role in the success of the marketing activity, influencing the marketing decision-making. Companies are made of people, and their behaviours and the owner/director influence the 'atmosphere' within the company, and consequently, the way people work.

Ideas and actions come from people who have to be coordinated, people who have their own needs, and people who, at the end of the day, can determine the success of the company, with their correct and responsible behaviour, or its fall, with irresponsible behaviour. Those people have to represent the company in its organic complexity. People should be given trust and respect and should be empowered to create moments of truth with customers [11].

The culture and values within a company determines its level of flexibility or rigidity and its ability to adapt. Several researchers [12, 23, 33, 47] maintain the importance of flexibility, speed of reaction and ability to identify opportunities and strengths. These aspects are simplified in SMEs because of the lack of a traditional theoretical framework, thus allowing more flexibility and a higher degree of potential adaptation.

The focus on marketing activity in general gives an advantage over the long term [53], and a long-term focus on marketing and branding strategies brings far bigger financial, strategic and managerial benefits than the costs involved to realise them. It appears that culture, this way, influences the ability to have a vision, the ability to see forward. In SMEs, the vision, if it exists, is in the entrepreneur.

Carson and Cromie [13] regard organisational culture as a set of inherited ideas, values and norms influencing the behaviour of the members of a company and consequently of the company itself. According to them, the 'carrier' of the culture is a person that plays the role of the culture 'acquirer', and in the case of SMEs, the 'carrier' is the business owner or director, by virtue of his/her visibility, power, influence and dominant role within the business. The carrier and his/her tendency to acquire more or less marketing culture for the firm has a strong impact on the direction the company takes, so that 'owners may deliberately ignore it, treat it unthinkingly and merely pay lip service to it, treat it moderately seriously, or treat it very seriously' [13].

The same authors state that the culture of a small firm influences the marketing planning activity, and they consider the approach of SMEs to marketing 'simplistic'. Nonetheless, this simplistic approach to marketing should not necessarily be considered bad marketing but just evidence that the attitude to the acquisition of marketing culture rises as an element of distinction or difference between SMEs and bigger companies.

Vision and values are elements of the culture of a firm. A constraint to the use of marketing information can be identified in the lack or presence of vision and values, whose orientation is not to the market. The culture affects the firm overall on issues such as customer focus, competitive strategies, and positioning that reflects on the potential SME growth. A culture in which vision and values push towards lack of pro-activity in terms of marketing focus might affect growth negatively. In this regard, small business owners might not have vision, because they might not have developed specific values inherent to their business philosophy. Sometimes a limited personal education might narrow a business owner's perspective on the outside world – thereby shading potential opportunities. In fact, in current marketing literature, there have been comments on the 'limited formal business education' of owner-managers and suggestions that small business problems and failures occur because of a lack of managerial skills and depth of knowledge, misuse of time, and lack of vision [13].

Several studies [4, 18, 29, 60] confirm that the entrepreneur's level of education is positively associated to the SME's survival and growth. Tyebjee et al. [59] are of the opinion that many companies present a chaotic organisation because they already struggle with operative issues (e.g., cash flow monitoring and production schedules settings) and end up losing sight of the outside world, their market, their customers' needs and wants, and where they should direct their marketing efforts.

In terms of attitude, small business owners and big firms managers differ in that in SMEs, there is a tendency to approach marketing with a negative attitude [13]: perceiving marketing as a potential cost, perceiving the management of distribution channels and sales as problematic areas requiring lots of efforts or, as defined by the authors, 'uncontrollable problems'. Different attitudes have been found in small business owners of different ages. We do not mean that age is necessarily an indicator of personal experience; nevertheless, in many cases, greater age is often associated with longer business experience. Often age, education and experience are somewhat related factors that shape the cognition of the small business owner.

A crucial characteristic in entrepreneurs is the cognitive style [1], i.e. 'the way of thinking about, and processing, vital information upon which decisions are made' [1]. This is connected to their personality but with their personal experience, too [24]. 'The style of the successful entrepreneur will of necessity be intuitive because of the characteristics of the environment in which they are operating. These characteristics are: incomplete information, time pressure, ambiguity, and uncertainty' [1].

Chell [15], in his behavioural study, maintains to this regard there is difference between business owners who do business to achieve a series of personal goals – e.g. higher income, a certain lifestyle as well as autonomy – and those business owners doing business with the purpose of growing a profitable business allowing them to cumulate wealth, as Sexton and Bowman-Upton [52] and Timmons [58] also point out. The last author defines the first ones as 'caretakers', who are characterised by having little strategic focus and little desire to achieve growth and to innovate; whereas the second ones are considered stereotypical 'entrepreneurs', thriving on change, able to come out with ideas and pushed by their adventurous spirit and proactivity to pursue opportunities. These entrepreneurs tend to present a restless behaviour, always active and pushed by curiosity.

Also age is an important factor in fostering growth [61]. Winter et al. [62] report that 'age and education of the home-based business owner, length of time in the home-based business and positive feelings by the business owner towards their work were all significant and positive predictors of being in business three years later'.

3.2 Entrepreneurial orientation

Despite the differences between entrepreneurs and owner-managers, the volatile and complex environment in which firms operate forces them constantly to renew their competencies or to create new sources of value. So different small business owners adopt different behaviours to sustain their livelihood. Volatility and complexities in the environment also mean increased competitiveness among firms, and consequently, the need for small business owners to find ways to survive on the marketplace. So in order to be more competitive, managers seek to improve organisational effectiveness by identifying and adopting strategic approaches (or orientations) to suit the firm's work practices [48], although in the case of small business owners this process might not be taking place at a totally conscious level.

Researchers have identified different 'strategic orientations', defined as the strategic directions or approaches a firm takes to encourage behaviours leading to the improvement of sustainable business performance [27], among which entrepreneurial orientation is one (along with market orientation and innovativeness). Nevertheless, the body of current research in marketing and management [6, 56, 63] focuses on market orientation as the competitive strategy with the greatest potential impact on a firm's performance, when this is compared to other strategies, such as entrepreneurial orientation or innovativeness. However, some studies [3, 17, 28, 40, 46] indicate that market orientation is not the only viable strategic orientation or approach, which suggests that other business strategies may also have considerable impact on competitive advantage and firms' performances.

However, before this last stream of research, in 1996, Lumpkin and Dess [42–43] introduced the concept of entrepreneurial orientation (also known as EO), defined as the 'strategy-making processes and styles of firms that engage in entrepreneurial activities' [43]. In their 1996 paper they conceptualised EO as a construct made of five main dimensions, namely autonomy, innovativeness, risk taking, proactivity and competitive aggressiveness. The authors describe these dimensions of EO in the following way [43]:

Autonomy is defined as independent action by an individual or team aimed at bringing forth a business concept or vision and carrying it through to completion.

Innovativeness refers to a willingness to support creativity and experimentation in introducing new products/services, and novelty, technological leadership and R&D in developing new processes.

Risk taking means a tendency to take bold actions such as venturing into unknown new markets, committing a large portion of resources to ventures with uncertain outcomes, and/or borrowing heavily.

Proactiveness is an opportunity-seeking, forward-looking perspective involving introducing new products or services ahead of the competition and acting in anticipation of future demand to create change and shape the environment.

Competitive aggressiveness reflects the intensity of a firm's efforts to outperform industry rivals, characterized by a combative posture and a forceful response to competitor's actions.

Although these are all dimensions of EO, it should be noted that they do not necessarily have to express altogether or in the same proportion, so that different combinations of the different dimensions create a unique EO mix typical of the single individual. Hence, different mixes of EO affect entrepreneurial behaviour in different ways.

An example of what we have said so far can be found in the competitive behaviour of two firms operating in the field of electronics: Sony and Panasonic (also known as Matsushita Electrics), as reported by Limpkin and Dess [42]:

> Sony, well known for its entrepreneurial spirit and R&D skills, aggressively pursues first-mover advantages from new-product innovation. ... Matsushita typically lets Sony and others innovate, but then takes a leadership position based on its skills in manufacturing and marketing ... that is, it incurs risks through capital investment in plant and equipment, is proactive by entering markets early in the product life cycle, and displays intense competitive aggressiveness through its strategies that are intended to build strong market share.

Therefore, small business owners can also have different mixes of EO, and this affects the way they run their firms, the long-term aims for their business, the tactical choices related to the allocation of resources, and overall, the ethos followed in their business activity.

3.3 Environment and opportunities

Entrepreneurs are well known for being able to identify opportunities that other people cannot identify. Entrepreneurs apparently have their own way of perceiving reality [9] which differs from non-entrepreneurs. They are able to identify opportunities for growth [14] and their thinking style is highly non-linear [31], meaning it is characterised by highly intuitive, creative and emotional processes, as opposed to rational and analytical processes.

Nevertheless, their decision-making is affected by what happens in the environment, as many entrepreneurs react very quickly to changes in the marketplace [16-17, 29, 39]. Entrepreneurial activity is affected by both an external environment, which influences entrepreneurial activity through political, social, economic and technological events, and an internal environment, which defines the boundaries for firms' operational capabilities and capacity. In what follows, we will discuss the external environment.

3.3.1 The external environment: institutional factors affecting SMEs

The external environment is something that SMEs can hardly control. The environment in which a firm operates influences all its activities, and often firms have to adapt to changing market conditions. In current marketing literature, there are several models of external environment; the best-known are the PEST (political, economic, social and technological factors) and PESTEL (political, economic, social, technological, environmental and legal factors). For full details on these models, we refer to classical marketing university textbooks [11, 25, 33, 35, 37-38, 47, 51].

In this section, we briefly present some considerations on how political, economic, social, and technological factors affect SMEs' activities. Institutions differ in different socioeconomic realities, as the interaction with the existing social environment can determine different institutional effects [4, 28]. An example of this could be a formal institution like a country's legal system: its effectiveness might depend on the level of corruption of the judiciary (values) or on the regulation-implementation gap (uncodified attitudes). This is an example of how the external environment might affect SMEs' livelihood. But, what do we mean by the term 'institution', and how does this affect SMEs' activities?

Institutions provide a 'behavioural framework of social compliance' within which firms and individuals make their choices [3, 13]. Individuals and organisations' behaviour is therefore influenced by the social norms that enable or constrain social behaviours [5], such as political systems, economical systems, legal systems, and the perception and protection of private property. On the other hand, informal institutions are those social frames that contribute to the creation of norms for communal peaceful cohabitation [10, 49], such as codes of conduct, values, beliefs, social norms, uncodified attitudes, and social networks.

From the institutional point of view, the world has increasingly become more open to quick changes as a result of 30 years of globalisation [23, 54]. These socioeconomic changes increased opportunities through a more enhanced interconnectedness amongst firms; however these changes also pushed SMEs to the need to react faster to changes in the marketplace, pushing them to adopt competition tactics based on differentiation. The development of a competitive advantage based on differentiation has become paramount to the survival of Western economies, due to the cost-leadership retained by the BRIC (Brazil, Russia, India and China) countries. International trade brought huge pressure on those firms that lacked competitiveness, and therefore, Western countries' political forces reacted to this pressure by trying to improve SMEs' ability to compete in the market through a series of initiatives, among them the recognition of the need for policies of economic growth that allow firms to grow. By manipulating the regulative (legislative) system, Western countries' governments tried to implement policies aimed at reducing fiscal pressure on SMEs, while increasing accessibility to capital through bank loans [22, 34, 45]. Despite the fact that in some places these policies were more or less effective [53], the creation of policies per se is a clear indicator of interconnectedness between the political and economic factors, and these do affect SMEs' activities.

In some cases, like in the UK, not all governmental policies benefit SMEs, and not all SMEs are encouraged to grow, given the limitations of unfavourable taxation policies:

> Small firms are usually unable to utilise the complex financial instruments used by large firms to exploit the benefits available from tax allowances on interest charges and depreciation. The adverse outcome for tax legislation has recently been demonstrated by the impact on small firms of the UK Government's decision to significantly alter the tax regime on capital gains [20].

Innovation also plays an important role in how firms' activities are affected [19]. Building innovation capability is not only important for economic survival [54], but also for fostering national and regional growth and welfare [6]. SMEs are particularly good at innovating in industries that are not capital intensive:

> The relative innovative advantage of large firms tends to be promoted in industries that are capital-intensive, advertising intensive, concentrated and highly unionised. By contrast, in industries that are highly innovative and composed predominantly of large firms, the relative innovative advantage is held by small enterprises' [2].

Technological factors can either improve or hamper firms' competitiveness, depending on the level of innovation with which firms engage. Therefore, to protect SMEs' innovation through effective IP (intellectual property) rights policies, it is important for political forces to undertake as many legislative efforts as possible, to grant the exclusivity of IP exploitation to SMEs while encouraging KT (knowledge transfer) activities [19].

Although universities and research institutions enable knowledge creation and transfer [15], the government's support for the development of innovation capabilities at local and national level, is essential, as it can manipulate firms' behaviours through the creation of policies enabling or hampering different activities. All these institutional factors affect the way business is conducted, as they shape the organisation of the society the firm operates in. SMEs cannot control these factors, many of which pose a potential threat to their survival; nevertheless, many SMEs can also find opportunities when the institutional environment changes, as some of the changes that take place within the regulative system (political and economic forces), the normative system (peoples' accepted behaviours), and the cultural system (social forces) might allow the firm to discover new opportunities to exploit. Maybe they find new markets for their products, or they might be pushed to improve their business processes in light of changes in the competitive scenario or in consumers' needs.

3.3.2 Competitors, suppliers, intermediaries and consumers

SMEs do not have control over the major institutional factors affecting their activities; however, they can influence their external environment when dealing with their supply chain stakeholders: competitors, suppliers, intermediaries and consumers. SMEs' management of their relationships within the supply chain can enhance the possibility to capitalise on opportunities that might arise by the ties firms create with each other. Opportunities can be found both up and down the supply chain.

When we look at opportunities identification upstream of the chain, current marketing literature argues that effective supply chain management practices are built on the holistic concept of development of strong partnerships', so on the cooperation on strategic activities. However, strong partnerships are based on trust among firms and on a high degree of information sharing with stakeholders. These best practices of supply chain relationships management contribute to the creation of competitive advantage, which, in turn, improves firm performance [18, 24, 26, 32, 36, 40, 57].

However, although current marketing literature suggests SMEs can achieve competitive advantage leveraging on the accessibility and mobilisation of resources through the use of social capital [1], several firms still operate within 'functional silos' [21], although this is not recommended, as it hampers the development of collaborations because of the inability to integrate business functions. In firms whose functional silos philosophy is dominant, communication is generally scarce, and this hampers collaborations where power structures often revolve around supply chain members' negotiation abilities, due to the lack of understanding of stakeholders' functional needs. Therefore, this lack of communication affects supply chain coordination levels and abilities [42, 52].

On the contrary, in those supply chains where information is shared amongst stakeholders and flows along the chain (and can be controlled at all stages), we observe optimal performance derived by effective cooperation [44]. Competition is weakened by stronger relationships along the chain. Furthermore, we also observe individual chain members' coordination can be achieved [44], provided that functional silos are broken down. Thus, optimal performance is given by the cooperation and collaboration of all stakeholders in the supply chain [43].

Some of the opportunities SMEs can achieve with supply chain integration include (1) reduced transaction costs, (2) improved inventory management, (3) the creation of entry barriers to new competitors and (4) reduced business opportunities loss caused by the lack of supply chain coordination (e.g., delayed deliveries and other similar problems arising in decentralised supply chains). As a result, contracts that facilitate vertical chain integration (top to bottom) improve buyer-supplier relationships (in many cases through profit-sharing agreements [8]) and appear to be an excellent choice to exploit the opportunities offered by vertical chain integration [55-56].

SMEs can also identify opportunities downstream the chain. In many industries, products are generally differentiated at the 'actual' level [48] (e.g., FMCGs, crude oil, gasoline, automotive, Internet services and telecommunications). In these cases, exclusive dealership is not uncommon [41], and consumers' transactional involvement is often low, with very little risk for unfulfilled promises, which encourages brand switching [27, 30].

SMEs should encourage brand loyalty, rather than brand switching. From a supply chain management point of view, these markets are generally characterised by the presence of cost-leaders; therefore, the competition is based on price. Such competition structure generates the need for low-cost sourcing to grant acceptable margins to the focus company, and little room is left for a Plan B, should something go wrong. Hence, SMEs could capitalise on differentiation by gaining better understanding of their consumers: current consumer-driven markets are more and more fragmented [50]. Although this increased fragmentation increases rivalry among firms [7], in markets characterised by a high heterogeneity, SMEs can capitalise on consumers' needs and wants to enable the elaboration of differentiation strategies.

Firms in general, SMEs in particular, must strive to know their customers, as failure to do so would be too costly, both in financial and economic terms. Porter [46] demonstrated that the key to success is the attention paid to final consumers. Listening to the final consumer enables the development of competitive advantage through the proposition of value, but there is also room for the improvement of production efficiency [12], given that a higher focus on the right consumers limits the waste of resources.

References

[1] Allinson CW, Chell E, Hayes J. Intuition and entrepreneurial behaviour. European Journal of Work & Organizational Psychology. 2000;Vol. 9 (No. 1): pp. 31–43.
[2] Anderson J. Local Heroes. Glasgow: Scottish Enterprise; 2005.
[3] Baker WE, Sinkula JM. The Complementary Effects of Market Orientation and Entrepreneurial Orientation on Profitability in Small Businesses*. Journal of Small Business Management. 2009;Vol. 47 (No. 4): pp. 443–64.
[4] Bates T. A comparison of franchise and independent small business survival rates. Small Business Economics. 1995;Vol. 7: pp. 377–88.
[5] Baumol WJ. Formal entrepreneurship theory in economics: Existence and bounds. Journal of Business Ventures. 1993;Vol. 83: pp. 197–210.
[6] Bigné E, Vila-López N, Küster-Voluda. I. Competitive positioning and market orientation: two interrelated constructs. European Journal of Innovation Management. 2000;Vol. 3 (No. 4): pp. 190–8.
[7] Burnes B. Managing Change. A Strategic Approach to Organizational Dynamics. London: Pitman Publishing; 1996.
[8] Burns P. Entrepreneurship and Small Business. 2nd ed. China: Palgrave MacMillan; 2007.
[9] Cannon T. Enterprise: Creation, Development and Growth. Oxford: Butterworth-Heinemann; 1991.
[10] Cantillon R. Essai sur la nature du commerce en general. London. Reissued for the Royal Economic Society in 1959: Frank Cass and Company Ltd; 1755.
[11] Carlzon J. Moments of Truth. New York: Ballinger Publishing; 1987.
[12] Carson, Cromie S, McGowan P, Hill J. Marketing and Entrepreneurship in SME's: An Innovative Approach. Englewood Cliffs, NJ: Prentice Hall; 1995.
[13] Carson D, Cromie S. Marketing Planning in Small Enterprises: A Model and Some Empirical Evidence. Journal of Consumer Marketing. 1990;Vol. 7 (No. 3): pp. 5–18.

[14] Chapman M. "When the entrepreneur sneezes, the organization catches a cold": A practitioner's perspective on the state of the art in research on the entrepreneurial personality and the entrepreneurial process. European Journal of Work & Organizational Psychology. 2000;Vol. 9 (No. 1): pp. 97–101.
[15] Chell E, Haworth J, Brearley S. The entrepreneurial personality: cases, concepts and categories. London: Routledge; 1991.
[16] Choueke, Armstrong RK. The learning organization in small and medium sized enterprises: a destination or a journey? International Journal of Entrepreneurial Behaviour & Research. 1998; Vol. 4 (No. 2): pp. 498–505.
[17] Cillo P, De Luca LM, Troilo G. Market information approaches, product innovativeness, and firm performance: An empirical study in the fashion industry. Research Policy. 2010;Vol. 39 (No. 9): pp. 1242–52.
[18] Cooper A, Woo C, Dunkelberg W. Entrepreneurship and the inital size of firms. Journal of Business Venturing. 1989;Vol. 4 (No. 5): pp. 317–32.
[19] Cromie S, Hayes J. Towards a typology of female entrepreneurs. The Sociological Review. 1988;Vol. 36 (No. 1): pp. 87–113.
[20] Deal TE, Kennedy A. Culture: a new look through old lenses. The Journal of Applied Behavioural Science. 1983;Vol. 19 (No. 4): pp. 498–505.
[21] Drucker P. Management Tasks, Responsibilities, Practices. New York: Harper & Row; 1974.
[22] Ely RT, Hess RH. Outline of Economics. New York: MacMillan; 1893.
[23] Gillinsky AJ, Stanny E, McCline RL, Eyler R. Does size matter? An empirical investigation into the competitive strategies of the small firm. Journal of Small Business Strategy. 2001;Vol. 12 (No. 2): pp. 1–13.
[24] Göbel S. Klaus B: The success story of an entrepreneur – a case study. European Journal of Work & Organizational Psychology. 2000;Vol. 9 (No. 1): pp. 89–92.
[25] Goffee R, Scase R. Class, entrepreneurship and the service sector: towards a conceptual classification. Service Industries Journal. 1983;Vol. 3: pp. 14–22.
[26] Gray C. Enterprise and Culture. London: Routledge; 1998.
[27] H. Gatignon, Xuereb JM. Strategic orientation of the firm and new product performance. Journal of Marketing Research. 1997;Vol. 34 (No. 1): pp. 77–90.
[28] Hakala H. Strategic orientations in management literature: three approaches to understanding the interaction between market, technology, entrepreneurial and learning orientations. International Journal of Management Reviews. 2011;Vol. 13 (No. 2): pp. 199–217.
[29] Hay RK, Ross DL. An assessment of success factors of non-urban start-up firms based upon financial characteristics of successful versus failed ventures. Frontiers of Entrepreneurship Research. 1989: pp. 148–58.
[30] Hayek FA. The use of knowledge in society. Studies in Philosophy, Politics and Economics. Chicago: University of Chicago Press; 1948.
[31] Hayek FA. The Sensory Order. Chicago: University of Chicago Press; 1952.
[32] Hayek FA. Competition as a Discovery Procedure. New Studies in Philosophy, Politics, Economics and History of Ideas. Chicago: University of Chicago Press; 1967.

[33] Hill J. A multidimensional study of the key determinants of effective SME marketing activity: part 1. International Journal of Entrepreneurial Behaviours & Research. 2001;Vol. 7(No. 5): pp. 171-204.
[34] Kets de Vries MFR. The entrepreneurial personality: a person at the crossroads. Journal of Management Studies. 1977;Vol. 14 (No. 1): pp. 34-57.
[35] Kirzner I. Competition and entrepreneurship. Chicago: The University of Chicago Press; 1973.
[36] Kirzner I. Perception, Opportunity and Profit: Studies in the Theory of Entrepreneurship. Chicago: University of Chicago Press; 1979.
[37] Kirzner I. (1997) Entrepreneurial discovery and competitive market processes: an Austrian approach. Journal of Economic Literature 35(1): 60-85.
[38] Kirzner I. (1999) Creativity and/or alertness: a reconsideration of the Schumpeterian entrepreneur. Review of Austrian Economics 11(1-2):5-17.
[39] Knight F. Risk, Uncertainty and Profit. Chicago: University of Chicago Press; 1921.
[40] Lee T-S, Tsai H-J. The effects of business operation mode on market orientation, learning orientation and innovativeness. Industrial Management & Data Systems. 2005; Vol. 105 (No. 3): pp. 325-48.
[41] Low MB, MacMillan IC. Entrepreneurship: past research and future challenges. Journal of Management. 1988;Vol. 14 (No. 2): pp. 139-61.
[42] Lumpkin GT, Dess GG. Clarifying the entrepreneurial orientation construct and linking it to performance. Academy of Management Review. 1996;Vol. 21 (No. 1): pp.135-72.
[43] Lumpkin GT, Dess GG. Linking two dimensions of entrepreneurial orientation to firm performance: The moderating role of environment and industry life cycle. Journal of Business Venturing. 2001;Vol. 16 (No. 5): pp.429-51.
[44] Miner JB. A psychological typology of successsful entrepreneurs. London: Quorum Books; 1997.
[45] Morgan G. Images of Organizations. London: Sage; 1997.
[46] Olavarrieta S, Friedmann R. Market orientation, knowledge-related resources and firm performance. Journal of Business Research. 2008;Vol. 61 (No. 6): pp. 623-30.
[47] Reijnders W, Verstappen P. SME en Marketing. Amsterdam: Kluwer; 2003.
[48] Rodríguez C, Carrillat F, Jaramillo F. A meta-analysis of the relationship between market orientation and business performance: evidence from five continents. International Journal of Research in Marketing. 2004;Vol. 21 (No. 2): pp. 179-200.
[49] Say JB. A treatise on political economy; or the production, distribution, and consumption of wealth. American edition, translated from the 4th French edition. Philadelphia: Claxton, Remsen & Haffelfinger; 1880.
[50] Schumpeter JA. Theorie der Wirtschaftlichen Entwicklung. Leipzig: Dunker und Humblat; 1911.
[51] Schumpeter JA. The instability of capitalism. Economic Journal. 1928;Vol 38 (151):361-386 [52] Sexton DL, Bowman-Upton NB. Entrepreneurship: Creativity and Growth. New York: MacMillan; 1991.
[53] Shocker AD, Weitz B. A Perspective on Brand Equity Principles and Issues. Cambridge: Marketing Science Institute; 1998.
[54] Slater, Narver. Marketing orientation and the learning organization. Journal of Marketing. 1995;Vol. 59 (July): pp. 63-74.

[55] Smith NR. The entrepreneur and his firm: the relationship between type of man and type of company. East Lansing: Michigan State University; 1967.
[56] Spillan J, Parnell J. Marketing resources and firm performance among SMEs. European Management Journal. 2006;Vol. 24 (No. 2): pp. 236–45.
[57] Stevenson HH, Roberts MJ, Grousebeck HI. New business ventures and the entrepreneur. Homewood, IL: Irwin; 1989.
[58] Timmons JA. New Venture Creation. Illinois: Irwin; 1990.
[59] Tyebjee TT, Bruno AV, McIntyre SH. Growing ventures can anticipate marketing stages. Harvard Business Review. 1983;Vol. 61 / Jan-Feb (No. 1): pp. 62–6.
[60] Ven AHVd, Hudson R, Schroeder DR. Designing new business start-ups: entrepreneurial, organizational and ecological considerations. Journal of Management. 1984;Vol. 10 (No. 1): pp. 89–107.
[61] Winter, Fitzgerald. Continuing the family owned homebased business: evidence from a panel study. Family Business Review. 1993;Vol. 6: pp. 4417–26.
[62] Winter M, Danes SM, Koh S-K, Fredericks K, Paul JJ. Tracking family businesses and their owners over time: panel attrition, manager departure and business demise. Journal of Business Venturing. [DOI: 10.1016/S0883-9026(03)00061-2]. 2004;Vol. 19 (No. 4): pp. 535–59.
[63] Zhou KZ, Gao GY, Yang Z, Zhou N. Developing strategic orientation in China: antecedents and consequences of market and innovation orientations. Journal of Business Research. 2005;Vol. 58 (No. 8): pp. 1049–58.

4
Entrepreneurial Cognition and Learning

4.1 Entrepreneurial cognition and Kolb's experiential learning

Entrepreneurial cognition is concerned with the 'knowledge structures' that people use to make assessments, judgements or decisions involving opportunity evaluation, creation and growth [1]. Current entrepreneurial cognition literature posits there is a relationship between individual's cognitive properties and his/her ability to identify, develop and exploit opportunities [1-5]. However, the ability to recognise opportunities is different in all people because everyone has a limited and fragmented perception of the world we live in, and everyone relies on heuristic mechanisms to make sense of this world [2, 6-8].

Current entrepreneurial cognition and learning reference models such as Kolb's entrepreneurial learning [9] model and Verkataramanan's learning processes model [10], consistently show us that opportunities can be identified if the entrepreneur has correct information and the right cognitive properties [11, 12]. Cognition is therefore shaped by the person-environment interaction. In environments characterised by information overload, for instance, high uncertainty or novelty, strong emotions, time pressure and fatigue are the by-products of bad entrepreneurial cognition (ENCO).

Since decision making and cognition are affected by the knowledge acquired through the learning process, it is necessary to highlight the fact that there is virtually no perfect information in the world we live in, making it difficult for anyone to acquire knowledge. This implies a reliance on experiential learning, which is, according to Kolb [9] an integrative process that combines previously gained knowledge, perception, cognition and experience.

However, the heterogeneity of human experiences characterises the difference amongst people in terms of knowledge structures. In fact, the corridor principle [13] tell us that previous experience is a critical factor for entrepreneurship in general, and in the identification of opportunities specifically [14–16].

Experiential learning theory shows us the existence of two different learning types [10]: the knowledge derived by recreation of experience and the knowledge derived by direct experience. According to the cognitive point of view, the first one takes place in a phase of comprehension, whereas the second one is an antecedent of comprehension and takes place during the phase of apprehension. Likewise, the work of Kolb [9] earlier and Corbett [4] later, allowed us to classify learning styles according to four fundamental learning mechanisms whose dimensions are the concrete experience (both in terms of feeling and thinking), the observation (which is a reflective process), and the experimentation (which is an active process). The resulting four learning styles are the accommodator, the diverger, the converger, and the assimilator. For further details, we refer to Kolb's work: 'Through their choices of experiences, people program themselves to grasp reality through varying degrees of emphasis on apprehension or comprehension' [9].

By using experiential learning frames to understand the opportunity identification process amongst entrepreneurs, we can also, by extension, understand the process of entrepreneurial action that follows the opportunity (or threat) identification. This is achievable by gaining insight on the interconnectedness among the attributes of the person-environment interaction, institutional processes and entrepreneurial activity.

4.2 Institutions and entrepreneurial behaviour

Shane [15] proved the influence of prior knowledge on opportunities, as it was found that differences in behaviour are given by knowledge asymmetries. While it is recognised that cognitive heuristics play an important role in entrepreneurial decision-making, entrepreneurs are more prone to biases [17]. Entrepreneurial cognitive scripts are consistent across cultures, but it is important to look at the individual's cognitive processing style [18], since entrepreneurs tend to prefer intuition over adopting an analytical approach, like managers do. Opportunities (or threats) are better identified intuitively; nevertheless, the environment we live in affects our learning process [19], and it is not unlikely that the processes of apprehension (i.e., the way we experience reality) and comprehension (i.e., the way we make symbolic sense of the reality we experienced) might play a role in determining entrepreneurial behaviour [9]. Entrepreneurs are therefore pushed by the strength of their own symbols, elaborated – thanks to comprehensive processes – to react in a peculiar manner to the identification of an opportunity or threat.

The antecedent to the symbolic elaboration of the experience is the way the experience per se is lived in the single individual in the apprehensive phase [20]. Variations in the institutional environment generate cognitive differences that ultimately dictate different behaviours, although these behaviours are moderated by personal characteristics such as gender and learning style [21], as well as by the type of learning that generates the scripts or knowledge structure the entrepreneurs consequently enacts [1]. In the case of gender, research [22] shows that female entrepreneurs in transitional economies often lack of support, have a stronger fear of failure, and are sometimes perceived as lacking competency for business.

Current institutional theory [23] and institutional economics [24] agree that both formal and informal institutions influence individuals' and organisations' decision-making. Institutions can be both formal and informal [25], and it is the formal ones that shape the way a nation is structured, through its regulative, normative and cultural-cognitive systems [23]. Examples are political, economic, and legal systems, and private property. Working within the framework provided by formal institutions, informal institutions contribute to the creation of norms for communal peaceful cohabitation [23, 26]. Examples are codes of conduct, values, beliefs, social norms, uncodified attitudes, and social networks. Formal institutions create cohesion in the social tissue of the nation and contribute to stability within the social environment. This stability enables the development of entrepreneurship.

The institutional environment can effectively create or destroy entrepreneurship in countries [27]. Institutions therefore provide a 'behavioural framework of social compliance' within which firms and individuals make their choices [28, 29].

Individuals and organisations' behaviour is therefore influenced by the social norms that enable or constrain social behaviours [30]. Good coordination of formal institutions creates societies whose social groups networks are characterised by weak ties [31]. Weak ties allow social groups to exploit opportunities that can be pursued through entrepreneurial behaviour because of the accessibility and openness of the networks [32].

However, in transitional economies, formal institutions often fail to function properly, so that political systems clash with economic systems, and legal systems and do not grant the required level of legality within a country [33]. This institutional failure generates a change in the institutional environment, which consequently affects entrepreneurs' cognition due to the alteration of the person-environment interaction. Differences in cognition therefore emerge due to the different experiences the environment offers and the instability of reliable information, which both decrease trust among transactions' partners [34]. This experience lived in the apprehensive phase of cognition is then re-elaborated in the comprehensive phase, where symbolic value is attached to the experience itself. For instance, Lim [21] reports that 'of particular relevance to entrepreneurship is a country's level of corruption, which is the extent to which public power is misused for private benefit in business transactions [35, 36]'. Therefore, the apprehensive phase of 'encountering corruption' corresponds to a shift from the 'rule of law' to the 'rule of man' in the comprehensive phase.

However, when institutional failure occurs, current studies [24, 37] show that informal institutions often manage to compensate for it, filling the institutional void that has been created [38-41]. Examples are the role that networking has played to bring benefits to network members in both transitional Russia [42, 43] – where it's used to solve inter-firm legal disputes while influencing the legal system – and in China [44, 45] – for getting easier access to the allocation of public resources.

Instead of simply focusing on the growth of their business, entrepreneurs in hostile environments have to learn how to survive and foster growth [46-48]. Their survival depends on their ability to identify both opportunities and threats before it is too late, as this might hamper their very same survival. Entrepreneurs therefore might react to some threats either by dropping from business or by fighting injustice back. The type of adaptive behaviours that is used will depend upon (1) the type of threat the entrepreneurial individual or the organisation faces; (2) the way cognitive processes react to institutional change; (3) moderating factors such as gender and learning style. In the current entrepreneurship literature [48-55], several entrepreneurial actions were reported as being manipulative of the person-institutional environment interaction.

4.3 Entrepreneurs' adaptation to the environment

The entrepreneur responds cognitively to the stimuli of the institutional environment. When the person-environment interaction takes place, different cognitive processes affect the way the entrepreneur perceives an opportunity or a potential threat. These stimuli then generate a sort of entrepreneurial resilience in the identification of both opportunities and threats. Depending on the learning style of the entrepreneur and his/her gender, as well as his/her ability to manipulate or exploit institutions in his/her favour, is a much better choice than exiting business.

Formal institutions – whether political, economic or legal – may pose threats to entrepreneurs. In the political environment, the failure to achieve clear-cut and transparent policymaking (or instability in the political system) generates uncertainty in the social environment [56]. Several authors have observed that bad governance generates high bureaucracy, posing a barrier for lean operations and affecting negatively firms' operational and transaction costs [48, 57–60]. As Aidis and Adachi suggest [48], entrepreneurs in transition economies often deal with regulations that turn out to be incoherent and volatile. Entrepreneurs might react to these threats by establishing adaptive mechanisms of defence based on the exploitation and manipulation of institutions such as personal networks, trust, and more or less legitimate actions, which mitigate the negative effects of bad governance or the inadequacies of unstable political systems.

Also, formal economic institutions can pose threats to entrepreneurs. Access to credit is often exclusively available to powerful, well-connected, bigger firms, rather than small and medium-sized enterprises, as the former are favoured by formal institutions [61, 62]. Since access to credit is so difficult to obtain (it often requires bribery) [42], it is necessary for the entrepreneur to adopt some sort of defence mechanism. The unclear and inconsistent application of taxation rules and the existence of hidden administration fees when dealing with public organisations, pose a threat to firms' liquidity and business planning [56]. Unclear regulatory systems and inaccessible licensing [63] pose other barriers. Entrepreneurs facing the threats posed by the economic environment might develop defence mechanisms based more or less on legitimate actions.

Also, dysfunctional legal systems do not contribute to entrepreneurship. For example, if property rights are not respected, then simple activities like medium- and long-term planning or the acquisition of resources become difficult [16, 63–65]. The threats coming from the legal environment identified in extant literature include potential private property 'expropriation' [65], legal decisions unenforced by courts and police [66, 67], ineffective or unguaranteed contracts [57, 68], mistrust of judiciary impartiality when dealing with legal disputes [66], and the competitive disadvantage in dealing for those entrepreneurs who do not bend rules [69]. Entrepreneurs who perceive themselves to be under threat from the legal environment may develop defence mechanisms such as different business strategies, capitalising on personal networks, trust, and enacting acquired informal codes of conduct.

Informal institutions are also a major factor in determining the social environment of the entrepreneur. Social norms, codes of conduct, values, networks and trust may be strong enablers or barriers to entrepreneurial behaviour. Values and beliefs are hard to change [24], and in some cases of transitional economies, a sudden change in formal institutional assets does not correspond to as quick a change in values and beliefs [37]. When the modifications become widely accepted by the majority of a population, the behavioural codes become social norms [70].

As mentioned above, networks can be both enablers and barriers to entrepreneurial activity, depending on how they affect business. 'Close' networks [71] can pose a threat to business when they 'bind certain groups together in ways that are undesirable for society as a whole, e.g., by reinforcing the practices of favouritism, nepotism, or ethnic hatred' [33]. However, networks can be used as a defence mechanism to protect a business from formal institutional voids by decreasing opportunistic behaviour [72] and granting access to resources [73] that are needed to survive or to minimise uncertainty. Networks are not only used to decrease opportunistic behaviour, but also to strengthen linkages with those individuals or organisations that retain power in order to achieve competitive advantage and personal gain.

The last threat posed by the social environment may derive from the misuse of trust. A generalised trust could describe a mental model [74] 'of what can be expected when dealing with people that someone does not have personalised information about' [33], whereas the misuse of trust generates a particular form of trust, which can be found among a closed network of people supporting each other through nepotism and corruption [75, 76]. Nevertheless, trust can also be adopted as a defence mechanism against the uncertainty caused by formal institutions, thus decreasing opportunistic behaviour [72] and increasing potential compliance with business agreements [77, 78].

We see that values, norms, codes of conducts, networks and trust are important informal institutions that affect entrepreneurial behaviour through the entrepreneurs' cognitive processes of apprehension, comprehension and experiential learning. The deinstitutionalisation process typical of transitional economies poses a threat to entrepreneurial activity by bringing instability into the social environment. Hence, informal institutions can be instrumental to the development of adaptive defensive actions that entrepreneurs in transitional economies can use to limit the negative effects of the threats posed by the institutional environment while increasing their chances for survival.

References

[1] Mitchell RK, et al. Toward a theory of entrepreneurial cognition: rethinking the people side of entrepreneurship research. Entrepreneurship: Theory & Practice. 2002; Vol. 27(No. 2): pp. 93–104.

[2] Baron RA and Ward, TB. Expanding Entrepreneurial Cognition's Toolbox: Potential Contributions from the Field of Cognitive Science. Entrepreneurship: Theory & Practice. 2004; Vol. 28(No.6): pp. 553–73.

[3] Busenitz LW and Lau, C-M. Growth Intentions of Entrepreneurs in a Transitional Economy: The People's Republic of China. Entrepreneurship: Theory & Practice. 2001; Vol. 26(No.1): pp. 5–20.

[4] Corbett AC, Experiential Learning Within the Process of Opportunity Identification and Exploitation. Entrepreneurship: Theory & Practice. 2005; Vol. 29(No. 4): pp. 473–91.

[5] Corbett AC and Hmieleski, KM. The Conflicting Cognitions of Corporate Entrepreneurs. Entrepreneurship: Theory & Practice. 2007; Vol. 31(No. 1): pp. 103–21.

[6] Hayek FA. The use of knowledge in society. In: Studies in Philosophy, Politics and Economics. University of Chicago Press: Chicago; 1948.

[7] Hayek FA. The Sensory Order. Chicago: University of Chicago Press; 1952.

[8] Hayek FA. Competition as a Discovery Procedure, in New Studies in Philosophy, Politics, Economics and History of Ideas. University of Chicago Press: Chicago; 1967.

[9] Kolb DA. Experiential learning: experience as the source of learning and development. Englewood Cliffs, NJ: Prentice Hall; 1984.

[10] Verkataraman S. The distinctive domain of entrepreneurship research. In: J.A.Katz.and R.H. Brockhaus, editors. Advances in Entrepreneurship, Firm Emergence and Growth. JAI Press. Vol 2 : pp. 119–38; 1997.

[11] Mitchell RK, et al. Cross-cultural cognitions and the venture creation decision. Academy of Management Journal. 2000; Vol. 43: pp. 974–93.

[12] Mitchell RK, et al. Are Entrepreneurial Cognitions Universal? Assessing Entrepreneurial Cognitions Across Cultures. Entrepreneurship: Theory & Practice. 2002; Vol. 26(No. 4): pp. 9–32.

[13] Ronstadt RC, The corridor principle. Journal of Business Venturing.1988; Vol. 3(No. 1): pp. 31–40.

[14] Ardichvili A, Cardozo R and Ray S. A theory of entrepreneurial opportunity identification and development. Journal of Business Venturing. 2003; Vol. 18(No. 1): pp. 105–23.

[15] Shane S. Prior knowledge and the discovery of entrepreneurial opportunities. Organization Science. 2000; 11(4): pp. 448–69.

[16] Shane S and Venkataraman S. The promise of entrepreneurship as a field of research. Academy of Management Review. 2000; Vol. 25 (No. 1): pp. 217–26.

[17] Baron R. Cognitive mechanisms in entrepreneurship: why and when entrepreneurs think differently than other people. Journal of Business Venturing. 1998; Vol. 13(No. 4): pp. 275–94.

[18] Corbett AC. Recognizing high-tech opportunities: a learning and cognitive approach. Frontiers of Entrepreneurship Research. 2002; Vol. 1(No. 2): pp. 49–61.
[19] Jung C. Collected Works of Carl Jung. Vol. 6. Princeton, NJ: Princeton University Press; 1977.
[20] Fiske ST and Taylor SE. Social cognition. Reading, MA: Addison-Wesley; 1984.
[21] Lim DSK, et al. Institutional Environment and Entrepreneurial Cognitions: A Comparative Business Systems Perspective. Entrepreneurship: Theory & Practice. 2010; Vol. 34(No. 3): pp. 491–516.
[22] Shinnar RS and Young CA. Hispanic immigrant entrepreneurs in the Las Vegas metropolitan area: motivations for entry into and outcomes of self-employment. Journal of Small Business Management. 2008; Vol. 46(No. 2): pp. 242–62.
[23] Scott WR. Institutions and Organizations. Thousand Oaks, CA: Sage; 2002.
[24] North DC. Institutions, Institutional change and economic performance. Cambridge: Cambridge University Press; 1990.
[25] North DC. Understanding the process of economic change. Princeton, NJ: Princeton University Press; 2005.
[26] Baumol WJ. Entrepreneurship: productive, unproductive, and destructive. The Journal of Political Economy. 1990; Vol. 98(No. 5): pp. 893–921.
[27] Aldrich HE and Wiedenmayer G. From traits to rates: an ecological perspective on organizational foundings, in Katz JA and Rockhaus RH editors. Advances in Entrepreneurship, Firm Emergence, and Growth. Greenwich, CT: JAI Press; 1993, pp. 145–95.
[28] Ahlstrom D and Bruton GD. An institutional perspective on the role of culture in shaping strategic actions by technology-focused entrepreneurial firms in China. Entrepreneurship Theory and Practice. 2002; Vol. 26(No. 4): pp. 53–70.
[29] Bruton GD, Fried VH and Manigart S. Institutional influences on the worldwide expansion of venture capital. Entrepreneurship Theory and Practice. 2005; Vol. 29(No. 6): pp. 737–60.
[30] Aldrich H and Fiol CM. Fools rush in? The institutional context of industry creation. Academy of Management Review. 1994; Vol. 19(No. 4): pp. 645–70.
[31] Burt RS. Structural holes and good ideas. American Journal of Sociology. 2004; Vol. 110(No. 2): pp. 349–99.
[32] Granovetter MM. The strength of weak ties. American Journal of Sociology. 1978; Vol. 78(No. 6): pp. 1360–80.
[33] Tonoyan V, et al. Corruption and entrepreneurship: how formal and informal institutions shape small firm behavior in transition and mature market economies. Entrepreneurship Theory and Practice. 2010; Vol. 34(No. 5): pp. 803–31.
[34] Whitley R. Divergent capitalism: the social structuring and change of business systems. New York: Oxford University Press; 1993.
[35] Bowen HP and Clercq DD. Institutional context and the allocation of entrepreneurial effort. Journal of International Business Studies. 2008; Vol. 39(No. 4): pp. 747–67.
[36] Soto HD. The mystery of capital: why capitalism triumphs in the West and fails everywhere else. New York: Basic Books; 2000.

[37] Helmke G and Levitsky S. Informal institutions and comparative politics: a research agenda. Perspective on Politics. 2003; Vol. 2(No. 4): pp. 725–40.
[38] Hughes KD, et al. Extending women's entrepreneurship research in new directions. Entrepreneurship Theory and Practice. 2012; Vol. 36(No. 3): pp. 429–42.
[39] Welter F. All you need is trust? A critical review of the trust and entrepreneurship literature. International Small Business Journal. 2012; Vol. 30(No. 3): pp. 193–212.
[40] Smallbone D and Welter F. Entrepreneurship and institutional change in transition economies: The Commonwealth of Independent States, Central and Eastern Europe and China compared. Entrepreneurship & Regional Development. 2012; Vol. 24(No. 3–4): pp. 215–33.
[41] Mair J and Marti I. Entrepreneurship for social impact: encouraging market access in rural Bangladesh. Corporate Governance. 2007; Vol. 7 (No. 4): pp. 493–501.
[42] Guseva A. Friends and foes: informal networks in the Soviet Union. East European Quarterly. 2007; Vol. 41: pp. 2–9.
[43] Ledeneva A. Russia's economy of favors: blat, networking and informal exchange. Cambridge: Cambridge University Press; 1998.
[44] Xin KR and Pearce JL. Guanxi: connections as substitutes for formal institutional support. Academy of Management Journal. 1996; Vol. 39(No. 6): pp. 1641–58.
[45] Yang K and Callahan K. Citizen involvement efforts and bureaucratic responsiveness: Participatory values, stakeholder pressures, and administrative practicality. Public Administration Review. 2007; Vol. 67(No. 2): pp. 249–64.
[46] Aidis R. and van Praag M. Illegal entrepreneurship experience: Does it make a difference for business performance and motivation? Journal of Business Venturing. 2007; Vol. 22(No. 2): pp. 283–310.
[47] Manolova TS, et al. The differential effect of men and women entrepreneurs' human capital and networking on growth expectancies in Bulgaria. Entrepreneurship Theory and Practice. 2007; Vol. 31(No. 3): pp. 407–26.
[48] Aidis R and Adachi Y. Russia: firm entry and survival barriers. Economic Systems. 2007; Vol. 31(No. 4): pp. 391–411.
[49] Bates T. A comparison of franchise and independent small business survival rates. Small Business Economics. 1995; Vol. 7: pp. 377–88.
[50] Brixy U and Grotz R. Regional patterns and determinants of birth and survival of new firms in Western Germany. Entrepreneurship & Regional Development. 2007; Vol. 19(No. 4): pp. 293–312.
[51] Collins J. Cultural diversity and entrepreneurship: policy responses to immigrant entrepreneurs in Australia. Entrepreneurship & Regional Development. 2003; Vol. 15(No. 2): pp. 137–49.
[52] Kariv D, et al. Transnational networking and business performance: Ethnic entrepreneurs in Canada. Entrepreneurship & Regional Development. 2009; Vol. 21(No. 3): pp. 239–64.
[53] Michael SC and Combs, JG. Entrepreneurial failure: the case of franchisees. Journal of Small Business Management. 2008; Vol. 46(No. 1): pp. 73–90.
[54] Tödtling F and Wanzenböck H. Regional differences in structural characteristics of start-ups. Entrepreneurship & Regional Development. 2003; Vol. 15(No. 4): pp. 351–70.

[55] Wilson N, Hogarth-Scott S and Watson K. Winners and losers: a study of the performance and survival of TEC supported new start businesses in West Yorkshire. In: Entrepreneurship Research Conference 1994, Kauffman Foundation. Boston, MA: Babson College.
[56] McMillan J and Woodruff C. The central role of entrepreneurs in transitional economies. Journal of Economic Perspectives. 2002; Vol. 16(No. 3): pp. 153–70.
[57] Aidis R, Estrin S. and Michiewicz T. Institutions and entrepreneurship development in Russia: a comparative perspective. Journal of Business Venturing. 2008; Vol. 23(No. 6): pp. 656–72.
[58] Berkowitz D and Holland J. Does privatization enhance or deter small enterprise formation? Economics Letters. 2001; Vol. 74(No. 1): pp. 53–60.
[59] Djankov S, et al. The regulation of entry. The Quarterly Journal of Economics. 2002; Vol. 117(No. 1): pp. 1–37.
[60] Peng Y. When formal laws and informal norms collide: lineage networks versus birth control policy in China. American Journal of Sociology. 2010; Vol. 116(No. 3): pp. 770–805.
[61] Smallbone D and Weiter F. The distinctiveness of entrepreneurship in transition economies. Small Business Economics. 2001; Vol. 16(No. 4): pp. 249–62.
[62] Hellman JS, et al. Measuring governance, corruption and state capture: how firms and bureaucrats shape the business environment in transition economies. In: World Bank Policy Research Working Papers 2312. Washington, DC: The World Bank; 2000.
[63] Parker SC. Law and the economics of entrepreneurship. Comparative Labor Law and Policy Journal. 2007; Vol. 28: pp. 695–715.
[64] Shane S. A general theory of entrepreneurship: the individual-opportunity nexus. Northampton, MA: Edward Elgar; 2003.
[65] Henrekson M. Entrepreneurship and institutions. Comparative Labor Law and Policy Journal. 2007; Vol. 28: pp. 717–42.
[66] Radaev, V. (2004). How trust is established in economic relationships when institutions and individuals are not trustworthy: The case of Russia, in J Kornai, B Rothstein and S Rose-Ackerman eds, Creating social trust in postsocialist transition, London: Palgrave Macmillan.
[67] Volkov V. Who is strong when the state is weak? Violent entrepreneurship in post-Communist Russia. Europe-Asia Studies. 1999; Vol. 51(No. 5): pp. 741–54.
[68] Feige E. Underground activity and institutional change: productive, protective, and predatory behavior in transition economies. In E Feige, editors. Transforming post-communist political economies. Washington, DC: National Academy Press; 1997.
[69] Rose, R. (2000). Uses of social capital in Russia: Modern, pre-modern, and anti-modern. Post-Soviet Affairs, Vol. 16(No. 1), 33–57.
[70] Axelrod R. An evolutionary approach to social norms. America Political Science Review. 1986; Vol. 84(No. 4): pp. 1095–111.
[71] Putnam RD, Leonardi R and Nanetti RY. Making democracy work: civic traditions in modern Italy. Princeton, NJ: Princeton University Press; 2000.
[72] Lambsdorff, J. G., Taube, M., and Schramm, M. (2004). The new institutional economics of corruption. London: Routledge.

[73] Ahlstrom D and Bruton GD. Venture capital in emerging economies: networks and institutional change. Entrepreneurship Theory and Practice. 2006; Vol. 30(No. 2): pp. 299–320.
[74] Denzau AT and North DC. Shared mental models: ideologies and institutions. Kyklos. 1994; Vol. 47(No. 1): pp. 3–31.
[75] Tonoyan V. Corruption and entrepreneurship: does trust matter? Journal of Transforming Economies and Societies. 2003; Vol. 10(No. 3): pp. 2–20.
[76] Tonoyan V, Perlitz M and Wittmann WW. Corruption and Entrepreneurship: Unwritten Codes of Conduct, Trust and Social Values. East-West Comparison. In: Zahra, C Davidsson, P, JFiet, J, Greene PG, Harrison RT, Lerner M, Mason C, Meyer GD, Sohl J, and Zacharakis A, editors. Frontiers of Entrepreneurship Research. Wellesley, MA: Babson College; 2004.
[77] Rose-Ackerman S. Trust and honesty in post-socialist societies. Kyklos. 2001; Vol. 54(No. 3): pp. 415–44.
[78] Rose-Ackerman S. Corruption and Government. Causes, Consequences, and Reform. Cambridge: Cambridge University Press; 1999.

5
Growth Strategies within an SME Context

The importance of growth to an SME consists in the ability of the company to survive major changes in its environment. This is the reason why companies in general, and SMEs in particular, should not point their strategies simply to survival, but should instead opt for business strategies aimed at enhancing growth.

An example can be drawn from physics: there is a difference between velocity and acceleration. A body can be moving on a certain imaginary route in a space at a specific velocity. However, a change in the conditions of space in which the body is moving (e.g., an increase in attrition) slows down the body. In order not to be slowed down (and eventually stopped), the body needs to increase the velocity of its march; therefore, it requires acceleration, i.e. the increase (positive growth) of velocity.

Growing firms are winners in the marathon of market competition. Although some firms might have a very low turnover (e.g., micro firms), those companies that experience high growth are in a much better situation than firms with high turnover that do not grow or experience a business decline (negative growth).

Although business growth is important to firms' future development, we should not assume that all small business owners pursue growth, or that they are necessarily capable of doing so. In fact, despite the view that 'growth of individual firms is the normal and desired development pattern' [63], in fact, some SMEs find several difficulties in achieving growth [121, 131].

These difficulties are often related to the business owner's objectives[36, 121] and the SME's external environment [109], and they are highly affected by the owner's variable receptivity to marketing. Some small business owners might simply show little receptivity for marketing and might not feel the need for growth/expansion.

Sometimes, negative experiences while attempting a business expansion, such as a serious drop in profits/revenue, might ultimately put the small business owner off from trying again [69].

5.1 Factors affecting SMEs' business growth

Not all business owners pursue growth strategies because the drivers pushing people to open and run small firm are different from one SME to another. Therefore, growth is affected by the prospective owner's attitude toward the business. However, there are several other factors affecting business growth in SMEs. Overall, the factors affecting growth can be summarised as internal and external to the SME.

The internal factors that affect growth, according to researchers in entrepreneurship and marketing, are culture, resources, business-owner characteristics, company size/maturity and networking availability. The external factors identified are attitudes towards marketing constraints and the competition.

5.1.1 Owner-manager's culture

In a business and management context, the word 'culture' means 'organisational culture'. This refers to the processes, beliefs and practices of firms. In this section, we focus on the small business owner's culture. In fact, if we want to understand what culture means in a small business context, where the owner controls the business, we have to start considering how the set of rules and moral beliefs we acquire from our environment affect our action in society.

We are born, live and work within a social context. Human society is made of different cultures and subcultures: you might be aware of diverse communities living in your town, sometimes characterised by common ethnic characteristics (e.g., the Italian, Chinese, African, Caribbean, and Indian communities), sometimes by special interests in specific topics (e.g., emos, who are fond of emotional rock music, goths, who characterised by their fondness for 'darkness', and hippies, whose tastes evolved into the New Age subculture).

Sociologically, culture is often define as 'a configuration of learned behaviours and results of behaviour whose component elements are shared and transmitted by the members of a particular society' [90]. There is also agreement among academics that culture is 'the collective programming of the mind which distinguishes the members of one category of people from another' [68].

Culture therefore entails 'learned and shared human patterns or models of living' [34] and 'these patterns and models pervade all aspects of human social interaction' [34]. Cultures define what shared behaviours are acceptable for societal cohabitation; in that sense, regulative and normative systems are supported by the underlying values and beliefs of the culture and dictate what behaviour is right or wrong.

Business performance is affected by culture, as the motivations, cultural background, aspirations and intentions of the business owner [12, 29, 35, 65, 79, 115] affect the way business is conducted. Therefore, different small business owners show different managerial styles and are motivated by different aspects of business life.

Some SME owners have no personal interest or belief in growth [132]; therefore, they show reluctance to engage in growth-stimulating activities such as increasing the number of employees working within their business [56] or dealing with specific tasks such as marketing [93].

Small business owners do not place importance on the main aspects of marketing theory [75], and growth is affected by the firm's marketing efforts. Marketing is context specific, and its effectiveness is affected by the nature of the industry in which the SME operates, products distribution, the business life stage (lifecycle), the different types of products/ services offered on the market, and the firm's management style.

The business owner's culture affects the level of customer orientation [96, 118], which has an impact on growth [57, 92, 96, 103, 117–119].

Religion is an aspect of culture that affects the way business is conducted. Religion is the acceptance of the existence of a superior being [46]. It is part of a society's view of the world and the basis for normative systems, as religions often dictate the moral obligations of those who belong to a specific religion. As indicated in Lindridge [89], 'religion covers a range of topics including beliefs, narrative, practices and symbolism that provide a sense of meaning to the individual's life'.

Religion, through its dictates of righteous behaviour and our sense of identity, is a strong driver for both consumers and business people. Consumers' choices are affected by religion; for example, Muslims purchase Halal food, Jews purchase Kosher food, Hindus do not cook beef, and in areas with a strong Asian presence the size of rice bags is bigger than in communities with no Asian population. Likewise, the way an SME is run is affected by the religious ethos of the small business owner.

Religion is often intertwined with its members' personal characteristics, such as ethnicity (some religions are spread more among specific ethnic groups), which also helps to keep a positive self-concept of oneself through identity and belonging to a specific social group [123], gender, as female members of different religions are more likely to take part in celebrations and services than males [94], and age [62], which often reflects generational differences (e.g., younger generations from immigrant backgrounds reportedly are more religious than their peers whose families do not have an immigration history). All of these factors affect the way religion is lived within a community or at a personal level.

While from a social policy perspective different cultures in a social system have to learn to cohabit in peace, this might require big efforts by the policymakers' point of view and by a marketing perspective, because the process of acculturation changes in the culture of a society when two or more different cultures connect and start symbolic exchanges[9–10], which causes changes in customs and traditions within the original society – enriches the diversity found in a society and improves the marketing opportunities that smart small business owners can identify and pursue.

5.1.2 Available resources

The lack of available resources is a constraint to SME marketing; the very same lack of resources is often constrains business growth, too. Often, business owners lack the skills to deliver on marketing [120] and have no resources to outsource specialised marketing expertise [37, 100, 130].

Firms' capacity, other than marketing capabilities, has impact on SMEs' growth. More specifically, the ability of a firm to grow through the exploitation of opportunities, better decision-making, and the determination and avoidance of potential mistakes made by the company in the decision-making process, as well as the implementation of the decisions taken [102], all enable of business growth. This is supported by some studies,[1] which confirm that, with an increase in marketing expertise, the growth rate of firms also increases.

Greater marketing expertise adds value to a company's marketing assets [43], especially on superior marketing knowledge.

However, marketing capability is related to the available resources in the company. The lack of resources identifiable in both financial and human capital has a negative effect on an SME's growth [25, 31, 104, 107].

Human capital is paramount to the growth of a company [108, 110]. It contributes to intellectual capital, which has a positive correlation with better performance in SMEs, regardless of the industry sector analysed [16]. This means that those firms that manage to hire the right personnel, with the right mix of skills, will also benefit from the contribution their staff will bring to their company by virtue of those skills.

Furthermore, in terms of resources, the lack of financial capital puts constraints on business decisions [32, 44, 104], while a larger amount of financial resources positively influences business performance, allowing the business owner to have more flexibility in strategic choices. Small business owners face the reality of working with limited resources, both in terms of financial and human capital.

5.1.3 Business-owner personal characteristics

Another factor affecting growth in SMEs is the business owner's personal characteristics, as he or she plays an important role, as reported by several authors [17, 80, 98, 105]: the business owner's life experience, values and beliefs, previous experience in managerial or business roles, level of education, and biological age are all considered important in current entrepreneurship and marketing literature. In what follows, we will have an overview on these main factors identified as affecting SMEs' growth.

Previous business experience has been shown to be an important factor for growth in SMEs [32, 42, 47, 122]. To this end, Peña [104] maintains,

> Entrepreneurial start-up experience is expected to increase the odds of venture success.... Entrepreneurs whose parents, relatives or friends have been through a business start-up process are acquainted with the endeavours of building a firm. By sharing the concerns of people close to them, entrepreneurs learn the intricacies of creating a business. Sometimes, entrepreneurs start a new firm based on the industry knowledge acquired from a previous job (i.e., knowledge about customers, suppliers, industry regulation, subsidies etc.).

Therefore, entrepreneurs' previous experience is an important aspect of their learning, often improving their business skills in later enterprises.

Although previous business experience is important, it is often also related to the gender of the small business owner. Different small business owners present different business experiences, and their genders are likely to affect their business experience and their views of the business world.

According to several authors [27, 49-50, 73], the desire for – or orientation to – growth is affected by the gender of the entrepreneur, with female business owners tending to pursue growth less frequently than males, due to their need to balance their work and family relationships. Male business owners exhibit a greater tendency to seek growth, which may often be uncontrolled, and therefore, not beneficial to the SME.

Furthermore, female-owned businesses tend to grow less than those owned by their male counterparts [30, 50]. However, all of the studies conducted on gender and entrepreneurship have underlined the poorer performance of businesses run by women[128] because the measures of success focused only on business size and turnover – without taking into account more context-specific elements, such as the female business owner's attitude about growth, her motivation for not pursuing it, the family/work balance, and greater caution shown among female business owners.

5.1.4 Company size and life stage

In terms of size and maturity, some authors [14, 73] agree that the size of the company and its age have an impact on growth – with older companies tending to perform better and presenting higher chances of survival. More recent studies [2, 53] show that the relationship between size and performance is not straightforward and should not be generalised because of its ambiguity, as the relationship between size and growth seems random.

In terms of strategy, the awareness of the different segments of the market, as well as appropriate distribution, has a positive impact on growth; this is confirmed by Sandberg's and Hofer's [111] study, in which they found that SMEs that focus on product differentiation outperform other start-up companies.

The same authors also consider geographical factors (e.g., where the company operates, ease of networking with consultants, suppliers and service providers, competitors and so on) as contributing to growth. Part of the strategy also involves attention to distribution strategies, as they are considered important to growth [97, 113, 124] in the sense that focused distribution in appropriate channels may foster growth or may waste financial resources.

Growth is affected by the firm's life cycle. SMEs and larger organisations have very similar life cycle structures. All these organisations have a first phase of business planning, which is characterised by the generation of the business idea, and a start-up phase, which is characterised by financial loss due to the investments undertaken to launch the business. Phases that follow are growth, characterised by improved sales and profits; maturity, characterised by slowed growth or stationary sales; and decline, characterised by the obsolescence of the products or brands the company proposes, and sometimes by the succession of ownership (through the sale or inheritance of the business), which often generates a new start and a recovery to a new growth phase.

In all this, it should be taken into account that SMEs also have an intermediate phase between the phase of growth and maturity [26]: 'organisational formalisation', in which the small business becomes formalised and adopts a specific legal form as well as managerial structure.

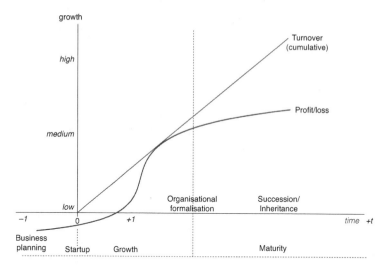

Figure 5.1 SME growth phases, adapted from Chaston [26]
Source: Author's own.

5.1.5 Competition and other marketing constraints

Some other factors affecting growth, which can also be classified as external factors, can be found in the effects of competition and the overall performance of the market in which the SME operates. Some markets, like China's consumer goods market, are very fast, as they are characterised by many competitors who come up with new products and brands fairly quickly, and the level of brand or product replication is very high. Differentiation is the core of these markets, but it is difficult to achieve. Other markets, such as train transportation, are not very fast. They are characterised by few competitors and little opportunity for differentiation.

Firms' growth is therefore partially affected by the type of market the firm operates in. Nevertheless, 'some small firms achieve high growth despite being in sectors where market conditions are unfavourable. Growth performance in small businesses has been found to be related to a number of factors, including

- a successful product-marketing strategy;
- how the managers create and exploit market opportunities and cope with difficulties;
- a greater propensity to follow a strategy of focused differentiation, and a lower propensity to compete on price. [69]

Another factor that affects an SME's growth is the way it faces the marketing constraints that present themselves during the business lifecycle. There are phases of crisis that the SME has to overcome in the transition between a growth stage and another [113]. Constraints on marketing activity account for part of the problem, by causing crises during the transition between one stage and another. Some constraints might result in increased competition, shifts in consumers' preferences, and more unfavourable economic and sociopolitical conditions that make it difficult to carry on with operations. All these may hamper firm growth during the transition phases from a stage to another, e.g., from start-up to established business.

5.2 The diversity of the drivers to growth

There are different reasons why small business owners decide to start their own firm. Most commonly, they pursue personal profits. However, financial performance is not necessarily a driver for all small business owners. Some like the independence of running a business, while others are obliged to do it following redundancy from their previous employment. Some see their business as a different and helpful way to spend their retirement. The motivations at the root of entrepreneurial action are many and depend on the small business owners' personality and personal situation, along with the pressures from the economic and social environment.

Despite the flexibility of SMEs' reactions to market changes[54], entrepreneurs or owner-managers can manage SMEs. These differ significantly in their managerial styles and their decision-making. Entrepreneurs are more inclined to take risks, and this affects their strategic attitudes. Entrepreneurs are opportunity seekers and show less inclination to plan [67]. Furthermore, their decision-making shows itself to be 'irrational and erratic' [58]. On the other hand, owner-managers tend to behave more rationally. They tend to take planning activities into consideration, and they control business processes as well as measuring performance [18]. Several studies [40, 80, 105] have dealt with entrepreneurs' characteristics; more in-depth information can be found in those publications.

We should not take it for granted that all entrepreneurs are motivated by seeking growth [61], as some might just run the business because of their lifestyle. In the case of female entrepreneurs, not all women search for growth:

> Research on the goals of men- and women-led ventures finds that woman business owners frequently pursue both economic and social

goals rather than economic goals only, which may detract from economic performance or growth [13]. Furthermore, women [38] are more likely than men to start businesses to achieve a work–family balance [91].

However, growing businesses not only contribute to the small business owner's wealth, but also to local economies. It is true that governments are interested in growing companies due to the local and national benefits related to business growth [85], but nevertheless, companies often need governmental support in order to be able to start, develop and grow. This is especially true in turbulent times, and some small businesses might need more governmental support when economic and social conditions deteriorate because also small business owners' morale gets worse with the increase of economic difficulties. Those small business owners who are strongly motivated to survive hard conditions should then think about how to add value to their products and brands through a better understanding of the market and through the implementation of differentiation or cost-leadership practices.

5.3 Differentiation versus 'me-too' strategies

In the previous sections, we highlighted the importance of growth to SMEs. Amongst different strategies of growth, SMEs often face the problem of differentiating. Differentiation strategies are very powerful in many markets, and are necessary in some (especially in very dynamic markets). Unfortunately, differentiation is not easy to achieve, as it requires a strong orientation to the market, a good understanding of consumers' profiles and preferences, and investment of resources in the design and implementation of marketing plans that involve market research, product development and marketing communication [19].

Current consumer markets are increasingly fragmented [114], and this increases competition amongst firms [4]. In fast markets (characterised by a high level of heterogeneity), consumers' needs and wants, as well as the drivers to purchase, need to be thoroughly understood by producers and processors in order to enable the elaboration of strategies of differentiation.

An example, taken from the food and drink industry, is the evolution of a commodity such as eggs: consumers can nowadays find organic, special feed and breed, free range, small, medium, large size, or high bird welfare eggs, and these eggs are branded or have their own label [71]. Firms in general, but SMEs in particular, must strive to know their customers, as failure to do so would cost too dearly to them, both in financial and economic terms.

The key to success is the attention paid to final consumers [106], which enhances the chance to achieve a competitive advantage through the provision of value to consumers. A better understanding of the final consumer also improves production efficiency [15], as evidence shows a positive, significant, and robust link between marketing orientation and firm performance [76]. As a consequence, it is of paramount importance for companies to take a customer-oriented approach in order to sustain their market share [82], and create "customer value" for different market segments [127].

Adding value to a firm's customer base means that consumer preferences, attitudes and behaviours should be monitored continuously to help develop attractive value propositions, as perceived by the consumers, and to reduce competitive pressure by proposing truly different ways to satisfy consumers' needs and wants.

Consumer decision-making is a complex process that may be affected by a variety of factors [77, 81, 86, 88, 112]. The drivers for consumer choices can be found both inside and outside the supply chain and are often tied to individuals' lifestyle, cognition and level of awareness about products. Whilst firms may have control over product attributes (e.g., taste, smell, look, packaging, brand name and label, among others) to appeal to consumers and influence their decision-making, no companies have control over consumers' purchase decisions, and SMEs often also lack a deep understanding of the market they operate in.

Personal factors (e.g., cultural background, product knowledge, perception, attitudes, socio-demographics and psychologyare uncontrollable characteristics, yet they play an important role in the purchasing decision and are at the basis of differentiation's success. SMEs should consider consumers' characteristics thoroughly when differentiating their offering. This point may seem obvious in a business to consumer (B2C) environment. In a business-to-business (B2B) context (in which customers are wholesalers and retailers), products are designed in line with these customers' specifications, rather than according to final consumers' preferences, but this might not be the best way of doing it, nor is it necessarily advantageous for the producing firm in the long run.

Nevertheless, in a B2C context, consumers play a major role in products' availability on the market, given their expressed demand. For many SMEs, it may be difficult to cater to this demand, given the high heterogeneity of consumers, so SMEs are often tempted to copycat products as a safe strategy for easy market penetration. In fact, it is quite common to find SMEs that pursue a 'me-too' strategy by copying existing products, rather than truly differentiating or innovating. However, me-too strategies are not effective in the long run because

> as markets become more competitive and trade customers more assertive, the number of "me-too" brands and stock-keeping units will diminish. Its growth linked to affluence and two-worker households, convenience-store retailing will accentuate the pressure on many "other than leading" brands because of its restricted shelf space. Supermarkets seeking growth by adding new categories will increasingly have to weed out those manufacturers' brands with less market share in traditional categories [11].

5.4 Marketing decision-making and performance: measures available to SMEs

SMEs generally cannot rely on data mining or marketing departments that can organise state- of-the-art market research. Their marketing know-how and available time, let alone financial resources, are very limited. Within an SME marketing context, growth is the sole output measure that can safely determine the year-on-year success of the firm, although other measures of performance exist.

5.4.1 Marketing decision-making influencing factors

Researchers [69] working on firm performance generally use growth as a reliable measure of performance, because without growth, SMEs cannot survive. Nevertheless, a firm's marketing decision-making is complex. Several factors interact in the process to generate a decision that might have either a positive or negative effect on the overall performance of the firm.

In what follows, we briefly describe how different factors affect the marketing decision-making and therefore performance, before turning our attention to some specific measures that can both support marketing decision-making and contribute to measure performance. First of all, amongst the initial observations on SMEs marketing decision-making, we have to consider that an entrepreneur's attitude towards external factors (e.g., customer needs/consumer wants, competitors' moves, relationship with suppliers and service providers) has a direct impact on marketing strategy [8, 99]. The more in tune businesses are with customer needs (e.g., rates of sale, profit margins, and waste levels) and consumer

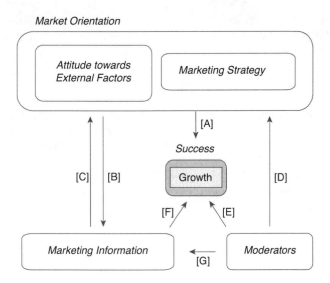

Figure 5.2 Frequency of purchase affecting marketing decision-making and performance within an SME context
Source: Author's own.

wants (e.g., product attributes and availability), the more likely they are to make changes to the marketing mix that are consumer- and customer-driven [45]. Also, the more they learn about their competitors' behaviour, the more likely they are to respond quickly and protect or grow their market share [45].

The better SMEs' relationships are with suppliers and service providers, the more likely they are to benefit from higher quality inputs and the level of service those SMEs often struggle to attract, due to their small size. The more knowledgeable they are about the range of support services provided by government agencies, the less likely they will be to expose themselves to excessive/unnecessary debt, and the more likely they are to benefit from grants and subsidies directed specifically at SMEs.

Small business owners' attitude towards external factors affects the marketing information construct [B] [45, 64, 125–126], and marketing information itself comprises three factors: source of information, frequency with which the information is acquired or used, and the type of information acquired or used. These three factors are affected by whether the company has any interest in its consumers and customers, competitors, suppliers and service providers. It should be considered that all these stakeholders provide important inputs at different stages of the marketing strategy development process [39, 64, 72, 74, 83, 87], and the acquisition of information from them might generate a feedback effect on market orientation [C], since more insight from the market could raise further the SME interest in acquiring information to support marketing decision-making processes, rather than operations (e.g., procurement, production, distribution and so on).

To this regard, much of the entrepreneurial marketing literature highlights SMEs' tendency to focus more on production and turnover (sales) rather than on marketing activity per se, which, in the short term, generates costs [6, 23, 28, 51, 66]. Many small business owners therefore fail to see the strategic aspects of engaging with marketing. Nonetheless, it has been long established that marketing in general, and branding in particular, are essential ingredients for enhancing the firms' long-term competitiveness, irrespective of their size [1]. Therefore, marketing intelligence is linked to marketing strategy, because they enable business growth by its power to inform marketing decision-making overall.

Marketing strategy comprises four different components: distribution strategy, segmentation awareness, targeting strategy and perceived brand awareness. Together, these components drive the marketing process and help the marketing decision-making, the outcome of which drives business growth [3, 24, 33, 48, 60, 116, 125, 129]. Marketing strategy has, therefore, a direct impact on a company's success [A], because growth is affected by all the factors contained in the marketing strategy [45, 64, 72].

However, creating a marketing strategy often requires access to marketing expertise. In fact, its presence or absence affects the ability to identify the most appropriate sources of information [E] [23, 70, 84] – whether it is primary or secondary, for instance – and the type of information needed [G], too, such as whether it is qualitative or quantitative in nature or relevant to a business's activities.

Management style affects the type of information sought and its frequency of use because of a higher or lower orientation to marketing [G] [78]. The funds allocated and the company analytical capability affect both the quality and quantity of information SMEs use [G] [22-23].

The internal factors of growth affect marketing strategy [D] in different ways: the management style affects the way the mangers direct the business and determine the areas the company should focus on, which therefore affects the level of segmentation awareness [6-7, 41, 55, 59]. Marketing expertise affects the way the marketing strategy is set up or conducted through the targeting strategy [1, 39, 51], with implications for the level and nature of marketing activity, and consequently, with an impact on growth. In addition, marketing resources affect the targeting strategy as well as the whole marketing strategy and the attitude toward external factors [22-24].

Also, the personal characteristics of the entrepreneur contribute to the generation of growth, as they have an impact on management style[56]. Younger owner-managers are likely to be less risk averse than older managers, and the latter are more likely to be resistant to change and autocratic in style, a characteristic that is also more likely to be present in managers with many years of business experience.

Business size is presented as having moderating effects on the marketing strategy [D] [69] and overall business growth [E], as well as on the use of marketing information [G]. Larger businesses are more likely to have more resources to support their marketing activities and have greater alignment of the different elements in the marketing mix: the right product at right price in the right distribution channel, targeting the right consumers [45, 69, 72]. Along with business size, we found the age of the business is also reported in the entrepreneurial marketing literature as affecting the use of marketing information [G] [48, 116, 125] – the more mature the business, the more likely it is to have been exposed to, and benefitted from, the use of marketing information.

A relationship between the internal factors and both the size and age of the business should also be noted [52, 125]. SMEs at different stages of development are likely to have different management styles, different levels of resources available for their marketing activities [5, 22-23, 54, 66, 70, 84, 133], and different capabilities to develop and execute the marketing strategy [D] [54].

A last factor affecting a firm's growth is the presence of a brand that distinguishes the business and its products in the market. Sometimes an owner-manager in a family may inherit the brand (along with the family business) from a previous generation, and both are already established in local markets. Other times, companies have not operated for long time to grant high awareness of their products, so brands are developed from scratch to address customers' and consumers' lack of awareness. However, for other owner-managers, having a brand is not important, so they focus on producing for and supplying own-label brand owners. Given this diversity of options, it is sensible to believe the presence of a brand may have an impact on the marketing strategy [D]; SMEs with an established brand will have very different requirements, capabilities and resources than those yet to establish a brand in their target market [101], thereby making brand owners potentially more eager to use marketing information to push brand awareness, market better, and achieve growth.

5.4.2 Measures to inform marketing decision-making and monitor performance

Following what has been described so far, and provided SMEs have the right mix of business owners' personal characteristics, market orientation, brand awareness and strategic views, we raise the following question:

> Can SMEs pursue, should they wish to, actions to focus their marketing decision-making, and then monitor the effectiveness of their business activity generally and their marketing activity in specific?

In fact, there are several different measures SMEs could use, both qualitatively and quantitatively, in order to guide their marketing decision-making and to assess their performance. Among the simple measures SMEs could look, at we find

- value growth (measured in terms of turnover, also known as sales' value)
- volume growth (measured in terms of sales' volume)
- frequency of purchase
- customer penetration
- repeat purchase
- sales per customer (both in terms of value and volume)
- consumers' ratings

In the case of those SMEs that operate as retailers, footfall is also helpful. All of these measures can help with the marketing decision-making and with an assessment of current firm performance. SMEs could also use a series of accountancy tools to determine their financial and economic strength and their actual position with respect to debtors and creditors in general, as well as to determine their stock and the allocation of resources within the firm. However, from a marketing point of view, decision-making benefits by the above mentioned measurements. If SMEs were becoming more aware of the use of these measures they would start their first steps into marketing intelligence.

In what follows, we describe the above measures within their strategic context, and in order to do so, we have to introduce a specific question for the firms who want to start engaging with marketing intelligence.

> What are the marketing opportunities for growth?

72 *Entrepreneurial Marketing for SMEs*

This is a simple question; nevertheless, it is critical for all those SMEs that are willing to engage with marketing intelligence. The question addresses the problem of market growth. Different markets have different dynamicity, as we have already seen, and all markets are not at the same stage of development and do not all move at the same speed.

It is possible to determine the growth rate of the market in a fairly simple way, when the data are available. However, the big problem for SMEs is that it is not always possible to determine the aggregate value or volume of sales for all their competitors. Therefore, it is not possible to most of the SMEs to determine whether the market they operate in is a high- or low-growth market. Governmental bodies often make these estimations and national Offices of Statistics in different countries generally estimate market growth.

Nevertheless, firms can determine market growth, both in terms of value and volume for their own products, and thereby understand which are high- and low-growth, giving them a simple but helpful measure of performance of the single products within their portfolio. SMEs can also compare growth by channel of distribution, identifying the fast-growing products when distributed in different channels, and so on. The growth in terms of value and volume is determined in the same way; however, to calculate value growth, we use the figures related to the turnover of the firm (i.e., the total amount of sales within a specific period of time) and to determine volume growth, we use the units sold. We also choose two periods of time, to determine the growth over a specific period whose boundaries are the first time period (i.e., time 1) and the second period (i.e., time 2). Then, the growth rate (Gr) is calculated the following way:

$$Gr = [(\text{total sales at time 2} - \text{total sales at time 1}) \div \text{total sales at time 1}] \times 100; \qquad (1)$$

So, for example, if we the value of sales in January amount to £20,000, and by the end of April, we reach £28,000, then the sales value growth rate is 40% over the first quarter of the year. The same applies to the growth rate in terms of volume (or units) of a specific product.

By knowing the growth rate of a specific product, SMEs can then measure the performance of specific products within our portfolio, or we might be interested in comparing different growth rates during the different periods of the year, so that we know when we could expect a fast increase in sales (and consequently prepare to supply more of a specific product) or find ways to incentivise consumption when we expect slow growth...or decide to take a holiday on a tropical island (Maldives?) when the growth rate of our products becomes does not justify our efforts.

We have now learnt that the very first opportunities for marketing are found in the type of market we are in. Ideally, we would all love to be operating in fast-moving, high-growth markets, but this is not always possible. Therefore, SMEs could try to answer this specific first question by trying to identify ways to either attract new consumers or get existing consumers to buy more often.

The first option – attracting new consumers – focuses on increasing market penetration, a measure calculated as a proportion of the people in a specific target who buy a specific product at least once in a specific period of time, with respect to the number of people who could possibly purchase it. Let us clarify this with an example: If my target consumers are university students between the ages of 18 and 22, we would then calculate the customer penetration (CP) for students as follows:

$$CP = (\text{students who bought the product} \div \text{total number of students in the area}) \times 100; \qquad (2)$$

So if we estimate that 25,000 students match the description of my target segment in my geographical area, then we know that if 2,750 students purchase my product at least once in, let us say, 3 months, we know that my CP is 11%. We can then record the customer penetration for that specific period (in this example, one-quarter of the year), and then compare how the penetration fluctuates over the quarters of the year.

If we find a specific pattern, we might then want to try to incentivise trial purchases amongst potential new customers in periods when customer penetration is particularly low. This tactic focuses on the stimulation of trial purchase amongst consumers. This could be achieved through promotional mechanics aimed at incentivising consumers to purchase, such as a price cut, although price promotions are not generally well suited for SMEs because they reduce income while increasing stock (in the case of unsold goods), and sometimes create waste (in the case of short shelf life or perishable goods). Other forms of promotion could be incentives in the form of gifts attached to the original product, and so on.

The second way to identify opportunities for growth lies in the increase of the frequency of purchase amongst existing consumers, so that they could buy more often than what they already do. This option looks at existing customers and aims to increase the purchase frequency to incentivise further consumption. The way to calculate it is really easy. The frequency of purchase over a specific period of time corresponds to the total number of purchases made over that specific period of time by a group of consumers.

The frequency of purchase helps us understand how often a specific product is purchased, and we might also use this information to compare usage across different target segments or across different products lines we supply. We might have customers who are heavy users, as opposed to light users, or we might spot differences in usage that are related to the customers' segments personal characteristics (e.g., age, gender, lifestyle and so on). We might also try to increase the frequency of purchase by stimulating further usage of the product or new usages for the same product. We calculate the frequency of purchase in the following way. Let us suppose we have 10 customers, and they purchase our product, Y, a certain number of times in one month. The following table shows how many times each customer bought product Y, and we add the number of times they purchased the product. In this case we add 4 + 2 + 4 + 4 +...+ 8 = 48 as shown in the Table 5.1.

In this case, now that we know the total purchases, we only have to divide that by the number of customers; let us call the frequency of purchase FP, so

FP = sum of the times the product was bought ÷
total number of people in the segment; (3)

This function gives us a number that is our frequency of purchase. In our example, FP= 4.8, meaning that the customers belonging to that specific segment purchase the product almost 5 times in a month. In order to determine whether this is a little or a lot, we will need to compare the figure with other segments and use our personal intuition and judgement. Purchasing bottles of water 5 times a month might be little in summer, whereas purchasing lobsters 5 times a month definitely is not a bad result –especially for the supplier of lobsters!

Table 5.1 Factors affecting marketing decision-making and performance within an SME context

Customer	1	2	3	4	5	6	7	8	9	10	Total: 10 people
Product Y	4	2	4	4	8	1	4	6	7	8	Total: 48 times

Source: Author's own.

Another helpful measurement, along with purchase frequency, is the sales per customer, which can be determined in terms of either value or volume and indicates the total expenditure in monetary terms and in terms of units purchased. The sales per customer in financial terms is the cumulative turnover generated by a specific customer segment, and the sales per customers in terms of volume consists of the cumulative number of units purchased by a customer segment within a specific period of time. The sales per customer are calculated in a similar manner to the frequency of purchase. Let us assume that we again have the same ten customers in a market segment. They purchase different quantities of different products in a given period of time and their total expenditure is a certain amount. We add the total expenditure per month, let us say, and then we divide by the number of customers in the segment. We obtain a measure of the average sale that each customer generates within a market segment. Let us call sales value per customer Va/C and sales volume per customer Vo/C.

$$\text{Va/C or Vo/C} = \text{sum of the value/volume} \div \text{total number of people in the segment;} \qquad (4)$$

In this specific case, our Va/C = £23 and our Vo/C = 2,300 units (see Table 5.2). It is helpful to know the sales per customers because, again, we can get an indication of the usage under the form of overall consumption of a specific customer group. We could then compare this consumption pattern against the personal characteristics of the customer segment, so we can determine consumers' expenditure against their available income, for instance.

The last helpful measure SMEs could use in trying to support their marketing decision-making is the repeat purchase. Although similar

Table 5.2 Sales per customer

Customer	1	2	3	4	5	6	7	8	9	10	Total:
											10 people
Value	£10	£20	£10	£30	£10	£50	£30	£40	£20	£10	Total: £230
Volume	200	100	400	200	300	100	100	200	300	400	Total: 2,300 units

Source: Author's own.

to the frequency of purchase, it differs by measuring the number of customers that have purchased a specific product at least twice within a specific period of time. So, while the frequency of purchase indicates how many products someone purchases in a specified period of time, the repeat purchase gives the SME an indication of how many customers purchase a specific product more than twice in a given period of time. Therefore, we say that repeat purchase is a measure of loyalty. It is calculated in a slightly different way from the frequency of purchase and the sales per customer. We calculate it in a similar manner to customer penetration. Let us consider a given product, Z, sold over a period of one month. We have the times the product was purchased by customers.

We add the number of people who purchased the product at least twice (highlighted in bold in the table 5.3), and we divide this number by the total number of people to obtain the repeat purchase (RP).

RP = (people buying at least twice ÷ total number of people in the segment) x 100; (5)

In our specific case, the RP = 60%, meaning that 6 people in 10 purchase the product more than twice in a given period of time. Ideally, we would like to identify those segments that have high repeat purchase, as we do not want to lose them because they are loyal. Instead, we want to reward them and increase their loyalty wherever possible. On the other hand, segments with low repeat purchase have little loyalty, and we might want to identify them so that we could work out ideas about how to improve their loyalty.

The next measure, consumers' ratings, supports marketing decision-making and evaluates the performance of a product or firm. Consumers' ratings indicate preference within given choices, about which consumers should express an opinion. These are the basis for perceptual maps: a graph that plots the preferences of many customers on two single products' attributes of reference. This is very common in market research,

Table 5.3 Repeat purchase

Customer	1	2	3	4	5	6	7	8	9	10	Total: 10 people
											Total X: 06 people
Product X	1	**3**	0	**4**	**2**	0	0	1	**5**	**2**	

Source: Author's own.

and someone may have stopped you on the street to ask you to take part in a survey. On that occasion, the person might have read some statements and asked you to express an opinion. Let us now see how SMEs can create their own surveying tool. In order to do so, we need some elements of the toolbox: a list of attributes of specific product characteristics (e.g., qualitative characteristics) and a rating scale.

The first is a list on which several attributes of the product we want to obtain ratings for are indicated, such as colour preference, usability, physical characteristics and so on. The second is a scale of numbers from 1 to 10 that indicates the level of appreciation of each attribute on the list. Generally, these are indicated together on a questionnaire that is administered to the customer, and it looks like as shown in Table 5.4.

In order to obtain a rating for all the customers, we need to select a sample (As a rule of thumb, if you manage to get about 100 customers to answer your questionnaire, that would be already good, but this is true if you are a very small SME. Optimally, you should really look at bigger samples, on the order of 300–400 questionnaires). Once all customers have completed their questionnaire, we insert the data in an Excel spreadsheet, with the rows indicating the customer number (e.g., customer no. 1, customer no. 2 and so on), and in the columns, our attributes (e.g., colour, size, portability). In the cell in which the rows and columns intersect, we report the rating we find in the questionnaire. The following table 5.5 shows you the imaginary ratings of 10 customers arranged in a rating dataset.

In the last row, we calculate the average of each column, so that we can get a general score for the attribute. At this point, we can do two things with our data: create a table that compares our customers to the benchmark (our average) or plot our perceptual maps.

Table 5.4 Example of rating scale

How do you rate the following?	Really bad		Quite bad		Either /or		Quite good			Great
	1	2	3	4	5	6	7	8	9	10
Colour				x						
Size							x			
Portability									x	

Source: Author's own.

Table 5.5 Example of a rating dataset

Customer no.	Colour	Size	Portability
1	5	1	5
2	8	2	5
3	2	3	6
4	4	4	5
5	5	3	4
6	9	2	9
7	9	5	0
8	8	6	9
9	7	3	8
10	6	2	3
average	6.3	3.1	5.4

Source: Author's own.

Let us first create a table that compares our customers' preferences by ordering all the data in ascendant order (from the smallest to the larger), first by colour, and then by customer number. We obtain the following:

Table 5.6 Comparison of customers' preferences to our average score

Customer no.	Colour
3	2
4	4
1	5
5	5
10	*6*
9	7
2	8
8	8
6	9
7	9
Average	6.3

Source: Author's own

Ideally, we would like to have many customers – rather than a few – expressing a high rating. We can see that an average of 6 out of 10 is already quite good, because it indicates customers, on average, like the colour. However, in light of this simple exercise, we can see that customers 3, 4, 1 and 5 do not like the colour of our product very much, whereas customers 9, 2, 8, 6 and 7 like it very much. Customer 10 likes our product perfectly in line with our average sample. If we collected a contact number for the customers, we could organise a focus group and invite them to discuss their opinions and let us know what colour they would like better and why. Teas and coffees are on us!

However, if we want a more general view of our customers' perceptions, we can opt for the second option and create a perceptual map. Perceptual maps are created by plotting all our customers' data on two dimensions that we choose. In this simple example, we use very simple dimensions, but larger organisations use sophisticated statistical techniques to determine these dimensions. If you are interested in these techniques, you could read Cacciolatti and Mar-Molinero's paper [20], which gives you an idea of what type of statistical analysis it is used to create dimensions that can be plotted to generate perceptual maps.

In our specific case, we derive the XY coordinates for each point by using ratings in our table. If we plot, for instance, colour versus size, we will define X=colour and Y=size. Therefore, customer no. 1 in the rating dataset will have coordinates x=5 and y=1, and so on. Once we have plotted all the maps, we will determine the cut-off points (or limits) that indicate where the average for the sample is, and we will include them in the plot as markers, so that we remember the average values. Now, with the markers, we have a point of reference on which firms have preferences below or above the average. If we want to plot it in Excel, we have to use a scatter graph and indicate as a series name 'customers', as values for the X-axis the values of the column denominated 'colour', and as values for the Y-axis the values of the column denominated 'size'. The graph is as shown in the Figure 5.3.

In this case, we can interpret the plot by saying that if we look at the overall picture, the greatest number of customers does not like the size of the product (as shown by the customers below the size horizontal reference line), although overall they are quite happy with the colour (as shown by the customers on the right of the colour vertical reference line). Therefore, further investigation should be conducted on the reasons why the size is not appealing to customers. Furthermore, a very small number of customers (numbers 7 and 8) are very pleased with both colour and size. The company could therefore explore the characteristics of those customers to whom the product strongly appeals.

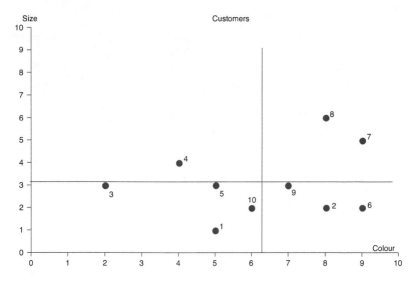

Figure 5.3 Perceptual map

Note:This map shows customers' ratings based on the colour and size dimensions; the vertical black line is the marker for the average rating for the attribute 'colour', whereas the horizontal black line is the market for the average rating for the attribute 'size'.

Source: Author's own

This was just an example of interpretation of the results; however, all sorts of interpretations can take place from perceptual maps. Most of the insight they provide can be helpful and easy enough for SMEs to raise important questions about their consumers' preferences and potential ways to focus their marketing decision-making, while monitoring the performance of their products.

A last measure, which especially applies to those SMEs who operate at the retail level, is the footfall, allows SMEs to understand the flow of people in a specific place at a given time. In its simplest form, the footfall consists of counting all the customers who pass by a specific place; however, the footfall might get more complicated when we need to count only people with specific characteristics based on gender, age and so on. By knowing the flow of people at specific times, we can then know when to run promotions. Footfall also improves SMEs' decision-making about the allocation of resources within the firm, so they are able to supply all customers at peak times, while they reduce the use of resources in slower periods.

References

[1] Aacker DA. Building Strong Brands. Bath: The Bath Press; 2002.
[2] Agarwal R, Audretsch DB. Does entry size matter? The impact of the life cycle and technology on firm survival. The Journal of Industrial Economics. 2001; Vol. XLIX (No. 1): pp. 21–43.
[3] Alsbury A. Quick Answers to Small Business Questions. Jay R, editor. London: Prentice Hall; 2001.
[4] Asp EH. Factors affecting food decisions made by individual consumers. Food Policy. 1999; Vol. 24 (No. 2–3): pp. 287–94.
[5] Barney J. Strategic factor markets: expectations, luck and business strategy. Management Science. 1986; Vol. 32 (No. 10): pp. 1231–41.
[6] Barney J. Firm resources and sustained competitive advantage. Journal of Management. 1991; Vol. 17 (No.1): p. 99.
[7] Barney J. Gaining and Sustaining Competitive Advantage. Reading: Addison-Wesley; 1997.
[8] Bennett RJ, Robson PJA. Intensity of interaction in supply of business advice and client impact: a comparison of consultancy, business associations and government support initiatives for SMEs. British Journal of Management. 1999; Vol. 10 (No. 4): pp. 351–69.
[9] Berry JW. Immigration, acculturation, and adaptation. Applied Psychology. 1997; Vol. 46 (No. 1): pp. 5–34.
[10] Berry JW. Conceptual Approaches to Acculturation. Washington DC: American Psychological Association; 2003.
[11] Berthon P, Hulbert JM, Pitt LF. Brand management prognostications. Sloan Management Review. 1999; Vol. 40 (No. 2): pp. 53–65.
[12] Bird B. Implementing entrepreneurial ideas: the case for intention. Academy of Management Review. 1988; Vol. 13 (No. 3): pp. 442–53.
[13] Bird B, Brush C. A gendered perspective on organizational creation. Entrepreneurship: Theory & Practice. 2002; Vol. 26 (No. 3): pp. 41–65.
[14] Birley S, Westhead P. Growth and performance contrasts between types of small firms. Strategic Management Journal. 1990; Vol. 11: pp. 85–100.
[15] Bonney L, Clark, R., Collins, R., and Fearne, A. From serendipity to sustainable competitive advantage: insights from Houston's Farm and their journey of co-innovation [Case Study]. Supply Chain Management: An International Journal. 2007; Vol. 12 (No. 6): pp. 395–9.
[16] Bontis N, Chua Chong Keow, W and Richardson S. Intellectual capital and business performance in Malaysian industries. Journal of Intellectual Capital. 2000; Vol. 1 (No. 1): pp. 85–100.
[17] Bracker JS, Keats BW, Pearson JN. Planning and financial performance among small firms in a growth industry. Strategic Management Journal. 1988; Vol. 9 (No. 6): 591–603.
[18] Brigham KH, De Castro JO, Shepherd DA. A person-organization fit model of owner-managers' cognitive style and organizational demands. Entrepreneurship Theory and Practice. 2007; Vol. 31 (No. 1): 29–51.
[19] Cacciolatti L, Garcia C and Kalantzakis M. (2015) Traditional food products: the effect of consumers' characteristics, product knowledge and perceived value on actual purchase. *Journal of International Food and Agribusiness Marketing, 0:1–22.*

[20] Cacciolatti L, Molinero CM. Analysing the demand for supply chain jobs through job advertisements. KBS Working Paper Series. 2013; Vol. 264 (January).
[21] Capron L, Hulland J. Redeployment of brands, sales forces, and general marketing management expertise following horizontal acquisitions: a resource-based view. Journal of Marketing. 1999; Vol. 63 (No. 2): 41–54.
[22] Carson, Cromie S, McGowan P, Hill J. Marketing and Entrepreneurship in SMEs: An Innovative Approach. Englewood Cliffs, NJ: Prentice Hall; 1995.
[23] Carson D, Cromie S. Marketing Planning in Small Enterprises: A model and some empirical evidence. Journal of Consumer Marketing. 1990; Vol. 7 (No. 3): 5–18.
[24] Carson DJ. The evolution of marketing in small firms. European Journal of Marketing. 1985; Vol. 19 (No. 5): pp. 7–16.
[25] Chandler GN, Hanks SH. An examination of the substitutability of founders human and financial capital in emerging business ventures. Journal of Business Venturing. 1998; Vol. 13 (No. 5): 353–69.
[26] Chaston I. Entrepreneurial Management in Small Firms: Sage Publications; 2009.
[27] Cliff JE. Does one size fit all? exploring the relationship between attitudes towards growth, gender, and business size. Journal of Business Venturing. 1998; Vol. 13 (No. 6): 523–42.
[28] Cohen WA, Stretch SM, editors. Problems in small business marketing as perceived by owners. Chicago, IL: Proceedings of Research Symposium on the Marketing/Entrepreneurship Interface; 1989.
[29] Cooper. Challenges in predicting new firm performance. Journal of Business Venturing. 1993; Vol. 8: pp. 241–53.
[30] Cooper, Gimeno-Gascon, Woo. Initial human and financial capital as predictors of new venture performance. Journal of Business Venturing. 1994; Vol. 9: pp. 371–95.
[31] Cooper, Gimeno-Gascon, Woo. Initial human and financial capital as predictors of new venture performance. Journal of Business Venturing. 2002; Vol. 9 (No. 5 [September]): pp. 371–95.
[32] Cooper A, Woo C, Dunkelberg W. Entrepreneurship and the inital size of firms. Journal of Business Venturing. 1989; Vol. 4 (No. 5): pp. 317–32.
[33] Cooper AC. The entrepreneurship – small business research. In: Kent S, D. Sexton and K. Vesper, editors. Encyclopaedia of Entrepreneurship. Englewood Cliffs, NJ: Prentice-Hall; 1982.
[34] Damen L. Culture Learning: The Fifth Dimension on the Language Classroom. Reading, MA: Addison-Wesley; 1987.
[35] Davidsson. Continued entrepreneurship: ability, need, and opportunity as determinants of small firm growth. Journal of Business Venturing. 1991; Vol. 6: pp. 405–29.
[36] Davidsson P. Continued Entrepreneurship and Small Firm Growth. 2nd ed. Stockholm: Ekonomiska Forskningsinstitutet; 1989.
[37] Davis CD, Hills GE, LaForge RW. The marketing/small enterprise paradox: a research agenda. International Small Business Journal. 1985; Vol. 3(No. 3): pp. 31–42.

[38] De Bruin A, Brush CG, Welter F. Introduction to the special issue: towards building cumulative knowledge on women's entrepreneurship. Entrepreneurship Theory and Practice. 2006; Vol. 30 (No. 5): 585–93.
[39] de Chernatony L, McDonald M. Creating Powerful Brands in Consumer, Service and Industrial Markets. 2nd ed. Oxford: Butterworth-Heinemann; 2001.
[40] Delmar F, Davidsson P. Where do they come from? Prevalence and characteristics of nascent entrepreneurs. Entrepreneurship & Regional Development. 2000; Vol. 12 (No. 1): 1–23.
[41] Dierickx I, Cool K. Asset stock accumulation and sustainability of competitive advantage. Management Science. 1989; Vol. 35 (No. 12): pp. 1504–11.
[42] Doutriaux J, Simyar F. Duration of comparative advantage accruing from some start-up factors in high-tech entrepreneurial firms. In: *Frontiers of Entrepreneurship Research*. N. Churchill (eds). Wellesley, MA: Center for Entrepreneurial Studies Babson College; 1987.
[43] Doyle P. Value-based marketing. Journal of Strategic Marketing. 2000; Vol. 8 (No. 4): 299–311.
[44] Duchesneau DA, Gartner WB. A profile of new venture success and failure in an emerging industry. Journal Of Business Venturing. 1990; Vol. 5: pp. 297–312.
[45] Dunn E. It's Marketing Jim, But Not As We Know It. London: dunnhumby; 2006.
[46] Durkheim E. The Elementary Forms of the Religious Life: Dover Publications; 2008.
[47] Dyke LS, Fisher EM, Reuber AR. An inter-industry examination of the impact of owner experience on firm performance. Journal of Small Business Management. 1992; (October): pp. 73–86.
[48] Ennis S. Growth and the small firm: using causal mapping to assess the decision-making process – a case study. Qualitative Market Research: An International Journal. 1999; Vol. 2 (No. 2): pp. 147–60.
[49] Fisher E. Sex differences and small-business performance among Canadian retailers and service providers. Journal of Small Business and Entrepreneurship. 1992; Vol. 9 (No. 4): pp. 2–13.
[50] Fisher E, Reuber R, Dyke L. A theoretical overview and extension of research on sex, gender, and entrepreneurship. Journal of Business Venturing. 1993; Vol. 8 pp. 151–68.
[51] Frank BG, Krake JM. Successful brand management in SMEs: a new theory and practical hints. Journal of Product & Brand Management. 2005; Vol. 14 (No. 4): pp. 228–38.
[52] Fuller PB. Assessing marketing in small and medium-sized enterprises. European Journal of Marketing. 1994; Vol. 28 (No. 12): pp. 34–49.
[53] Geroski PA. What do we know about entry? International Journal of Industrial Organization. 1995; Vol. 13: pp. 421–40.
[54] Gilmore A, Carson D and Grant K. (2001a) SME marketing in practice. *Marketing Intelligence & Planning* 19 (1): 6–11.
[55] Grant RM. Contemporary Strategy Analysis: Concepts, Techniques, Applications. 2nd ed. Cambridge: Blackwell; 1995.

[56] Gray C. Business independence – impediment or enhancement to growth in the 1990s? 13th National Small firms' Policy and Research Conference; Harrogate, UK;1990.
[57] Greenley GE. Market Orientation and Company Performance: Empirical Evidence From UK Companies. British Journal of Management. 1995; Vol. 6 (No. 1): p. 1.
[58] Gustafsson V. Entrepreneurial Decision-Making: Thinking Under Uncertainty. In: Carsrud AL, Brännback M, editors. Understanding the Entrepreneurial Mind. New York: Springer; 2009, pp. 285–304.
[59] Hamel G, Prahalad CK. Strategic intent. Harvard Business Review. 1989; Vol. 67 (No. 3): pp. 63–78.
[60] Hanks SH, Watson CJ, Jansen E, Chandler GN. Tightening the life-cycle construct: a taxonomic study of growth stage configurations in high-technology organizations. Entrepreneurship: Theory & Practice. 1993; Vol. 18 (No. 2 [Winter]): pp. 5–30.
[61] Hansen B, Hamilton R. Factors distinguishing small firm growers and non-growers International Small Business Journal. 2011; Vol. 29 (No. 3): pp. 278–94.
[62] Harker K. Immigrant generation, assimilation, and adolescent psychological well-being. Social Forces. 2001; Vol. 79 (No. 3): pp. 969–1004.
[63] Havnes PA, Senneseth K. A panel study of firm growth among SMEs in networks. Small Business Economics. 2001; Vol. 16: pp. 293–302.
[64] Hayward M. Customers Are for Life, Not Just Your Next Bonus. London: dunnhumby; 2005.
[65] Herron L, Robinson R. A structure model of the effects of entrepreneurial characteristics on venture performance. Journal of Business Venturing. 1993; Vol. 8: pp. 281–94.
[66] Hill J. A multidimensional study of the key determinants of effective SME marketing activity: part 1. International Journal of Entrepreneurial Behaviours & Research. 2001; Vol. 7 (No. 5): pp. 171–204.
[67] Hisrich RD, Peters MP, Shepherd DA. Entrepreneurship. 6th ed. New York: McGraw-Hill Irwin; 2005.
[68] Hofstede G. National Cultures and Corporate Cultures. In: Porter LASaRE, editor. Communication between Cultures. Belmont, CA: Wadsworth; 1984.
[69] Hogarth-Scott S, Watson K, Wilson N. Do small businesses have to practise marketing to survive and grow? Marketing Intelligence & Planning. 1996; Vol. 14 (No. 1): pp. 6–18.
[70] Huang X, Brown A. An analhysis and classification of problems in small business. International Small Business Journal. 1999; Vol. 18 (No. 1): pp. 73–85.
[71] Hughes D. European Food Marketing: Understanding consumer wants; the starting point in adding value to basic food products. The Agricultural Ecomomics Society and the European Association of Agricultural Economists. December 2009; Vol. 8 (No. 3): pp 6–13.
[72] Humby C. Brand is Dead, Long Live the Customer. London: Dunnhumby; 2005.

[73] Kalleberg A, Leicht K. Gender and organizational performance: determinants of small business survival and success. Academy of Management Journal. 1991; Vol. 34 (No. 1): pp. 136–61.
[74] Keller KL. Conceptualizing, measuring, managing customer-based brand equity. Journal of Marketing. 1993; Vol. 57 (No. 1): pp. 1–22.
[75] Kenny B, Dyson K. Marketing in Small Business. London: Routledge; 1989.
[76] Kirca AH, Jayachandran S, Bearden WO. Market orientation: a meta-analytic review and assessment of its antecedents and impact on performance. The Journal of Marketing. 2005; Vol. 69 (No. 2): pp. 24–41.
[77] Knight JG, Holdsworth DK, Mather DW. Country-of-origin and choice of food imports: an in-depth study of European distribution channel gatekeepers. Journal of International Business Studies; 18 January 2007; Vol. 38 (No. 1): pp 107–25.
[78] Kohli AK, Jaworski BJ. Marketing orientation: the construct, research propositions, and managerial implications. Journal of Marketing. 1990; Vol. 54 (April): pp. 1–18.
[79] Kolvereid L. Growth aspirations among Norwegian entrepreneurs. Journal of Business Venturing. 1992; Vol. 7: pp. 209–22.
[80] Kotey B, Meredith GG. Relationships among owner/ manager personal values, business strategies, and enterprise performance. Journal of Small Business Management. 1997; Vol. 35 (No. 2): 37–64.
[81] Kotler P, Armstrong G, Saunders, J, Wong, V. Principles of Marketing. 4th European ed. Harlow: Financial Times Prentice Hall; 2005.
[82] Kotler P, Keller K. Marketing Management: New York, USTA: Prentice Hall; 1991.
[83] Kotler PH. Marketing Management: Analysis, Planning, and Control. 7th ed. Englewood Cliffs, NJ: Prentice-Hall; 1991.
[84] Kraft FB, Goodell PW. Identifying the Health Conscious Consumer. Newbury Park, CA: Sage; 1989.
[85] Kuratko D. Entrepreneurship: Theory, Process and Practice. Mason, OH: South Western Educational Publishing; 2008.
[86] Lancaster KJ. A new approach to consumer theory. The Journal of Political Economy. 1966; Vol. 74 (No. 2): pp 132–57.
[87] Levitt T. Marketing myopia. Harvard Business Review. 1960; Vol. 38 (No. 4): pp. 45–56.
[88] Levitt T. Marketing success through differentiation of anything. Harvard Business Review. 1980; Vol. 58 (No. 1): pp 83–91.
[89] Lindridge A. Are we fooling ourselves when we talk about ethnic homogeneity? The case of religion and ethnic subdivisions amongst Indians living in Britain. Journal of Marketing Management. 2010; Vol. 26 (No. 5–6): pp. 441–72.
[90] Linton R. The Cultural Background of Personality. Oxford, England: Appleton-Century; 1945.
[91] Manolova TS, Brush CG, Edelman LF, Shaver KG. One size does not fit all: entrepreneurial expectancies and growth intentions of US women and men nascent entrepreneurs. Entrepreneurship & Regional Development. [doi: 10.1080/08985626.2012.637344]. 2011 2012/01/01; Vol. 24 (No. 1–2): 7–27.

[92] Matsuno K, Mentzer JT, Aysegul O. The effects of entrepreneurial proclivity and market orientation on business performance. Journal of Marketing. 2002; Vol. 66 (No. 3):18–32.
[93] Mayes DG, Moir C. The growth of small firms in the UK. Competition and Markets. Basingstoke: Macmillan; 1990, pp. 41–62.
[94] McCullough ME, Tsang JA, Brion S. Personality traits in adolescence as predictors of religiousness in early adulthood: findings from the Terman Longitudinal Study. Personality and Social Psychology Bulletin. 2003; Vol. 29 (No. 8): pp. 980–91.
[95] McDougall PP, Covin JG, Robinson Jr RB, Herron L. The effects of industry growth and strategic breadth on new venture performance and strategy content. Strategic Management Journal. 1994; Vol. 15 (No. 7): pp. 537–54.
[96] Narver JC and Slater SF. (1990) The effect of market orientation on profitability. *Journal of Marketing* 54 (4): 20–35.
[97] Nevins JL, Money RB. Performance implications of distributor effectiveness, trust, and culture in import channels of distribution. Industrial Marketing Management. 2008; Vol. 37 (No. 1): 46–58.
[98] O'Farrell, Hitchins. Alternative theories of small firm growth: a critical review. Environment and Planning. 1988; Vol. 20: pp. 365–82.
[99] O'Farrell PN, Hitchens DMWN. Producer services and regional development: key conceptual issues of taxonomy and quality measurement. Regional Studies. 1990; Vol. 24 (No. 2): pp. 163–71.
[100] Oakey R. Innovation and the management of marketing in high technology small firms. Journal of Marketing Management. 1991; Vol. 7 (No. 4): pp. 343–56.
[101] Olins W. Olins on Br@nd. London; 2007: Thames and Hudson.
[102] Pasan M, Shugan SM. The Value of Marketing Expertise. Management Science. 1996; Vol. 42 (No. 3 [March]): pp. 370–88.
[103] Pelham AM, Wilson DT. A longitudinal study of the impact of market structure, firm structure, strategy, and market orientation culture on dimensions of small-firm performance. Journal of the Academy of Marketing Science. 1996; Vol. 24 (No. 1 [Winter]): p. 27.
[104] Peña I. Intellectual capital and business start-up success. Journal of Intellectual Capital. 2002; Vol. 3 (No. 2): pp. 180–98.
[105] Perry C, Meredith G, Cunnington H. Relationship between small business growth and personal characteristics of owner-managers in Australia. Journal of Small Business Management. 1988; Vol. 26 (No. 2): pp. 76–9.
[106] Porter M. Competitive Advantage, Creating and Sustaining Superior Performance. New York: Free Press; 1985.
[107] Romer PM. Capital Accumulation In The Theory Of Long Run Growth. Working Paper: University of Rochester – Center for Economic Research (RCER);1988.
[108] Roos J, Roos G, Edvinsson L and Nicola C. Dragonetti. (1997) *Intellectual Capital. Navigating in the New Business Landscape*, London: Macmillan Press.
[109] Rosa P. Entrepreneurial processes of business cluster formation and growth by 'habitual' entrepreneurs. Entrepreneurship Theory and Practice. 1998; Vol. 22 (No. 4): pp. 53–88.

[110] Sánchez, P, Chaminade, C and Olea, M (2000) Management of intangibles. An attempt to build a theory. *Journal of Intellectual Capital* 1 (4): 312–27.
[111] Sandberg WR, Hofer CW. Improving new venture performance: the role of strategy, industry structure and the entrepreneur. Journal of Business Venturing. 1987; Vol. 2 (No. 1): pp. 5–28.
[112] Schiffman L, Bednall, D., O'cass, A., Paladino, A., Ward, S., and Kanuk, L. (2008) Consumer Behaviour. In: Lewis S (ed.) *Consumer Behaviour.* French Forest NWS, Australia: Pearson Education, pp. 29–7.
[113] Scott M, Bruce R. Five stages of growth in small business. Long Range Planning. 1987; Vol. 20 (No. 3): 45–52.
[114] Senauer B, Asp, E,, Kinsey, J. Food Trends and the Changing Consumer. 2006 ed. St. Paul: Eagan Press; 1992, pp. 320–1.
[115] Sexton D. Growth decisions and growth patterns of women-owned enterprises. Women-Owned Businesses. New York: Praeger; 1989, pp. 135–50.
[116] Simpson M, Padmore J, Taylor N, Frecknall-Hughes J. Marketing in small and medium sized enterprises. International Journal of Entrepreneurial Behaviour & Research. 2006; Vol. 12 (No. 6): pp. 361–87.
[117] Slater, Narver. Does competitive environment moderate the market orientation – performance relationship? Journal of Marketing. 1994; Vol. 58 (No. 1): pp. 46–55.
[118] Slater, Narver. Marketing orientation and the learning organization. Journal of Marketing. 1995; Vol. 59 (July): pp. 63–74.
[119] Slater, Narver. The positive effect of a market orientation on business profitability: a balanced replication. Journal of Business Research. 2000; Vol. 48 (No. 1): 69–73.
[120] Smallbone D. Success and failure in new business start-ups. International Small Business Journal. 1991; Vol. 8 (No. 2): pp. 34–45.
[121] Storey DJ. Understanding the Small Business Sector. London: Routledge; 1994.
[122] Stuart RW, Abetti PA. Impact of entrepreneurial and management experience on early performance. Journal of Business Venturing. 1990; Vol. 5: pp. 151–62.
[123] Tajfel H, Turner JC. An integrative theory of intergroup conflict. The social psychology of intergroup relations. 1979; Vol. 33: p. 47.
[124] Thomas AR, Wilkinson TJ. It's the distribution, stupid! Business Horizons. 2004 2005; Vol. 48 (No. 2): pp. 125–34.
[125] Tyebjee TT, Bruno AV, McIntyre SH. Growing ventures can anticipate marketing stages. Harvard Business Review. 1983; Vol. 61 (No. 1 [Jan–Feb]): pp. 62–6.
[126] Urde M. Brand orientation: a mindset for building brands into strategic resources. Journal of Marketing Management. 1999; Vol. 15 (No. 1–3): pp. 117–33.
[127] Van Trijp H, Meulenberg M. Marketing and consumer behaviour with respect to foods. In: Meiselman HL, MacFie HJH, editors. Food Choice, Acceptance, and Consumption. London, UK: Blackie; 1996. p. 264–92.
[128] Venkatraman N, Ramanujam V. Measurement of business performance in strategy research: a comparison of approaches. Academy of Management Journal. 1986; Vol. 11 (No. 4): pp. 801–14.

[129] Wai-sum S, Kirby DA. Approaches to small firm marketing. European Journal of Marketing. 1998; Vol. 32 (No. 1/2): pp. 40–60.
[130] Weinrauch DJ, Mann OK, Robinson PA, Pharr J. Dealing with limited financial resources: a marketing challenge for small business. Journal of Small Business Management. 1991; (October): pp. 44–54.
[131] Wiklund J. Small Firm Growth and Performance. Jönköping: Jönköping International Business School; 1998.
[132] Wilson N, Hogarth-Scott S, Watson K. Winners and losers: a study of the performance and survival of TEC supported new start businesses in West Yorkshire. Entrepreneurship Research Conference; Babson College, Boston, MA: Kauffman Foundation; 1994.
[133] Wong HY, Merrilees B. A brand orientation typology for SMEs: a case research approach. Journal of Product & Brand Management. 2005; Vol. 14 (No. 3): pp. 155–62.

6

The Role of Structured Marketing Information in SMEs' Decision-Making

Marketing decisions are critical to firms' business success. However, competitive markets are characterised by asymmetry of information; therefore, the level of uncertainty of firms' outcomes when operating in a market makes it difficult to make the right decisions. Firms need information to support their decision-making.

Glazer defined market information [33] as 'data that have been organized or given structure – that is, placed in context – and endowed with meaning'. The definition is much more generalised than Moorman's [54]:

> Market information refers to external information that cuts across all functional areas of the firm rather than the more delimited marketing information that suggests it applies only to marketing departments. The substantive content of market information is broad enough to include what is known as a result of experience and primary or secondary research studies.

Cacciolatti et al. [9] define marketing information as 'structured data, usable within a marketing context and that has been voluntarily sought and systematically collected'. Some examples include all internal (related to the organisation, the marketing mix, business and marketing strategies and tactics adopted, internal resources available and so on) and external (related to the customers, competitors, other stakeholders as well as external resources available and the market dynamics and economic trends) information.

Most of the studies [23, 33, 47, 87] related to marketing and information (both processing and utilisation of marketing information) focused on decision-making processes – and the decision makers only – rather than marketing processes and their effect on growth.

A big contribution has been made by several authors [23, 37, 50, 53, 55–56] about the effects of organisational characteristics and structures of business owners' use of marketing information – although they are not directly linked to a marketing perspective in an SME context and definitely not related to the effect of the information utilisation on growth.

Some other studies have been conducted on the relationship between marketing planning and performance – measured as sales growth – finding that more independent [65], bigger [74] and high-growth companies [2] tend to perform better – however, these studies did not focus on the information collection process as factors impacting growth. Other studies, such as those by Dollinger [27] and Brush [5], have been defined by Peters and Brush [63] as 'inconclusive'. Moorman [54] agrees, arguing that research so far has not demonstrated empirically how information processes impact business performance, with the only exception being Kohli and Jaworki's [38, 45] study, which examines the consequences of a company's market orientation on business performance but without including the potential effect of the acquisition and processing/utilisation of information that may, we argue, have an impact on the marketing processes [15, 22, 26].

Information, in general, is believed to play an important role in SMEs, as those that collect and analyse marketing information can make more informed decisions in their planning activity [70, 75]. Collecting information allows the company to reduce uncertainty in their business activities [1] and enables the company to add value to its supply chain [40]. 'Information is now critical for the management and growth of business value. Knowledge about competitors and customers is essential to understand the future direction of business development' [46] and monitoring the marketing environment is important, if not critical, to companies' success [36, 71, 77].

Though SMEs tend not to plan their business activities formally [61], there is evidence that those companies that engage with formal planning tend to have higher success than those companies that do not [17, 31, 62]. In principle, the more information the entrepreneur has, and the better its quality, the easier it should be for the business owner to minimise risk when planning marketing activities and implementing ideas.

Furthermore, research in planning has tested the relationship between an SME's level of planning and the success or failure of the company. SMEs show little formal planning [62]; therefore, information is not playing an important role in those companies, and this is seen as a barrier to growth [81]. Moorman [54] shows that the information-utilisation processes are predictors of new product performance, timeliness and creativity in the company, maintaining that competitive advantage in the company is strictly related to how information is used. Several authors [17, 31, 61] have maintained these findings: those companies where business is planned formally tend to be more successful than others.

Despite it being shown that SMEs prefer informal and unstructured information-collection methods [5-6, 69], it seems those small firms that opt for formal planning demonstrate better performance than those that are not planning [27]. However, the collection of information and planning may be affected by an SME's level of development [64, 83].

It is important for small firms to collect information regarding 'size and growth rate of markets, purchasing characteristics of consumers, competitors' products and prices, and general demographic, economic, and industry needs...Moreover, these sources note that there are distinct differences in information types and sources' [63]. This information-collection process is referred to as 'environmental scanning' [28]. The structure information collected includes data on suppliers, buyers, competitors and trends – national, global, economic, socio-cultural and technological.

Despite many SMEs' perception that marketing information is unimportant [35, 51, 64] and the informal and unstructured process of marketing information collection, SMEs using marketing information show a propensity to use secondary, rather than primary, sources of information [85], and marketing ideas that were developed by informal verbal exchanges.

As per the types and sources of marketing information used by SMEs, the extant literature identified information related to market channels [39]; the most used sources of information/advice being family and friends [18], customers [69] and competitors [5-6], indicating a preference for information obtained through informal but trusted channels. The type of information acquired through different channels plays an important role in the entrepreneurial marketing decision-making, and information utilisation is closely correlated to business performance [8-9].

6.1 The relationship between business growth and information use

Marketing allows companies to generate value for the consumer, hence contributing directly to business growth [30]. However, several studies have shown that marketing in SMEs is often unstructured or not fully understood [49], that often there is lack of marketing expertise [46], as many owner-managers are not formally trained in marketing, and resources are generally limited [32]. This way the potential development of the marketing function may be constrained. An improvement in marketing decision-making can be achieved through marketing intelligence [76].

However, in order to improve marketing decision-making, it is important to support the decision-making process with accurate information (provided that information on markets is asymmetrical by definition). Marketing intelligence, therefore, enables the company to collect information about both the internal and external environment that can be used to improve the accuracy and precision of the marketing decisions. It also allows the company to react faster to changes in the market or environment [43], because small business owners can make decisions on their own and more swiftly.

Whether a company engages in marketing intelligence depends on their market orientation [67]. Market-orientated firms tend to make use of marketing intelligence, while non-market orientated companies tend not to collect information that way. [43]. Small companies in general gain knowledge by sharing information [14] collaboratively with companies in their sector or industry in industrial clusters or community partnerships.

However, even market-oriented companies often find acquiring information difficult [89], as the quantity and variety of information is wide, with data relating to suppliers, buyers, customers or consumers, competitors, and socioeconomic trends [63]. Nevertheless, the information collected can help with the identification of opportunities [86], and can reduce uncertainty in business activities [40], because firms can make more informed decisions [70]. However, not all companies make good use of formalised marketing information, and both SME's and owner-managers' personal characteristics may play an important role in explaining the different usage of marketing information. Furthermore, some companies use different types and sources of information.

6.2 Types, source and frequency of information use

Current entrepreneurship literature on the acquisition of information and environmental scanning focuses on the sources of information utilised by companies [72]. However, further research on the utilisation of information by firms 'may clarify issues associated with the recognition and exploitation of economic opportunity' [72]. This focus of current literature on sources neglects the focus on information utilisation, per se, with a clear lack of contributions about what types of information are most used by firms and how. There is also an overall lack of agreement amongst researchers on the formal definition of marketing information. Cacciolatti et al.'s [9] definition of marketing information includes, but is not limited to, both internal (related to the organisation, the marketing mix, business and marketing strategies and tactics adopted, and internal resources available) and external information (related to customers, competitors, and other stakeholders, as well as available external resources, market dynamics and economic trends).

The definition of what to include in the concept of marketing information is fundamental if we want to gain a better understanding of information utilisation in firms. In fact, different companies have different market orientations, showing different attitudes towards the use of marketing information. A clear definition of marketing information is therefore helpful to frame the studies of information utilisation within specific boundaries drawn by the definition of marketing information itself.

Depending on the types and sources of information acquired, companies with more formalised marketing information available can make better informed decisions [70] because, in fact, they know more about their market, reduce uncertainty in their business activities, because they potentially know what to do and what to avoid doing, and add value to their supply chains [40] by providing their customers and consumers with what they really need or want. But what types of information do they need to make better decisions? And from what sources?

The types and sources of marketing information used by SMEs are mostly informal [39]. However, we argue that SMEs need formalised marketing information, which includes data on suppliers, buyers, competitors and national, global, economic, sociocultural and technological trends [63]. Accurate information should be seen as important because it is helpful to the company (as it is instrumental to its decision-making), but this importance may be influenced by several SME characteristics, such as the type of marketing strategy adopted, the size of the company, and consequently, the available resources that can be invested in order to acquire information. Nevertheless, marketing information could also include internal data relative to the performance of the firm (e.g., turnover, sales growth, innovation related information, new products launches, and so on).

In the same way, the quality and reliability of the source of information used should be instrumental to the SME marketing decision-making process and may contribute to a higher or lower use of information.

Thus, this may be true for customer-orientated firms, as non-customer oriented SMEs may not see the value of marketing information.

Amongst entrepreneurs, the most frequently used sources of information (often non-formalised) are family and friends [18], customers [69] and competitors [5–6]. Among the different sources of information firms use, we might also find market reports from marketing companies, governmental agencies and statistical services, category or trade associations, and specialised press or sector publications, as well as consultants.

Those companies that use formalised marketing information show a preference for secondary, rather than primary, sources of information [85]. This is understandable, as most SMEs have few resources (both in terms of financial and human capital) to engage in primary research and data collection. This point could be related to the level of proactivity the SME shows, since the chosen source is affected by how proactive the owner-manager is in seeking further business insight.

Ideas are often developed from informal verbal exchanges, and the closest sources of information for the company to access consist of those related to market channels [39], family and friends [18], customers [69] and competitors [5–6]. However, not all firms segment their market in the same way, and the type of source used may be affected by the strength of consumers' segmentation awareness in the SME. Perhaps business-owners need to adopt a systematic, skilful way of collecting, analysing and monitoring certain amounts of quality information from the marketplace in order to minimise risk when planning marketing activities. It seems sensible to propose that the more marketing information is used to support decision-making, the greater the probability is that the company will make the right choices within their competitive environment. However, this may be dependent upon both SMEs' characteristics and business owners' personal characteristics.

6.3 Marketing intelligence: SMEs' and owner-managers' characteristics

Although marketing intelligence has been proven to be important to support marketing decision-making and to foster growth, a market orientation is needed to be able to engage with marketing intelligence. The market orientation of a firm is affected by the personal characteristics of the small business owner, as well as some organisational characteristics typical to the SME, such number of employees and organisational structure. This affects whether marketing intelligence takes place in the firm, and if it does, the way that it is conducted.

Previous studies on market intelligence focused on organisational characteristics rather than personal characteristics [23, 37, 50, 53, 55-56]. Among the SME organisational characteristics, current marketing and entrepreneurial literature indicates important characteristics affecting information utilisation: size, time, scope and scale of operations, business strategy, and customer orientation.

If we look at the SMEs' organisational characteristics, firm size appears to be important with regard to both the marketing and entrepreneurship literature. Small companies do not have all the resources (both human and financial capital) which are available to larger organisations. Therefore, larger firms can formally access marketing information and have trained personnel available to analyse data and extract relevant information. Size should not be determined according to the relative quantitative size as defined by standard classifications determined by governmental bodies [12], because other qualitative characteristics than mere size metrics should be taken into consideration in order to gain a clearer idea of a firm's size.

Among the qualitative characteristics to take into consideration are 'the scope and the scale of operations, the independence and the nature of their ownership arrangements, and their management style' [12]. The more resources that are available to a firm, the higher the likelihood is that the information is used frequently, provided the firm acquires useful information and is able to identify its value.

Other than size, the lack of time dedicated to the scanning and utilisation of information may hamper information use. If it is taken into consideration, the time and money that the SME should spend in order to obtain enough information to make better decisions engaging with marketing intelligence may simply not be considered feasible by the firm [90]. This may be particularly true in smaller firms, which lack human capital (expertise, know-how and dedicated personnel) and financial capital (cash availability). Furthermore, the legitimacy of the firm in the environment and their level of expertise might be a barrier to the identification of the right sources of information, because SMEs often use informal networks to acquire it, and informal networks need time to be built and nurtured.

Another characteristic of organisations that affects information utilisation is the scope and scale of operations (including distribution). Information is needed in cases of uncertainty, and the moment of expansion of business operations is critical, as the marketing decision-making needs as much accurate information as possible in order not to interfere with the right scaling (either up or down) of existing operations. A mistake in the scope and scale of operations might increase costs, due to increased stock in the warehouse or a loss of business because they were unable to supply enough goods to customers. The scope and scale of operations are connected to the presence or absence of resources, and, to a certain extent, to the overall business strategy. In fact, business strategy affects the choice of marketing strategy that is adopted. In SMEs, quite often the marketing strategy is not reflected in a traditional theoretical marketing framework, and marketing activities are 'simplistic, haphazard, often responsive and reactive to competitor activity' [12].

Also, the business strategy pursued affects the engagement with marketing intelligence. Generally, marketing intelligence is associated with differentiation strategies rather than cost-leadership. Marketing decisions made by owner-managers or entrepreneurs are often based on intuitive ideas and common sense, rather than on formal data. Entrepreneurs and owner-managers differ in their strategic approach, due to differences in motivation, attitude and cognition [52, 66, 73]. However, SMEs are not totally incompatible with marketing [88], even in the case when the owner-manager is a generalist, without much marketing expertise [32]. In fact, SMEs have higher flexibility when it comes to adapting quickly to changes in both the market and the competitive environment. Information, therefore, becomes of critical importance to SME marketing strategy [7], and at the same time, an appropriate marketing strategy is based on marketing information.

A study by Beal [3] proved that the frequency of use of information is positively related to the SMEs strategic alignment with their environment (about which they need information to operate). By the strategic point of view, SMEs can achieve competitive advantage when using marketing information to inform their decision-making [54]; however, this advantage can be achieved just by SMEs engaging in information acquisition. SMEs without a strategic approach may not consider the acquisition of information, and this may be an indication of a lack of customer orientation [8-10].

Understanding consumers' needs is the starting point for good value creation practices and a valuable asset regarding marketing productivity [42]. Market-orientated companies generate greater marketing intelligence [57], because through it, they can gain 'a deep understanding of customers, such as their purchasing habits, psychological makeup and lifestyles [and] can…conduct better market segmentation and find new niche markets' [41].

Customer-orientated firms demonstrate a stronger focus on the customer (who purchases the product or service) or consumer (who consumes the product or service) and need marketing information in order to differentiate their offering for consumers, as well as to position themselves against competitors [41].

With regards to the business owner's personal characteristics, current literature suggests information utilisation is affected by gender, age, education, marketing expertise, previous experience, and entrepreneurial orientation.

If we look at the small business owners' personal characteristics, current marketing and entrepreneurship, we find literatures are supportive of the idea that information utilisation is affected by gender [4, 29, 34, 68]. Men and women acquire information differently [25], and the different way information needs are determined also affects the ability to identify marketing opportunities [13]. Gender not only affects the type of information sought, but also the source from which information is accessed and its frequency of use. Women's access to information is often hampered by existing male-dominated networks [84], and the types of networks women and men use are different, as is their cognition, with women appearing to be more meticulous in the type and frequency of use of information [10].

Another characteristic affecting information utilisation is the age of the owner-manager, which is often related to their work experience [78], although an old age is not always associated with lots of experience. Different ages correspond to different risk aversions, financial constraints, technological and market competencies [16], and networks: 'Sometimes entrepreneurs will consciously seek out information from certain individuals believed to have a contribution to make; on other occasions information will be gleaned subconsciously' [32]. Age affects the quality and quantity of social capital (networks and linkages) and therefore, the access to information [21].

Education is another characteristic affecting information utilisation, and it is related to innovative thinking [44]. Although educated business owners are more likely to have the knowledge, skills and contacts that may enable business, only a small percentage of graduates become entrepreneurs [20]; therefore, education is not the basis for entrepreneurship, although educated entrepreneurs might take advantage of their knowledge. Better knowledge does not translate necessarily into better entrepreneurial behaviour. Nevertheless, sometimes better educated business owners may be more skilled at identifying what type and source of information is more helpful to support their marketing decision-making. Less educated small business owners do struggle more than educated ones when trying to make sense out of abstract information.

A mix of education and experience is marketing expertise. It enables firms to engage with market intelligence, and those business owners who are better at marketing in general are more customer-focused and search for more detailed information about the marketplace [48, 59]. The lack of marketing expertise may also concretise in the inability to identify the right information sources [11] that would therefore limit SMEs' information use. Furthermore, given the constraints on their resources, SMEs do not have the possibility of outsourcing marketing expertise; therefore, many SMEs simply do not engage with marketing or, if they do it, it is informal and unplanned.

Marketing expertise often comes from previous working experience in the marketing field, and previous experience affects marketing capabilities in general [60]. More specifically, Tuominen et al. [80] support the notion that marketing capabilities are determined by the knowledge accumulated over the years working in the firm. In marketing research, they identify a core firm capability affected by cumulative working experience [79]. Previous experience matured within the same sector is generally beneficial to the success of business ventures.

A last characteristic affecting the engagement with marketing intelligence is entrepreneurial orientation (EO), a disposition or behaviour [19]. Some authors [82] believe EO is 'a firm-level disposition to engage in behaviours...that lead to change in the organisation or marketplace' involving 'risk taking, innovativeness, proactivity, autonomy and competitiveness', while others [58] accept the view that EO is a 'set of distinct but related behaviours that have the qualities of innovativeness, proactivity, competitiveness, risk taking and autonomy'. EO affects learning in firms [19], and entrepreneurially oriented small business owners learn from both the internal and external firm environments [24]. EO appears to be a behaviour, rather than a disposition, since learning is a cognitive action that requires conscious information use, and an enhanced EO pushes entrepreneurs to search and gather more information to support their marketing decision-making.

References

[1] Aguilar FJ. Scanning the Business Environment. New York: Macmillan Publishing; 1967.
[2] Andrus DD, Norvell DW, McIntyre P, Milner L. Marketing Planning in Inc., 500 Companies. In: Hills G, editor. Research at the Marketing/Entrepreneurhsip Interface. Chicago, IL: University of illinois at Chicago Press; 1987, pp. 215–31.

[3] Beal RM. Competing effectively: environmental scanning, competitive strategy, and organizational performance in small manufacturing firms. Journal of Small Business Management. 2000; 38 (1): 27–47.
[4] Bird B, Brush C. A gendered perspective on organizational creation. Entrepreneurship: Theory & Practice. 2002; 26(3): 41–65.
[5] Brush CG. marketplace information scanning practices of new manufacturing ventures. Journal of Small Business Management. 1992; Vol. 30 (4 [October]): pp. 41–53.
[6] Brush CG, Peters MP. Market information scanning practices of new service ventures: the impact of owner/founder experience. Entrepreneurial Management Working Paper 92 3 11992.
[7] Butler J, Keh H, Chamornmarn W. Information acquisition, entrepreneurial performance and the evolution of modern Thai retailing. Journal of Asian Business. 2000; 16(2): 1–23.
[8] Cacciolatti L, Fearne A. Marketing intelligence in SMEs: implications for the industry and policy makers. Marketing Intelligence & Planning. 2013; 31(1): 4–26.
[9] Cacciolatti L, Fearne A, Ihua B, Yawson D. Types, Sources and frequency of use of formalised marketing information as a catalyst of SME growth. Journal of Strategic Management Education. 2012; 8(1): 1–24.
[10] Cacciolatti L, Wan T. A study of small business owners' personal characteristics and the use of marketing information in the food and drink industry: a resource-based perspective. International Journal on Food System Dynamics. 2013; 3(2): 171–84.
[11] Callahan T, Cassar M. Small business owners' assessments of their abilities to perform and interpret formal market studies. Journal of Small Business Management. 1995; 33(4): 1–9.
[12] Carson D, Cromie S. Marketing planning in small enterprises: a model and some empirical evidence. Journal of Consumer Marketing. 1990; Vol. 7(No. 3): 5–18.
[13] Chaganti R, Parasuraman S. A study of the impacts of gender on business performance and management patterns in small businesses. Entrepreneurship Theory and Practice. 1996; 21(2): 73–5.
[14] Clark J. Entrepreneurship and diversification on English farms: Identifying business enterprise characteristics and change processes. Entrepreneurship & Regional Development. 2009; 21(2): 213–36.
[15] Clark KM, Fujimoto T. Product Development Performance: Strategy, Organization, and Management in the World Auto Industry. 1991. Boston: Harvard Business School Press.
[16] Colombo MG, Delmastro M. Technology-based entrepreneurs: does internet make a difference? Small Business Economics. 2001; 16(1): 177–90.
[17] Conant JS, White C. Marketing program planning, process benefits and store performance: an initial study among small retail firms. Journal of Retailing. 1999; Vol. 75 (No. 4): pp. 525–41.
[18] Cooper A, Woo C, Dunkelberg W. Entrepreneurship and the initial size of firms. Journal of Business Venturing. 1989; Vol. 4 (5): pp. 317–32.
[19] Covin JG, Lumpkin GT. Entrepreneurial orientation theory and research: reflections on a needed construct. Entrepreneurship: Theory & Practice. 2011; 35(5): 855–72.

[20] David P, Gary P, Paul J, Christopher M, Brychan T. Graduate entrepreneurs are different: they access more resources? International Journal of Entrepreneurial Behaviour & Research. [DOI: 10.1108/13552551111114932]. 2011; 17(2): 183–202.

[21] Davidsson P, Honig B. The role of social and human capital among nascent entrepreneurs. Journal of Business Venturing. 2003; 18(1): 301–31.

[22] Day GS. Learning about Markets. Cambridge, MA: Marketing Science Institute1991.

[23] Deshpande R, Zaltman G. Factors affecting the use of market research information: a path analysis. Journal of Marketing Research. 1982; Vol. 19 (1 [February]): pp. 14–31.

[24] Dess GG, Ireland RD, Zahra SA, Floyd SW, Janney JJ, Lane PJ. Emerging issues in corporate entrepreneurship. Journal of Management. 2003; 29(1): 351–78.

[25] DeTienne DR, Chandler GN. The role of gender in opportunity identification. Entrepreneurship: Theory & Practice. 2007; 31(3): 365–86.

[26] Dickson PR. Toward a general theory of competitive rationality. Journal of Marketing. 1992; Vol. 56 (January): pp. 69–83.

[27] Dollinger M. Environmental contact and performance of the smaller firm. Journal of Small Business Management. 1985; Vol. 23 (January): pp. 24–30.

[28] Fahey L, King WR. Environmental scanning for corporate planning. Business Horizons. 1977; Vol. 20 (August): pp. 61–71.

[29] Finkelstein S, Hambrick DC. Top management team tenure and organizational outcomes: the moderating role of managerial discretion. Administrative Science Quarterly. 1990; 35(3): 484–503.

[30] Fornell C, Rust RT, Dekimpe MG. The effect of customer satisfaction on consumer spending growth. Journal of Marketing Research. 2010; Vol. 47(No. 1): pp. 28–35.

[31] Gaskill LR, Van Auken HE, Manning RA. A factor analytic study of the perceived causes of small business failure. Journal of Small Business Management. 1993; Vol. 31 (No. 4): pp. 18–31.

[32] Gilmore A, Carson D and Grant K. (2001) SME marketing in practice. *Marketing Intelligence & Planning* 19 (1): 6–11.

[33] Glazer R, Steckel J, Winer R. Locally rational decision making: the distracting effect of information on managerial performance. Management Science. 1992; Vol. 38 (February): pp. 212–26.

[34] Hambrick DC, Mason PA. Upper echelons: the organization as a reflection of its top managers. Academy of Management Review. 1984; 9(2): 193–206.

[35] Hills GE and Narayana CL. (1989) *Profile Characteristics, Success Factors, and Marketing in Highly Successful Firms*. Wellesley, MA: Babson College Conferrence on Entrepreneurship, pp. 69–80.

[36] Hisrich RD, Peters MP. The need for marketing in entrepreneurship. Journal of Consumer Marketing. 1992; Vol. 9 (September): pp. 43–7.

[37] Hutt MD, Reingen PH, Ronchetto JR. Tracing emergent processes in marketing strategy formation. Journal of Marketing. 1988; Vol. 52 (1 January): pp. 4–19.

[38] Jaworski BJ, Kohli AK. Market orientation: antecedents and consequences. Journal of Marketing. 1993; Vol. 57 (July): pp. 53–71.

[39] Johnson JL, Kuehn R. The small business owner/manager's search for external information. Journal of Small Business Management. 1987; Vol. 25 (3 June): pp. 53–60.
[40] Kaplan JM, Warren AC. Patterns of Entrepreneurship. 2nd ed. Hoboken, NJ: John Wiley & Sons, Inc.; 2007.
[41] Keh HT, Nguyen TTM, Ng HP. The effects of entrepreneurial orientation and marketing information on the performance of SMEs. Journal of Business Venturing. [DOI: 10.1016/j.jbusvent.2006.05.003]. 2007; 22(4): 592–611.
[42] Keller KL. conceptualizing, measuring, managing customer-based brand equity. Journal of Marketing. 1993; Vol. 57 (No. 1): pp. 1–22.
[43] Kirca AH, Jayachandran S, Bearden WO. market orientation: a meta-analytic review and assessment of its antecedents and impact on performance. The Journal of Marketing. 2005; 69(2): 24–41.
[44] Koellinger P. Why are some entrepreneurs more innovative than others? Small Business Economics. 2008; 31(1): 21–37.
[45] Kohli AK, Jaworski BJ. Marketing Orientation: The construct, research propositions, and managerial implications. Journal of Marketing. 1990; Vol. 54 (April): pp. 1–18.
[46] Levy M, Powell P. Strategies for Growth in SMEs. Oxford: Elsevier Butterworth-Heinemann; 2005.
[47] Mahajan J. The overconfidence effect in marketing management predictions. Journal of Marketing Research. 1992; Vol. 24 (August): pp. 329–42.
[48] Matsuno K, Mentzer JT, Aysegul O. The effects of entrepreneurial proclivity and market orientation on business performance. Journal of Marketing. 2002; 66(3): 18–32.
[49] McCartan-Quinn D, Carson D. Issues which impact upon marketing in the small firms. Small Business Economics. 2003; 21(2): 201–13.
[50] Menon A, Varadarajan PR. A model of marketing knowledge use within firms. Journal of Marketing. 1992; Vol. 56 (4 October): pp. 53–71.
[51] Meziou F. Areas of strength and weakness in the adoption of the marketing concept by small manufacturing firms. Journal of Small Business Management. 1991; Vol. 29 (August): pp. 72–8.
[52] Mitchell RK, Busenitz L, Lant T, McDougall PP, Morse EA, Smith JB. toward a theory of entrepreneurial cognition: rethinking the people side of entrepreneurship research. Entrepreneurship: Theory & Practice. Winter 2002; 27(2): 93–104.
[53] Mohr J, Nevin JR. Communication strategies in marketing channels. Journal of Marketing. 1990; Vol. 54 (4 October): pp. 36–51.
[54] Moorman C. Organizational market information processes: cultural antecedents and new product outcomes. Journal of Marketing Research. 1995; 32(3): 318–35.
[55] Moorman C, Deshpande R, Zaltman G. Factors affecting trust in market research relationships. Journal of Marketing. 1993; Vol. 57(1 January): pp. 81–101.
[56] Moorman C, Zaltman G, Deshpande R. Relationships between providers and users of market research: the dynamics of trust within and between organizations. Journal of Marketing Research. 1992; Vol. 29 (3 August): pp. 314–29.

[57] Morgan NA, Vorhies DW, Mason CH. Market orientation, marketing capabilities, and firm performance. Strategic Management Journal. 2009; 30(8): 909–20.
[58] Pearce JA, Fritz P, Davis PS. Entrepreneurial orientation and the performance of religious congregations as predicted by rational choice theory. Entrepreneurship Theory and Practice. 2010; 34(1): 219–48.
[59] Pelham AM, Wilson DT. A longitudinal study of the impact of market structure, firm structure, strategy, and market orientation culture on dimensions of small-firm performance. Journal of the Academy of Marketing Science. Winter 1996; 24(1): 27.
[60] Pérez-Cabañero C, González-Cruz T, Cruz-Ros S. Do family SME managers value marketing capabilities' contribution to firm performance? Marketing Intelligence & Planning. 2012;30(2): 116–42.
[61] Perry R. The relationship between written business plans and the failure of small businesses in the US. International Journal of Retail and Distribution Management. 2000;Vol. 39 (No. 3): pp. 201–8.
[63] Peters MP, Brush CG. Market information scanning activities and growth in new ventures: A comparison of service and manufacturing businesses. Journal of Business Research. 1996; 36(1): 81–9.
[64] Robinson RB, Pearce JA. Research thrusts in small firm strategic planning. Academy of Management Review. 1984; Vol. 9 pp. 128–37.
[65] Rudelius W, Hartley SW, Gobeli DH. Managerial Activities in Independent and Corporate Sponsored New Ventures. In: Parker LA, editor. Research at the Marketing/Entrepreneurship Interface. Chicago, IL: The University of Illinois at Chicago Press; 1989, pp. 63–74.
[66] Shane S. A General Theory of Entrepreneurship: The Individual-Opportunity Nexus. Northampton, MA: Edward Elgar; 2003.
[67] Shapiro BP. What the hell is 'market oriented?' Harvard Business Review. 1988; 66(6): 119–25.
[68] Singh SP, Reynolds RG, Muhammad S. A gender-based performance analysis of micro and small enterprises in Java, Indonesia. Journal of Small Business Management. 2001; 39(2): 174–82.
[69] Smeltzer LR, Fann GL, Nikoliasen VN. Environmental scanning practices in small business. Journal of Small Business Management. 1988; Vol. 26 (3 [July]): pp. 55–62.
[70] Spender JC, Kessler EH. Managing the uncertainties of innovation: extending Thompson. Human Relations. 1995; Vol. 48 (No. 1): pp. 35–56.
[71] Stevenson H, Roberts M, Grousbeck HI. New Business Ventures and the Entrepreneur. Homewook, IL: Richard D. Irwin Inc.; 1989.
[72] Stewart WH, May RC, Kalia A. Environmental perceptions and scanning in the United States and India: convergence in entrepreneurial information seeking? Entrepreneurship: Theory & Practice. 2008; 32(1): 83–106.
[73] Stewart WJ, Roth P. Risk propensity differences between entrepreneurs and managers: a meta-analytic review. Journal of Applied Psychology. 2001; 86(1): 145–53.
[74] Stoner CR. Planning in small manufacturing firms: A survey. Journal of Small Business Management. 1983; Vol. 21 (1 [January]): pp. 34–41.
[75] Thompson JD. Organizations in Action: Social Science Bases of Administrative Theory. New York: McGraw-Hill; 1967.

[76] Thong JYL. Resource constraints and information systems implementation in Singaporean small businesses. Omega. [DOI: 10.1016/S03050483(00)00035-9]. 2001; 29 (2): 143–56.
[77] Timmons JA. New Venture Creation. 2nd ed. Homewood, IL: Richard D. Irwin Inc.; 1985.
[78] Tocher N, Rutherford MW. Perceived acute human resource management problems in small and medium firms: an empirical examination. Entrepreneurship: Theory & Practice. 2009; 33 (2): 455–79.
[79] Tuominen M, Möller K, Anttila M. Marketing capability of marketing oriented organizations. 28th EMAC Conference Proceedings; Berlin, 1999. p. 680–700.
[80] Tuominen M, Möller K, Rajala A. Marketing capability: a nexus of learning-based resources and a prerequisite for market orientation. 26th EMAC Conference Proceedings; Warwick, 1997, p. 1220–40.
[81] Vesper K. New Venture Strategies. Englewood Cliffs, NJ: Prentice Hall Inc.; 1990.
[82] Voss ZG, Voss GB, Moorman C. An empirical examination of the complex relationships between entrepreneurial orientation and stakeholder support. European Journal of Marketing. 2005; 39 (9/10): 1132–50.
[83] Vozikis GS, Mescon TS. Marketing and Management Problems over Stages of Organizational and Exporting Development. In: Hills G, editor. Research at the Marketing/Entrepreneurship Interface. Chicago, IL: The University of Illinois at Chicago Press; 1987, pp. 214–31.
[84] Weiler S, Bernasek A. Dodging the glass ceiling? Networks and the new wave of women entrepreneurs. The Social Science Journal. 2001; 38 (1): pp. 85–103.
[85] Weinrauch DJ, Mann OK, Robinson PA, Pharr J. dealing with limited financial resources: a marketing challenge for small business. Journal of Small Business Management. 1991; October: pp. 44–54.
[86] Westhead P, Ucbasran D, Wright M. Information search and opportunity identification: the importance of prior business ownership experience. International Small Business Journal. 2009; Vol. 27 (No. 6): pp. 659–79.
[87] Wilton PC, Meyers JG. Task, expectancy, and information assessment effects in information utilization processes. Journal of Consumer Research. 1986; Vol. 12 (March): pp. 469–86.
[88] Wong HY, Merrilees B. A brand orientation typology for SMEs: a case research approach. Journal of Product & Brand Management. 2005; Vol. 14 (No. 3): pp. 155–62.
[89] Yeoh P-L. A conceptual framework of antecedents of information search in exporting: Importance of ability and motivation. International Marketing Review. 2005; Vol. 22 (No. 2): pp. 165–98.
[90] Zahra SA, Neubaum DO, El-Hagrassey GM. Competitive analysis and new venture performance: understanding the impact of strategic uncertainty and venture origin*. Entrepreneurship: Theory & Practice. 2002; 27(1): 1–28.

7
Internationalisation Strategies

7.1 Internationalisation: enablers, motives and models

7.1.1 Enablers of internationalisation

In spite of several years of economic crisis in the Eurozone that pushed firms all over the world to reengage with international marketing strategic thinking [1], globalisation brought lots of opportunities to SMEs. These have been generated by some changes in the business environment, and three major forces enabled SMEs to access internationalisation opportunities, entering this way in direct competition with larger organisations [2, 3].

While marketing and entrepreneurship literature maintained in the past that only MNEs had the proper characteristics to operate on international markets, more recent evidence [4–6] shows that size is not correlated with export intensity, exporting SMEs are heterogeneous [7], and their structures and orientations [8] are often very different one from each other.

In current SME and international marketing literature, it is widely acknowledged that three main forces drive the internationalisation of a company [9]; first is the decrease in price to access and use technology that allows connectivity [10], both intended to connect people and locations. Improvements in information technology and telecommunications allow a wider and quicker spreading of information about opportunities at the international level [11]. Telecommunications eliminated the physical frontiers and allowed people around the world to connect and share information, thereby improving business opportunities.

The second force that changes internationalisation opportunities and strategies is a radical change in different countries' institutional environment. Changes in international economic policy led to a gradual but constant demolition of trade barriers, facilitated by financial deregulation. Therefore, the agreement among countries to undersign treaties that allow more freedom in the circulation of goods and people (e.g., within the EU) allowed an improvement of innovation capabilities and capacity in firms.

The third force that played an important role in shaping internationalisation opportunities consists of world economic

restructuring and liberalization that followed the fall of socialism in Russia and Central/Eastern Europe, as well as the geographical expansion of markets in Asia, particularly China. These previously closed areas are now new markets and magnets for investment, opening further opportunities for growth and investment [9].

Internationalisation characterise our business reality. The impact of these three main forces on firms' internationalisation process is greater on SMEs than on larger organisations, which have consolidated experience in internationalisation; however, this is totally new to SMEs. These forces gave SMEs the opportunity to achieve internationalisation and enter into competition with larger players. SMEs are now active players who not only manage to compete with large companies successfully, but also to push economic growth through their exports [12].

Given the opportunities that emerged with the effect of lower technological costs, a dismantling of financial barriers and trade barriers, and the emergence of new markets, new opportunities are available to SMEs, and these can be pursued by small business owners within the measure of entrepreneurs' motives for internationalisation.

7.1.2 Motives of internationalisation

In SMEs, the entrepreneur's personal characteristics deeply affect the direction of the business. Likewise, when discussing the internationalisation of SMEs, we have to consider that the personality of the small business owner plays an essential role in determining whether the company will engage with internationalisation activities or would rather keep operating in the domestic market.

Business growth in a company often corresponds to the need for expansion of its business activities; therefore, both the concepts of growth and internationalisation are linked [13, 14]. Research, so far, has focused on the internationalising of SME's activities and operations [15–17], and on network analyses [18–20]. However, the commonality amongst the different studies is that internationalisation is driven by either proactive or reactive motives.. For a full and detailed discussion of internationalisation motives in a more general context, we refer to Hollensen [21].

Proactive motives are profit and growth goals, managerial urge, technology competence / unique product, knowledge of a foreign market opportunity, and economies of scale. Proactive motives for internationalisation are drivers for expansion [22]. Sometimes organisations increase their sales and their profits, and, along with that, they move their signpost in turnover targets and realise that internationalisation is often a quick and viable way to grow profits. Therefore, there may be a situation when the board of directors of a company (or the entrepreneur and his/her close collaborators) decide to boost the firm growth rate and – by the effects of some managerial urge – opt for engaging with foreign markets. This managerial urge is often motivated by the competitive scenario of the business environment the SME operates in and, in some areas of business, SMEs may move into a market and benefit from the first mover advantage.

Along with financial motives, we can find the need for complementarity in technological competencies, for instance, when an SME finds a potential partner in another country which has complementary capabilities with respect to the focus company. The collaboration of the two firms on different aspects of the business venture can help them increase efficiency and effectiveness in their operations, with an integration of technical knowledge, skills, manufacturing operations and know-how and knowledge of the local foreign market.

Often, the ownership of a patent, which gives the firm a competitive advantage, is a strong economic motive for internationalisation, as this would give access to new markets other than the domestic one and potentially help the company to foster growth in more than a single market. In fact, if the internationalising firm provides the technical expertise to design the product and its manufacturing processes, the local company in the foreign market often focuses on manufacturing and distributing the product, due to their knowledge of the local market.

Finally, another economic motive for internationalisation is the necessity of creating economies of scale which allow the internationalising SME to benefit from lowering manufacturing costs and expanding production and distribution in the foreign market [23]. However, along with these proactive models, we can find some reactive motives:

- Competitive pressures
- Domestic market: small and saturated
- Overproduction or excess of inventory
- Excess capacity
- Unsolicited foreign orders

Sometimes the competitive pressure in the domestic market is too high, and the firm has no alternatives other than opting for internationalisation. Also, along with fierce competition and the need for the company to find a niche market abroad, in very small domestic markets, the demand for a specific product can be unsustainable with respect to the offer of that specific product; therefore, the market saturates quickly because it is too small. In such cases, then, the company has no alternative and is pushed to react to the current market situation and opt for internationalisation.

While in some cases high competition or saturation of a small market are motives prompting the company to internationalise, we also see that sometimes the overproduction of a specific product or an overall excess of inventory cannot be distributed or sold within the domestic market. Again, in such cases, firms may start looking at exporting to other markets that may well be able to absorb the excess in production.

Finally, sometimes firms do not think of internationalising until they get an unsolicited order from abroad. This may allow the opening of an opportunity to initiate exports towards a different country. Likewise, internationalisation may be also motivated by the personal networks of the small business owner or by the entrepreneur's personal experience dealing with a specific country.

7.1.3 Models of internationalisation

Most of the current models for internationalisation of firms were developed for multinational enterprises (MNEs) or large organisations. Currently, the basis for the internationalisation of the individual firm can be found in the work developed by researchers in the areas of organisation behaviour and decision-making theories [24, 25], or in trade theories, which offer a market perspective [26], although the market perspective on SMEs internationalisation is often affected by theories rooted in economic studies such as Dunning [27] or Mahoney and Pandian [28].

While the focus of current research on SMEs internationalisation is on the market perspective, highlighting the economic aspects of internationalisation, rather than offering a more entrepreneurial perspective, current research on internationalisation developed different stages of understanding of the phenomenon, depending on the size of the firms studied [9]. For instance, Ruzzier reports, [9]

> Although global strategies, strategic international alliances, and problems of diversification and control are concepts frequently encountered, the discussion focuses almost exclusively on large firms or the

so-called multinational enterprises (MNEs). Small entrepreneurial business research is more concerned with various stages (or export development models) of internationalization. In spite of the gap between the two lines of research, both build on the foundations of organization theory, although significant differences have resulted. Attempts to apply theories developed or based on large firms may lead to relatively awkward results when applied to smaller businesses as ideas develop for large firms do not necessarily work in a small business setting.

In what follows, we quickly mention the main theories and approaches to internationalisation commonly acknowledged in marketing and entrepreneurship literature; however, we also point out these approaches are mainly built on the assumption of size. We then discuss a different perspective in a bit more detail; international entrepreneurship, which was proposed to accommodate SMEs internationalisation. This is a list of the main models of internationalisation currently found in the literature:

- Uppsala internationalisation model (U-model)
- Innovation-related model (I-model)
- Network approach
- Resource-based approach
- International entrepreneurship

The Uppsala model is named after a group of Northern European scholars who were referred to as the Uppsala School in the 1970s. The Uppsala model was developed by Johanson and Vahlne [29-31]. According to Ruzzier [9],

> In this dynamic model, internationalization of the firm is seen as a process of increasing a company's international involvement as a result of different types of learning. According to the model, the authors propose that the general and experiential market knowledge and resource commitment of firms (state aspects) affect commitment decision and current business activities (change aspects). The change aspects, in turn, increase the market knowledge and stimulate further resource commitment to foreign markets in the subsequent cycle...This model implies that firms increase their international involvement in small incremental steps within those foreign markets in which they currently operate. Firms will then enter new markets lying at a greater "psychic distance" due to differences in languages, education, business practices etc. (p. 482).

In this type of model, the focus is on the resources allocated to internationalisation and the level of commitment to the venture [32].

The second approach to explain the dynamics of internationalisation is proposed by the I-model, developed by Cavusgil [33, 34] and revived by Gankema et al. [35]. The I-model conceptualises the internationalisation process as composed of five aspects (or stages), which involves considering the following:

- Domestic marketing
- Pre-export
- Experimental involvement
- Active involvement
- Commitment involvement

All these aspects affect entrepreneurial decision-making, and, despite the lack of resources typical of small firms, global firms internationalise because of a specific mix of orientations and strategies determining their success in international markets.

The third approach to internationalisation is the network approach developed by Johanson et al. [36] and then revised by several other authors [19, 37, 38]. This model belongs to the category of stage theories, and was originally developed because

> international interdependence between firms and within industries is of great and increasing importance. Analyses of international trade, international investments, industrial organisation and international business behaviour attempt to describe, explain and give advice about these interdependencies... we discuss explanations of internationalisation of industrial firms with the aid of a model that describes industrial markets as networks of relationships between firms. The reason for this exercise is a belief that the network model, being superior to some other models of "markets", makes it possible to consider some important interdependences and development processes on international markets (p. 287) [39].

Ruzzier indicates [9]

> In the model of Johanson and Mattson (1993) the emphasis is on gradual learning and the development of market knowledge through interaction within networks. A firm's position in the network may

be considered both from a micro (firm-to-firm) or a macro (firm-to-network) perspective. From the micro perspective, complementary as well as competitive relationships are crucial elements of the internationalization process. In other words, firms are interdependent both through co-operation and competition. Both direct (involving partners in the network) and indirect (involving firms that are not partners in the network) relations within networks need to be taken into account when analysing macro relationships (p. 484).

Another approach to internationalisation is the resource-based approach, which capitalises on a whole body of theory related to the RBV (resource-based view) of the firm. Given the vast body of literature in this specific area, there are only a few seminal studies [40–42] and some more recent ones [43–45] that we refer readers to.

Ultimately, the approach that deserves more attention – because it focuses specifically on SMEs – has been adopted in international entrepreneurship. The main criticism of the previous models lies in their MNE focus. One criticism of the resource-based approach is that it does not account for individuals' strategic choices or radical change [46], while current literature recognises the importance of entrepreneurial in the marketplace [47].

International entrepreneurship is an intersection of international business and entrepreneurship as [48] 'cross-border business activity is of increasing interest to entrepreneurship researchers, and accelerated internationalization is being observed in even the smallest and newest organizations' (p. 902). International entrepreneurship is currently seen as a

> combination of innovative, risk-seeking behaviour that crosses national borders and is intended to create value in organization.... International entrepreneurship will be labelled a research approach to the internationalization of SMEs from the entrepreneurial perspective, which best integrates all the relevant approaches to internationalization with entrepreneurship, as a composite part of SMEs' internationalization [9] (p. 489).

7.2 Internationalisation strategies

Internationalisation strategies are well known in current marketing and entrepreneurship literatures, with good textbooks summarising past and current theories on internationalisation strategies and market entry modes (e.g., Hollensen) [21].

Recent research on internationalisation strategies in an SME context [49, 50] indicates that for SMEs, the process is highly dynamic and takes place at different stages of the development of international activities:

Most research on a firm's internationalisation process considers it to be an expansion of activities, i.e., entry into new markets and use of increasingly resource intensive internationalisation modes (Johanson and Vahlne, 1977). We add to this by considering that firms may also divest or de-internationalise (see Fletcher, 2001; Welch and Luostarinen, 1988; Benito and Welch, 1997; Pauwels and Matthyssens, 1999; Crick, 2004), i.e., withdraw from markets and use lower resource commitment modes (p. 1450) [49].

In an SME context, internationalisation strategies are modes of operating in a foreign market. Sometimes internationalisation is a synonym for international market [49] in that 'a change in strategy, thus, occurs when a firm changes in which markets it conducts business, or when it changes which modes are used' (p. 1451). Agndal and Chetty [49] recognise four main types of strategies SMEs use in international markets: market expansion, market contraction, new high commitment mode, and new low commitment mode.

Market expansion refers to a mode that allows the SME to enter a new market, while market contraction refers to withdrawal from it. The new high commitment mode takes place when an SME starts a process of internationalisation in a mode unfamiliar to the company that requires the employment of further resources. In low commitment mode, resources are divested and reallocated to lower the resource commitment to internationalisation.

While previous studies argued a sequential and incremental approach to SMEs' internationalisation, current literature maintains,

In such a context, the findings from earlier studies into the internationalisation of SMEs may no longer be totally applicable (Bilkey & Tesar, 1977; Cavusgil, 1984; Johanson & Vahlne, 1977; Johanson & Wiedersheim-Paul, 1975; Pavord & Bogart, 1975). For example, the "stage" models of internationalisation, suggest that SMEs enter overseas markets in a systematic and sequential way, evolving towards riskier means of market penetration and more demanding countries once domestic sales had been well established and enough management learning (experience) and resources have been acquired. Hence, companies evolve from being non-exporters to becoming large experienced exporters in several stages, depending on the respective authors' classifications (Andersen, 1993; Coviello & McAuley, 1999; Leonidou & Katsikeas, 1996). These studies, however, have been criticised for not fully capturing the complexity of the realities of internationalising SMEs, especially in the high-technology sectors, where environmental variables change constantly (Bell, 1995; Bell, Crick, & Young, 1998; Bell & Young, 1998; Knight & Cavusgil, 1996; Turnbull, 1987) (p. 169) [50].

More recently, it was found that the strategies mentioned above are affected by SMEs' ability to network. Crick and Spence [50] argue,

Networks are strongly relied upon by SMEs at the beginning of a firm's internationalisation, in particular to select and expand into foreign markets as they facilitate the acquisition of experiential knowledge about these markets (Lindqvist, 1997). Face-to-face encounters with potential business partners and clients, business representatives and ordinary citizens allow internationalising SMEs to get a feel for the market, to gain insight in to how business is conducted, to demonstrate interest, and to start the building of trust (Wilson & Mummalaneni, 1990). Networks also speed internationalisation by providing synergistic relationships with other firms, small and large, which complement each other's resources at various stages in the value chain (Dana, Etemad, & Wright, 1999; Jones, 1999). A number of private and public initiatives to help SMEs position themselves in appropriate networks have been developed and therefore the role of advisors and policy makers should not be overlooked. For example, trade associations organise various activities aimed at facilitating contacts between domestic and foreign business executives. Subsidised government programmes for SMEs also encourage the establishment of networks that may result in knowledge development and joint activities (Spence, 2000; Welch, Welch, Young, & Makino, 1997). Consequently, it can be argued that certain elements of the networking approach to business strategy can explain firms' internationalisation. (p. 171)

Therefore, SMEs' internationalisation strategies should always be considered with respect to the social role the SME plays in its business environment.

References

[1] Beinhocker E, Davis I, Mendonca L. The 10 trends you have to watch. Harvard Business Review. 2009; 87 (7/8): pp. 55–60.
[2] Friedman TL. The World is Flat: A Brief History of the Twenty-First Century. 2006, London: Macmillan;
[3] Ghemawat P. World 3.0: Global Prosperity and How to Achieve It. 2011, Boston, MA: Harvard Business Press.
[4] Calof JL. The relationship between firm size and export behavior revisited. Journal of International Business Studies. 1994, 25(2); pp. 367–87.
[5] Philp NE. The export propensity of the very small enterprise (VSE). International Small Business Journal, 1998; 16 (4): pp. 79–93.
[6] Fernández Z, Nieto MJ. Internationalization strategy of small and medium-sized family businesses: some influential factors. Family Business Review. 2005; 18 (1): pp. 77–89.
[7] Julien P-A et al. A typology of strategic behaviour among small and medium-sized exporting businesses. A case study. International Small Business Journal. 1997; 15 (2): pp. 33–50.
[8] Julien P-A, Ramangalahy C. Competitive strategy and performance of exporting SMEs: An empirical investigation of the impact of their export information search and competencies. Entrepreneurship Theory and Practice. 2003; 27 (3): pp. 227–45.
[9] Ruzzier M, Hisrich RD, Antoncic B. SME internationlization research: past, present, and future. Journal of Small Business and Enterprise Development. 2006; 13 (4): pp. 476–97.
[10] Acs, Z. (2006). How is entrepreneurship good for economic growth?. Innovations, 1(1), 97–107.
[11] Acs ZJ, Morck RK, and Yeung B. Entrepreneurship, globalization, and public policy. Journal of International Management. 2001; 7 (3): pp. 235–51.
[12] Coviello NE, McAuley A. Internationalisation and the smaller firm: A review of contemporary empirical research. MIR: Management International Review. 1999; pp. 223–56.
[13] Buckley PJ. International technology transfer by small and medium sized enterprises. Small Business Economics. 1997; 9 (1): pp. 67–78.
[14] Buckley PJ, Chapman M. A longitudinal study of the internationalisation process in a small sample of pharmaceutical and scientific instrument companies. Journal of Marketing Management, 1997. 13(1–3): pp. 43–55.
[15] Korhonen H, Luostarinen R, Welch, L. Internationalization of SMEs: Inward-outward patterns and government policy. MIR: Management International Review, 1996; 36(4) pp. 315–29.
[16] Zhou L, Wu W-P, Luo X. Internationalization and the performance of born-global SMEs: the mediating role of social networks. Journal of International Business Studies. 2007; 38(4): pp. 673–90.
[17] Hollenstein H. Determinants of international activities: Are SMEs different? Small Business Economics. 2005; 24 (5): pp. 431–50.
[18] Madsen TK, Servais P. The internationalization of born globals: an evolutionary process? International Business Review. 1997; 6(6): pp. 561–83.

[19] Coviello N, Munro H. Network relationships and the internationalisation process of small software firms. International Business Review. 1997; 6 (4): pp. 361–86.
[20] Oviatt BM, McDougall PP. Defining international entrepreneurship and modeling the speed of internationalization. Entrepreneurship Theory and Practice. 2005, 29 (5): pp. 537–54.
[21] Hollensen S. Global Marketing: a Decision-Oriented Approach. Madrid, Spain: FT Prentice Hall, 2010.
[22] Westhead P et al. Internationalization of SMEs: a research note. Journal of Small Business and Enterprise Development. 2002; 9 (1): pp. 38–48.
[23] Westhead P, Wright M, Ucbasaran D. International market selection strategies selected by 'micro'and 'small'firms. Omega. 2002; 30 (1): pp. 51–68.
[24] Cyert RM, March JG. A Behavioral Theory of the Firm. Englewood Cliffs, NJ; 1963.
[25] Pitelis CN. A behavioral resource-based view of the firm: the synergy of Cyert and March (1963) and Penrose (1959). Organization Science. 2007; 18(3): pp. 478–90.
[26] Havnes P-A. Dynamics of small business internationalisation. A European panel study, Norway: Agder Research R&D Report no. 6/2003, 2003. "http://www.storre.stir.ac.uk/browse?type=affiliation&value=Stirling+Management+School" Stirling Management School.
[27] Dunning JH. The eclectic paradigm of international production: a restatement and some possible extensions. Journal of International Business Studies. 1988; 19(1); pp. 1–31.
[28] Mahoney JT, Pandian JR. The resource–based view within the conversation of strategic management. Strategic Management Journal. 1992; 13 (5): pp. 363–80.
[29] Johanson J, Vahlne J-E. Management of foreign market entry. Scandinavian International Business Review. 1992; 1 (3): pp. 9–27.
[30] Johanson J, Vahlne J-E. The internationalization process of the firm-a model of knowledge development and increasing foreign market commitments. Journal of International Business Studies. 1977; 8(1): pp. 23–32.
[31] Johanson J, Vahlne J-E. The Uppsala internationalization process model revisited: From liability of foreignness to liability of outsidership. Journal of International Business Studies. 2009; 40 (9): pp. 1411–31.
[32] Andersen O. On the internationalization process of firms: a critical analysis. Journal of International Business Studies. 1993; 24(2): pp. 209–31.
[33] Calantone RJ, Cavusgil, ST, Zhao, Y. Learning orientation, firm innovation capability, and firm performance. Industrial Marketing Management. 2002; 31 (6): pp. 515–24.
[34] Knight GA, Cavusgil ST. Innovation, organizational capabilities, and the born-global firm. Journal of International Business Studies. 2004; 35 (2): pp. 124–41.
[35] Gankema HG, Snuif HR, Zwart PS. The internationalization process of small and medium-sized enterprises: an evaluation of stage theory. Journal of Small Business Management. 2000; 38(4): pp. 15.
[36] Johanson J et al. Internationalization in industrial systems–a network approach. Strategies. 1988; pp. 287–314.

[37] Chetty S, Holm DB. Internationalisation of small to medium-sized manufacturing firms: a network approach. International Business Review. 2000; 9 (1): pp. 77–93.
[38] Bell J. The internationalization of small computer software firms: A further challenge to "stage" theories. European Journal of Marketing. 1995; 29 (8): pp. 60–75.
[39] Hood N, Vahlne J-E. Strategies in Global Competition: Selected Papers from the Prince Bertil Symposium at the Institute of International Business. 2013, London: Routledge.
[40] Wernerfelt B. A resource–based view of the firm. Strategic Management Journal. 1984; 5 (2): pp. 171–80.
[41] Foss NJ. The resource-based perspective: an assessment and diagnosis of problems. Scandinavian Journal of Management. 1998; 14 (3): pp. 133–49.
[42] Penrose ET. The Theory of the Growth of the Firm. Oxford: Oxford University Press; 1995.
[43] Peteraf MA. The cornerstones of competitive advantage: a resource–based view. Strategic Management Journal. 1993; 14 (3): pp. 179–91.
[44] Rugman AM, Verbeke A. Edith Penrose's contribution to the resource–based view of strategic management. Strategic Management Journal. 2002; 23 (8): pp. 769–80.
[45] Kor YY, Mahoney, JT. Edith Penrose's (1959) contributions to the resource-based view of strategic management. Journal of Management Studies. 2004; 41(1): pp. 183–91.
[46] Andersson S. The internationalization of the firm from an entrepreneurial perspective. International Studies of Management & Organization. 2000; 30(1): pp. 63–92.
[47] Hitt, MA et al. Strategic entrepreneurship: Entrepreneurial strategies for wealth creation. Strategic Management Journal, 2001. 22 (6–7): pp. 479–91.
[48] McDougall PP, Oviatt BM. International entrepreneurship: the intersection of two research paths. Academy of Management Journal. 2000; 43(5): pp. 902–6.
[49] Henrik A, Sylvie C. The impact of relationships on changes in internationalisation strategies of SMEs. European Journal of Marketing. 2007; 41(11/12): pp. 1449–74.
[50] Crick D, Spence M. The internationalisation of 'high performing' UK hightech SMEs: a study of planned and unplanned strategies. International Business Review. 2005; 14(2): pp. 167–85.

8
Value Propositions: How to Build SMEs' Offering

Marketing developed in the second half of the nineteenth century. Several models were proposed over time by researchers in universities, in order to understanding how marketing works. Amongst the most common models are the 4 Ps of marketing, which was extended to 7 Ps for an industrial context, the 7 Cs of communication, and so on. You have already studied these in modules like introduction to marketing or marketing communications. Some extensions of these models are often taught in universities in modules like international marketing, marketing strategy or marketing management. Within the SME context, we could talk about the 4 Ps; however, it would be restrictive and a bit too rigid when looking at the loose and unstructured marketing that characterises SMEs. With SMEs, it is more appropriate to talk about 'value propositions'.

Value propositions are important to gain competitive advantage, as SMEs' strategies are based on 'a differentiated customer value proposition. Satisfying customers is the source of sustainable value creation' [19]. Value propositions are those offerings that are perceived as valuable in the consumers' perspective (and not necessarily from the firm's point of view), and that rely on the perception of value. A value proposition is defined as 'an analysis and quantified review of the business benefits, costs and value that a company can deliver to prospective customers and consumers' [4]. Value, as perceived by the consumer, is

> the consumer's overall assessment of the utility of a product based on perceptions of what is received and what is given. Though what is received varies across consumers (i.e., some may want volume, others high quality, still others convenience) and what is given varies (i.e., some are concerned only with money expended, others with time

and effort), value represents a trade-off of the salient give and get components [42].

Value propositions are aimed at specific and remunerable target segments: 'For the entrepreneur, the value proposition anticipates and is organized to serve markets that can comfortably afford the new product or service, and is thus designed to create financial profit' [24]. We can see, therefore, that value propositions are a mix of tangible goods, service level and communication. In fact, while the traditional concept of product is often referring to tangible goods that are exchanged in a one-off transaction, value propositions embed the idea of 'relationship with the customer' in their conceptualisation as 'the value proposition derives from the most generic definition of service: a promise to perform a deed on behalf of the customer' [36]. Furthermore, current literature indicates clearly that value propositions are conceptually different from traditional offerings rooted in the 4Ps concept, as 'for many firm offerings, the core value proposition is explicitly its combination of goods and services, and the market space for these offerings continues to increase' [36].

Value propositions, therefore, should be clearly targeted, communicate effectively, and deliver promises consistently. As we have seen in other chapters of this book, markets in general are increasingly fragmented, and there is huge pressure on firms, especially SMEs, to differentiate and add value whenever possible. Markets overtime became more refined, and competition got much tougher. The reason why value propositions should be clearly targeted lies in the differences amongst consumer segments. If we divide the market into groups of people with common characteristics (a market segment), we can easily see that some segments of the market have a preference for upmarket products, some for low-market products, and some others (often a great deal of people) have a preference for well-known and established mainstream products and brands. Likewise, when we observe various segments of the market, we can see differences in disposable income, lifestyle and stages of life. All these consumers have very different perceptions of value; these – not the firm's – should be reflected in our value propositions, which should clearly target specific market segments.

Likewise, value propositions should be communicated to the consumers in a clear way. Competition is tough, and consumers are bombed continuously with messages from competing companies. All these messages are sent to the consumers in different ways: media advertising (e.g., TV, radio and press), the slogans you find on billboards on the road, as well as all the information on packaging in the aisles of the supermarket. We are continuously exposed to information, and all these messages create confusing 'noise', so the message or statement about a product, brand or company should be clearly spelled out.

Lastly, value propositions that are clearly targeted and communicated effectively in order to sustain value overtime also have to deliver the promises made to consumers consistently. This means that if SMEs propose products to the market with specific characteristics and specific 'benefit bundles' (i.e., the aggregate of all benefits deriving from the purchase and usage of that specific product), the perceived benefits to consumers should be consistent with the message the SME communicates to them. It is important to remember that the consumers' perception of value matters. In what follows, we will try to understand the concept of value as perceived by consumers.

8.1 Understanding the concept of 'value'

Many markets are consumer-driven and highly competitive; innovation is essential for firms to succeed. It is not accessible to all firms and is especially a struggle for SMEs. However, SMEs can add value to their propositions. It should be noted that consumer demand is increasingly fragmented, meaning that more and more, people are not happy with 'standard' products; they want specific, distinctive features and request highly personalised products.

SMEs often suffer from a lack of resources and skills to run all business processes smoothly enough to achieve a high level of personalisation. Thus, it may be more difficult for them to satisfy consumers' increasing demand for products. In the case of the food and drink industry, an example of refinement of the market is the creation of the specialist food category (e.g., organic, free range, 'free from'). This new market was generated from a fragmentation of the ordinary commodity-based food and drink market.

An adequate understanding of consumers' needs becomes critical to SMEs' marketing success, as they are increasingly pushed to deliver value to consumers. But where are the roots of this value idea?

The concept of value creation first emerged with Michael Porter [30] in the context of larger organisations. He proposed the 'value chain' in his writings about competitive advantage [14, 29], which is still leading firms' strategies all over the world today.

According to Porter, firms have primary activities (the functions of a firm) and some supportive activities. Examples of primary activities are inbound logistics, operations, outbound logistics, marketing and post-sale service. Supportive activities include infrastructures, human resource management, technology development and procurement-related activities. All these activities enable firms to pursue and develop a competitive advantage [11, 29], provided they manage to fine tune their performance with specific market aims: that is, they pursue either cost-leadership or differential – and therefore high-quality – leadership.

However, firms' competitive advantage depends on their performance of those primary and supportive activities [11–12, 29]. So firms have to be able to manage both the way resources are allocated to their business activities and external relationship with the other stakeholders of their supply chain. You can see the complexity of managing all different primary and supportive activities taking place at the same time in a firm, and on top of that, the need to manage relationships with supply chain stakeholders. You would get confused, would you not?

In spite of the need for managing all these activities, what firms in general often forget is that the main driver of all their activities aimed at achieving competitive advantage derives from consumers, so they have the first place in the development of a business strategy [6, 14]. Therefore, value creation results from a series of linked activities that add value for each chain member [14], but with a strong consumer focus. These activities must be aligned with – and responsive to – their customers' needs (the actors buying a product) as well as those of the final consumers (the actors consuming the product).

It is critical to understand how to create value; however, we should first try to understand how the value perception mechanism works in consumers. The main elements of the value equation are the following, as shown in current research [4, 8, 20, 28]:

Value = benefits – costs – risk

Consumers perceive value as the benefits derived from the purchase of a specific product, and these benefits are weighed against costs and risk.

The benefit is the solution to a specific problem the consumer has. The problem could consist of a specific shopping mission, such as a child who asks for a particular type of toy, or the consumer who wants to get a chilled drink on a very hot summer day. The problem might also arise from a specific occasion, like the purchase of a painkiller when someone has a headache, or getting a last-minute gift to make up for not remembering a girlfriend's birthday. Another type of problem could simply be satisfying a desire; this is what happens, for instance, during an impulse purchase. Shoppers face different types of problems every day, and the solutions bear an absolute benefit that generates value in the perception of the consumer.

However, the benefits derived from the solution to a specific problem are balanced against the costs of the transaction. Costs can be both financial and economic. The price is a type of financial cost – the major cost the consumer weights against the benefits of the product. However, there are also some economic costs involved, such as the time it takes to go to the shop to purchase the product, whether it is easy or difficult to find the product, whether we might get stuck in traffic or have to search for a car park for ages, and so on. These represent the opportunity-cost. These are all costs that bulk up on the negative side of the scale and will be weighed against the benefits.

Among the bulk of negative attributes we can also find the risk. Risk is related to the possibility of encountering unfulfilled promises. Thus, a consumer might not purchase a specific brand or product because of the risk of cognitive dissonances, or because of the lack of credibility of the company producing it. Also, the potential lack of availability of the product contributes to a negative consumers' perception.. Therefore, the overall perception of value is affected by the benefits derived by solving a problem; however, it is weighed against existing costs and risk.

For SMEs, it is important to understand what different market segments perceive as valuable, so they can learn how to adapt value propositions in light of consumers' perceived value. In what follows, we will describe the importance of segmenting the market.

8.2 Segmenting the market

Market segmentation is critical to better understand consumers Because 'one of the prime reasons for conducting market research is to try to foretell the outcome of upcoming events, whether it be an election, a brand launch or a new service' [9]. The introduction of the concept of 'market segment' [31] has been received enthusiastically by both academics and practitioners because segmenting consumers improves the firm's understanding of an apparently complex and impenetrable customer base.. Based on the assumption that it is possible to identify groups of consumers with common behavioural characteristics according to specific criteria within a certain market, it necessarily follows that customers in submarkets will behave in similar ways.

The two main accepted theories about segmentation methods consist of demographics (with its shifting version corresponding to geodemographics) and bespoke systems or psychographics. Geodemographic classification and segmentation is a recent tool used by marketers to get insights and knowledge about their customers. Formulated about 20 years ago, it is still in its infancy, and many things need to be improved to get a tool that would enable a better understanding of the markets we are looking at. Geodemographics is 'the study of the population types and their dynamics as they vary by geographical area' [5]. The geographical area size usually used is the neighbourhood. But more specifically for marketing geodemographics help to get a better – although fixed – snapshot of the most important population represented in a given place. The outcomes and the results produced help to establish predictions about the future behaviour of consumers who are defined by common characteristics.

The formal academic definition of segmentation, rooted in an economic perspective, is 'viewing a heterogeneous market as a number of smaller homogeneous markets, in response to differing preferences, attributable to the desires of consumers for more precise satisfaction of their varying wants' [31]. Although the concept was initially developed for larger organisations, SMEs have the tools to engage with segmentation, if they are willing to do so. Its importance lies in understanding who buys what and why.

The fundamental concept behind segmentation is the impossibility of having a product or service that fits everyone. Just as there is more than one size of clothes or shoes, for other products, one single product cannot possibly satisfy all people. There is a need for some differentiation, and as we have already seen in other chapters of this book, the success of a differentiation strategy depends on the different characteristics of heterogeneous groups of consumers.

Nevertheless, firms benefit from standardisation, which is the process of homogenising the offering to consumers to capitalise on scale production. So they face a dilemma: on the one hand, they cannot satisfy everyone, and on the other hand, they should offer everyone something special and personalised.

Firms, therefore, need to find a way to group consumers in a large customer base into homogeneous groups. The main approaches to segmentation in marketing are socio-geo-demographic and psychographic segmentation methods. Let us briefly describe both of them.

Socio-geo-demographic methods include geographic segmentation, which is the categorisation of consumers by geographical attributes such as nations, states, regions, towns, and neighbourhoods. Often marketers use postal codes to group geographical areas. This geographical approach can be integrated with data on the demographic (e.g., age, gender, ethnicity, employment status), social (e.g., cultural background, social class) and economic (e.g., disposable income, home or car ownership) conditions of consumers.

8.3 Socio-geo-demographic segmentation

The appearance of geodemographics dates back to the middle 1970s in both the UK and the United States (for the purpose of this book, we will concentrate on the UK), and the father of this method is Richard Webber [35], who managed to analyse census data to establish a ward-level classification (i.e., a statistical technique using an algorithm called 'Ward') of the market, which remained confidential until its presentation at the Market Research Society in 1979.

An interested audience made it possible for the discipline to grow. Webber developed ACORN – A Classification of Residential Neighbourhoods [33]. In the 1980s, the addition of the electoral register to the classification permitted even better identification of the people living in specific households. At the beginning of the 1980s, competition in the market started with the emergence of new competing classifications such as PINPOINT in 1983. The second most important classification after ACORN appeared in 1986, again developed by Webber, who named it MOSAIC. It not only incorporated census-based data but also took into consideration a number of additional data items, such as the presence of company directors and the percentage of changes of address, in electoral composition [13].

This innovation in the way data were handled brought a great change to firms that engaged with marketing intelligence. Formerly, the cost to obtain raw census data was a barrier to the market for a long period of time; however, when the census data became free, and these new tools of segmentation were developed, companies saw it as an opportunity to enter previously unknown markets. Later on, the integration of non-census variables (such as lifestyles and survey findings) was the next most important development occurring in this industry at that time [13].

Improvements to computer methods and easier digitalisation of data, as well as the incorporation of lifestyles data in segmentation methods, made the techniques and classifications more reliable. Finally, in the late 1990s, different companies proposed a few numbers of general classifications. Although the fathers of the techniques were primarily academics, they have all moved into business and commercial areas. Moreover, until recently, academicians seemed uninterested in the development of a rigorous statistical treatment to improve the systems currently in use and to design better classifications [27]. However, since 1997, it seems academia has experienced a revival in its interest in geodemographics, because both the public sector and academics have realised the strategic importance of understanding the market better [23].

The geodemographics market has changed in the last decade, and now, although the number of companies has remained almost the same, we can distinguish major and minor players in the area. Although in 1997, 12 companies were licensed to use census data, CACI and Experian (formerly CCN) were and remain the uncontested leaders of the geodemographics segmentation tools market. MOSAIC and ACORN are the most used and share between them 80% of the market activities [26, 33]. Let us now understand what type of methodology lies behind these segmentation tools.

8.4 Demographic and geo-demographic segmentation methodology

The main assumption on which geodemographics is based can be basically summarised as, You are where you live!

Therefore, the rationale behind geodemographics lies in the fact that it is commonly accepted that people living close to one to another are more likely to have and display the same characteristics, attitudes and behaviours than people living farther away. Although this is not always true, in many cases, we can assign people to a neighbourhood, and we can distinguish amongst the populations of the neighbourhoods.

The variables taken into consideration by this principal stream of segmentation methods relate mainly to the socio-geo-demographic aspects of consumers' characteristics. Some examples of these variables can be found in demographic dimensions such as age, gender, income or social class, as well as in household composition, area of residence or business-related indicators – counting, for instance, the number of employees and business establishments in a specific area, vehicle use and availability, length of residence, and so on. It is important to look at these characteristics in order to evaluate the composition of a given geographical area because, as has been observed, 'the social context in which people live did have a significant effect on their consumption patterns as well as their attitudes, and values' [16].

However, geodemographics are not only based on spatial proximity: neighbourhoods far away one from another (such as the ones in the suburbs of large cities) could display similar (if not the same) characteristics to those in geographical areas which are farther away. Therefore, geodemographics group neighbourhoods that overall have common features, creating a measure of proximity that is only based on the similarity in the consumers' profiles, rather than on real geographical proximity. Geographical patterns are built to help understand processes that identify and build patterns within very complex data structures. Identifying these patterns can be difficult because the linkages between data categories are often characterised by complex information and their classifications are hard to define.

Nevertheless, socioeconomic patterns do not occur in isolation, and geodemographics enable detailed knowledge of consumer behaviour. This is an important step forward in knowledge acquisition with respect to the elaboration of reductionist models of consumer identity (as they were used in the past). Geodemographics do make some inferences of unobserved behaviour based on residential location [15], and although it should not be seen as a definite statistical method for hypothesis testing, it has often shown its commercial validity as an exploratory tool.

Geodemographic segmentation adds a geographic dimension to traditional demographic analysis by grouping together small areas whose inhabitants present similar demographic profiles, and theoretically [9], there is a distinction between ordinal and nominal classification systems. Geodemographics are not included in the standard demographics as an ordinal system, to the extent that it does give a sense of order to put into relation distinct variables that are apparently related, such as social level and age. An ordinal variable is one whose values can be arranged in an increasing or declining order (e.g., 33 years is more than 22 years). On the other hand, nominal variables are purely qualitative, and their values cannot be ordered (e.g., blue, green, red). Nominal variables are better handled with clustering techniques, rather than factoring techniques, in multivariate statistics. Geodemographics and multivariate value systems are considered nominal and more difficult to use because, as a precondition, they require classification according to a common discriminator (e.g., the area of residence), which does not necessarily always mirror reality.

Demographic and geodemographic systems are based on prejudice and on the interpretation of the researcher, since the way of formulating assumptions is based on variables that are not always dependent on each other. One example is the social grade parameter, which is linked directly to wealth, though in reality, other variables influence social status, such as educational level.

The basic foundations and methodology used to build any geodemographics classification is based on cluster analysis. Clustering is a difficult task to manage because it relies on decisions made throughout the process of statistical analysis, and indeed, at each step, the choice has an impact on the final classification obtained. The research design must be rigorous when using clustering techniques; otherwise, there is the risk of incurring biases that might yield misleading results.

Clustering relies on finding a balance between objective and subjective choices; furthermore, there is also equilibrium to be found between data-led and predictive solutions, the number of clusters desired, and the treatment of poorly classified classes that should also be taken in consideration when clustering. In order to be acceptable, a classification must be reliable; we must ensure the reproducibility of the results. Still, some authors [16] support the idea that geodemographic clustering is a process of trial and error, and that personal experience in classifying has a great impact on the results.

In a critical review of national classifications [10], less rigorous judgement was supported, in that a 'greater degree of openness involved make the classification more honest', and therefore, the fact that the results are reproducible and stable is already a sufficient condition to accept the quantitative method and consider the classification reliable. To be reliable and efficient, all classifications should include an abnormal cluster, in which clusters that are too different from the others are grouped. If this cluster does not exist, it would mean that those clusters would distort the clusters in which they are included, by over- or underrepresenting some of the population's features.

The classifications already available nowadays have the advantage of being mutually exclusive and exhaustive: in other words, a particular individual will belong to one, and only one, neighbourhood type, and all the individuals in the sample will get the same treatment [7]. However, when using large datasets, like in the case of the census, the risk of multicollinearity (i.e., the probability of having all variables correlating amongst themselves) is really high, and this is a major barrier in a cluster analysis. Highly correlated variables are inclined to repeat a lot of the information that is contained within just one variable [37], without allowing a clear pattern to emerge. It is therefore important to include in the clustering methodology an intermediate step of 'statistical thinking', where the number of variables, as well as their nature (ordinal, nominal or continuous) and correlation are assessed.

8.4.1 Classification features

There are currently different systems of geodemographic classifications, all with different features. The first type of system is about the number of cluster groups and subgroups that are obtained as a result of a particular statistical method used. Depending on the approach used, one could predict the number of clusters obtained. However, there seems to be little or no agreement as to how many clusters exist within the UK overall. It would seem that the only way to select the number of clusters is to try and run the classification obtained on a well-known area and look at the results to see whether they are representative of the area that was taken into consideration.

In order to determine the ideal number of clusters, some statistical work was performed that consisted of calculating distances amongst them, and it indicated 50 to 70 clusters. However, the study concluded that the chosen range does not explain all the differences amongst clusters [10]; therefore, more clusters would be needed. However, at the time of the study, ACORN was using fewer clusters than the number proposed by the study, so researchers found themselves facing the dilemma of having some clusters that were too small to explain meaningful patterns of behaviour in the population, but facing complications to increasing the number of clusters because of constraints in their computational capacity. In response, researchers started comparing the existing systems in order to determine which would be most reliable and representative of reality.

When comparing ACORN and Super Profiles, the creator of the latter method found that when testing it against ACORN, the differences in the results obtained were 'far smaller than expected' [27]. In an empirical piece of research conducted by the marketing company 'dunnhumby' [18], the effectiveness of existing systems was measured. The analysis involved drawing 'gains charts' (the proportion of a reached target on the proportion of the population selected to reach the target), and researchers concluded, after analysing one hundred product fields this way, that there was no definite conclusion about the best system.

The choice of a highly reliable system is in many ways an academic exercise, as these classification systems should be seen, from a commercial point of view, as generic, while offering similar power in their explanatory abilities [18]. Another interesting study [16] tried to assess whether the investment in such systems was worth it, as opposed to conventional segmentation and classifications with traditional household-level demographics. The results support the hypothesis that the inclusion of the type of neighbourhood in a demographic analysis enhances the knowledge when compared to demographics alone. According to the study, three independent variables – i.e., age, gender, and type of neighbourhood – are complementary to each other [16]. In ACORN and MOSAIC, classification differences in consumption, lifestyle or cultural values are the basis of the mapping of market positions, and they do not depend just on consumers' economic status [7]. In what follows, we give more detail on ACORN, MOSAIC and CAMEO segmentation methods.

ACORN by CACI

This method was created by Webber, while he worked at Consolidated Analysis Centers, Incorporated (CACI). It was the first geodemographic tool to appear on the market. ACORN categorised 1.9 million UK postcodes using over 125 demographic statistics within England, Scotland and Wales and employing 287 lifestyle variables. The classification system of ACORN contained 56 types of households split into 14 groups classified within 5 categories. The last version of ACORN was updated in 2004, when the 2001 census data was released, and it considered the fact that consumers' habits and behaviours had changed over a decade.

CACI classification used a two-stage method. The first step consisted of sorting out the postcodes crossing them with both the census and other databases. Each variable was tested against the overall contribution to the whole sample. Variables' interaction and correlation is also evaluated in order to select and include data that allow as much discrimination and targeting power as possible., In the second step, information about those areas where the census was supposed to match consumers' profiles was assessed. This is in fact characteristic of the ACORN system, the ACORN classification is tested against the data released by the census for convergent validity. In terms of layout, the classes are ranked according to an economic hierarchy, although the system is built according to predominant patterns of consumption.

MOSAIC by Experian

Experian constructed the MOSAIC system. Essentially, it is a consistent segmentation system that covers over 400 million of the world's households, and it does this by using local data from 25 countries. MOSAIC identified 10 types of residential neighbourhoods that can be found in each of the countries. The classification is built on a good understanding of consumers' segments. It analyses UK social trends and involves extensive fieldwork and market research to interpret the segments obtained through the statistical modelling. The methodology used to build the MOSAIC classification is characterised by seven steps [16]:

- The selection of the potential input data is done through a careful choice of non-census databases. It allows getting finer levels of

geographic detail than census and helps to update the clusters more often than every 10 years.
- The data are recorded by transforming information and storing data in a manageable way, so to guarantee the use of the correct data at all times.
- The data are evaluated and importance is given to the distribution of the variables, which are grouped with statistical techniques of multivariate data analysis. This step could involve PCA (Principal Component Analysis) or other factoring technique, in order to isolate the most important variables. PCA can in certain cases remove redundant information, but there is the risk of shadowing possibly helpful information.
- All data are weighted in order to reflect the appropriate importance of each variable, as a reflection of the composition of the population.
- Data are clustered: There are two approaches, either top-down (initial saturated model) where at each step the number of clusters is reduced until you reach an appropriate solution (which is evaluated subjectively), or by allocating and reallocating variables iteratively (i.e., by a sequence of random attempts) after an initial specification of the number of desired clusters in the final solution.
- Clusters are arranged hierarchically, in order to optimise their distances (i.e., the Ward method). This involves assessing the effectiveness of the solution proposed (usually by testing the classification on an area familiar to the researcher), as it determines which clusters are over-influenced or underweighted by population density.
- Visual summaries are created for the groups that were built. In this final step, graphical output visually describes the complexities of the different clusters.

Given the wide use of non-census data, the resulting clusters are likely to be data-specific, and there is the risk of inaccuracy in the collected data. However, it should be noted that in most of fieldwork activities, it is impossible to collect complete data for 100% of the cases; therefore, some corrective measures have to be adopted to account for potential non-response bias [13].

CAMEO

This classification tool is slightly different because it integrated geodemographics with psychographics. CAMEO lifestyle segments classify every UK household into 81 distinct marketing types. Each type is identified by a 3-digit code, which represents 7 age bands, 9 levels of income and affluence, and 14 life stage and lifestyle groups.

Value Propositions: How to Build SMEs' Offering 129

The information is collected from the census, Household Council Tax Band and property valuation data, consumer credit data, and residency data from the electoral roll. In total, 58 neighbourhood types are defined, and 10 key marketing groups created. This socio-geo-demographic classification system allocates residential postcodes to marketing groups, such as 'poorer family and single-parent households' and categories, like 'young and older households in housing association and mortgaged homes' capitalising on a mix of socio-economic as well as geographic profiling.

8.4.2 Socio-geo-demographic segmentation strengths and weaknesses

In the previous section, we described different types of socio-geo-demographic segmentation tools. Some are purely geo-demographic in nature, and as we saw, CAMEO also includes some psychographic specifications. Although a thorough description of psychographic segmentation will follow, let us now look at the strengths and weaknesses of geo-demographic segmentation methods.

Strengths

Among its strengths, geodemographics contributes to improving survey design and sampling because of the 'ability to link together different data sets, provided that these have been geo-coded' [25]. The creation of consumer profiles is aimed at generating new business through direct mailing. Although academics brought this marketing and segmentation technique to the world, it rapidly became more important commercially. De facto academics have hardly been able to assess its real efficiency and have merely seen it as a tool that could work most of the time, but that would not grant 100% reliability.

Companies providing these classifications warn their clients that it is not a 100% match to reality; it is only a model that tries to represent some general patterns that can be observed within a statistical population. Because of this, geodemographics have been the target of much criticism; however, in the realm of marketing and segmentation, we should recognise that every method has its weaknesses and its advantages. None is perfect. In what follows, we will describe some weaknesses of geodemographics.

Weaknesses

Probably, the most cited weakness of geodemographics consists in that this technique assumes that specific trends at the aggregate level (i.e., the population considered as a mass of more or less homogeneous people) are also true at the individual level, this is known in the academic literature as the ecological fallacy [5]. This means that geodemographics are at best the 'representation of the crude average tendencies and trends of the population' [5] and they only take into account average values (i.e., the expected values of a distribution) and ignore outliers, which represent potential attitudes at the extremes of a distribution [5]. It is therefore too reductive to use the 'average' values with respect to behaviour, because the variation in consumption could level out the behaviours of specific groups, such as the elderly or teens.

Finally, some might argue that geodemographics' classifications are not precise enough at the household level, and that they only produce 'clouds' that overlap, rather than 'clusters' of given areas; differences *within* classes are usually larger than differences *between* classes [38]. The counterargument is that geodemographics are the fruit of a cluster-based analysis. The use of cluster analysis presents a complex challenge because it requires several methodological choices that determine the quality of a cluster solution. Due to this partial recognition, geodemographics suffer from critiques that try to deny the usefulness of the method. If we take the example of variables like store location, we can also draw attention to the fact that external factors, such as competition effects, are not taken in consideration when conducting the analysis. Therefore, geodemographics might be very data-noisy, in which random factors dominate. Consequently, it matters little whether the classification is good or bad, or whether there are major sources of error, because even the best classifications have failed to take into account those very uncertain variables like store location and competition intensity [10, 27].

Furthermore, the fact that census data is updated only every 10 years is the source of conflicting arguments about geodemographics. Most of the time, the data is quite old because fully based on census data, and for obvious reasons, this makes this method inapplicable in situations in which markets present dynamicity,. On the one hand, people tend to move more often nowadays, and family shapes could change a lot in a little period of time (children leave home, working people retire, and so on). On the other hand, people moving in and moving out of a neighbourhood have a high probability of being similar in many aspects: people tend to live close to the ones who look the most like they do, and in that sense, it is argued, the overall aspect and shape of the neighbourhood remains fairly constant. Among its weaknesses, in classifying neighbourhoods, this method classifies only at the neighbourhood level, and not individuals or household. It is also inefficient because it lacks the option for good age targeting, since age is not always symptomatic of certain behaviours.

Finally, geodemographics presents only information about households' *probability* of purchasing, not whether the household *has* purchased or not. The majority of the users have a poor understanding of the data, and differing postcode systems at the international level present further barriers to the extension of this method to multinational and international contexts. Demographic variables alone are not able to identify the peculiarities of submarkets, since personal value systems are not taken into account as much as brand preference. This means that not all consumers belonging to a segment have the full range of preferences assigned to the segment itself, or hold the same values in their lives [22]: you can easily earn as much as your neighbour, be approximately the same age, and have the same or similar family composition, but still show different product and brand preferences, as well as different consuming patterns.

8.5 Psychographic segmentation

The second main theory of segmentation, which is accepted worldwide, is psychographics. It is employed as method when, under certain circumstances, geodemographics seemed too unreliable. The basic assumption of this method is, you are what you do!

> Many forms of segmentation exist but, as marketing knowledge advances and competition increases, the need for more precise segmentation tools becomes greater. For many products and services which are highly related to the "self" concept or with which the consumer is highly involved, psychographics can represent a good way to achieve this increased precision [25].

The word 'psychographics' often appears to be abused because the current literature points out a difference between bespoke systems including lifestyle and cognitive style, and psychographics. If observed in a deeper way, psychographics is related to the mental attitude of the customer, and it differs slightly from the other bespoke methods, which are more cognition-related. This means it includes all the variables related to the perception of reality and the systems of values in a subject. It differs from other bespoke systems, such as lifestyle and cognitive style, since

> The term "psychographic" [refers to] studies that place comparatively heavy emphasis on generalized personality traits. Analysts who have

preferred the term "lifestyle", on the other hand, have tended to focus either on broad cultural trends or on needs and values thought to be closely associated with consumer behaviour [39].

With regard to lifestyle, some of the variables are derived from demographics, such as the expert analyst using information about gender, age and social status to interpret the life stage of the consumers' group. However, this analysis is complicated by the influence of consumers' heterogeneous and irrational behaviour under given conditions.

The concepts of lifestyle and life stage are rooted in the observation that consumers' behaviour is affected more by the way the person is (their personal characteristics) rather than by the consumer's role or status in sociological terms. Hence, one of the main problems with this method limits the details a researcher can obtain about people's lifestyles. To compensate for this absence of information, among the psychographic segmentation styles, one focuses on cognition and looks at patterns of behaviour based on the possible thinking patterns of consumers, focusing on their ways of feeling and perceiving reality. It is connected, in a way, to lifestyle segmentation, but if it is true that lifestyle expresses variables of behaviour and preferences within a specific market segment, lifestyle itself is not a valid indicator of the cognitive perceptions of the shopper. In light of this information, what are the main strengths and weaknesses of psychographics? In what follows, we will describe them.

8.5.1 Psychographic segmentation strengths and weaknesses

Psychographics and bespoke systems present some advantages with respect to geodemographics. They comprise data sources that are much more updated. These data are freshly withdrawn from the databases of other companies (e.g., insurances, banks, retailers, and so on). This independence from census data makes the analysis of fresher and more personalised information at individual, or household, level possible. Personality and lifestyle are taken into account, and behavioural elements such as brand preference can be used as key factors in the development of new brands or new products, provided resources are allocated and aimed to develop effective product strategies.

Psychographics link purchase patterns to psychological attitudes. When dealing with lifestyle variables, a major problem is that lifestyle systems are based on behaviour, so it is possible to misunderstand lifestyles and cognitive styles in those customers who present behavioural parallelisms, or when there is an overlap of characteristics. This should be taken into consideration in any segments' analysis if conducted by making practical use of lifestyle or cognitive variables. This limit in the precision of definition has to be reminded especially when a cognitive contrast is highlighted by the analysis, in order to grant homogeneity in the segment choice [2].

Another problem, which is somewhat related to the previous one, is, if these consumers who share behavioural parallelisms (but with cognitive contrast) should be taken into account, which strategy is the best to pursue in regard to such misleading segments? Judgement is fundamentally difficult, but a possible solution could be found in the conciliation of these clashes with the use of 'sequential segmentation', which means 'segmenting first on the basis of consistencies in overt behaviour, then on the basis of congruence in cognitive style' [2].

We can conclude that psychographics is a useful segmentation method in which practitioners in the industry have put their hope to better mitigate risk and to better understand consumers' perceptions. Before psychographics, the perception of risk among consumers was not able to be assessed: in professional services, for example, it helps to measure whether the perception of psychosocial and financial risk is higher in different market segments, and it has been used whenever the need to understand the mental attitude of consumers is relevant to decision-making.

Unfortunately, a big limitation of psychographics is the connected to the reliability of the segment because the analysis itself starts with an already imperfect series of data and with assumptions about cognitive characteristics that are difficult to measure. In order to compensate the limitations in the measurement of cognitive variables, behaviour segmentation is an extension of lifestyle and cognitive styles segmentation methods.

8.5.2 Behavioural segmentation

A type of psychographic segmentation is behavioural segmentation; two criteria have been identified as characteristic of it [3]. The first criterion to segment markets is based on the behaviour of consumers, namely to the 'consumer response to a given marketing plan at a given point in time, or to change in the levels of marketing effort over time' [3]. The marketing plan, at a given point in time, represents the whole set of marketing stimuli over a specific period of time and where the change in the levels of marketing effort over time is intended to bring a degree of elasticity to the consumers' response to the changes in the set of stimuli.

For the first criterion, an example of descriptor could be the quantity purchased for a product or brand, the reaction to the product, i.e., brand loyalists against switchers or repeated purchases vs. first trial or non-purchasers. The second criterion offers a reflection on whether consumer response is influenced by one single behavioural element, such as the frequency of consumption of a determined brand, or by a multivariate behavioural element, such as the identification of predispositions to one specific behaviour or another. In the case of a single behavioural criterion,

> Direct association between marketing stimuli and response…would be difficult due to lack of control over external factors affecting response. Therefore, response is measured at a given point in time and consumer characteristics are associated to behaviour to serve as market segment descriptors, thus guiding in the selection of marketing stimuli [3].

On the other hand, in the case of behaviours presenting a multivariate response at a given point in time, different behavioural classifications can be applied in order to segment consumers according to their preference of one brand or product instead of another, for example. Another possibility is the segmentation of customers based on product categories, grouping them by similarities in their consumption behaviour, i.e., by finding out who, among the consumers, has the tendency to purchase a specific product or brand with more frequency. Some other important influences on individual choice include the 'development of "group type" characteristics (such as group cohesiveness, autonomy, intimacy, polarization, stability, flexibility, etc.)' [40].

8.5.3 Considerations on variables selection and on segmentation use

Given the differences between socio-geo-demographic and psychographic segmentation methods, and their ability to interact with each other to allowing overlapping, it would be important to make some considerations on the selection of variables and on the use of segmentation in general.

Variables selection

The choice of the variables employed in the segmentation analysis determines the net distinction between these two main streams methods. The effectiveness of the method of segmentation of the market is related to the ability to select proper bases and descriptors, the first ones representing the dependent variables (the output of the function) and the latter the independent ones (the input of the function). 'In a multidimensional market, companies can increase profitability by utilizing market segmentation.... Segmentation variables must be considered in light of their measurability, availability, reliability and ability to uncover the characteristics of each market segment' [22].

There is need for contextualisation because each method can be more effective if used in one industry instead of another. Therefore the explanatory power of segmentation methods is affecting by the context of the data sources. Geodemographics better apply to industries presenting quite a stable structure, where changes are very slow, rare and dynamicity is not on the dictionaries of the companies operating on the market. On the other hand psychographics better apply to more chilli pepper-flavoured markets; such could be technology, holidays and the food and drink industry.

As a matter of fact, the selection of the variables used to show the characteristics of the segments themselves requires good, common sense knowledge of the industry, since they are highly subjective [17], and judgement should be made according to the experience of the analyst. Furthermore,

> the process of identifying segments necessitates a thorough analysis of the entire market, not only focusing on the customer's needs and shopping habits but also providing knowledge of changing market conditions and competitive actions. This knowledge enables the retail organization to identify those segments that offer the most promising opportunities in relation to the organization's strengths and situational determinants [32].

All researchers seem to encourage pragmatism: 'a common reason for [segmentation studies'] lack of applicability is preoccupation with the techniques and method of segmentation is that in too many instances marketing researchers have failed to analyse the marketing environment and competitive structure before applying their favourite methodological approach' [41]. The idea is widespread that segmentation has to be seen as a system of several variables influencing decisions, rather than an individual analysis, as proposed with psychographics:

> The marketing literature recognizes that most purchase and consumption behaviour involves more than a single individual (the social context of, and influence on, purchase and consumption behaviour). Yet most of the empirical market segmentation (as well as consumer

behaviour and marketing) studies ignore this premise and, with few exceptions, center on the individual as the sole unit of analysis [40].

Different theories are applied and implemented according to the sector of activity and the company's objectives. A possible solution to the dilemma lies in the statement: 'There is no good or bad method'. The truth is that some methods can be more appropriate than others, given certain conditions in the market and industry. According to Kotler [21], in order to maximise the usefulness of the market segments, four basic characteristics – measurability, substantiality, accessibility and actionability – have to be searched for. The use of segmentation methods guarantees similarity for segment members', even if this similarity does not imply that all the members of the segment necessarily have to respond uniformly to the same marketing stimuli. So, the choice of a demographic or psychographic system will implicitly push practitioners to take into consideration the marketing mix inputs and consumer responses to specific stimuli, but most importantly, they have to try to understand what kind of outcome is desired.

Demographics or geodemographics will give more pre-concept, measurable, objective outcomes than psychographics or other bespoke systems, which are based on consumer attitudes, values, ways of thinking and lifestyles. Subjective decisions from practitioners are based on the search for the compromise between increased sample homogeneity and its accessibility, with the purpose of identifying the optimal number of segments. This step has not been undervalued because the choice of the segmentation method and the desired outcome influences the way decisions are made within the company and has repercussions on strategies and tactics.

All decision-making systems are positively or negatively affected by an appropriate or wrong decision. Even if further advantage will derive from an increase in the quality of the hardware and software that will allow more and more complex computations to take place [40], the potential key for success, independent of the complexity of the segmentation, lies in the ability of practitioners to interpret the results and create their own guidelines to operationalise the design, execution, and correct and fruitful evaluation of the most appropriate marketing strategy. They will also have to balance the knowledge from statistics and data analysis with the practitioners' knowledge of the product. This idea is strengthened by the concept that the interpretation of the results of segmentation research, when turned into creative and possibly profitable ideas, presents a rich profile of potential target segments that could enlarge the scope of the firms' strategies.

Segmentation use

The use of different segmentation methods is affected by different factors, such as the type of industry and costs, which have to be taken into considerations while designing a market segmentation system. Actual academic literature does not deal a lot with this issue, but academics are sometimes pushed not to forget that financial and economic efficiency is an important aspect that affects segmentation methods' use, as these are related to the practitioners' daily bread.

Collecting data is often costly, despite the new technologies that allow firms to speed up communication and data computation. Costs are directly related to the size of the sample; by increasing it, the accuracy also increases, but so do costs. Although it is a double-edged blade, higher reliability involves higher costs, and it's a mistake to think that design and analysis considerations present only minimal cost implications. Therefore, the statistical choice for the analysis does not have a strong impact on the structure of the costs themselves, but a wrong sampling could knock down the enthusiasm of the most energetic practitioner in terms of costs. Computer-based multivariate statistical techniques present some advantages in terms of analysts' time; however, 'in most segmentation studies the cost of research design and analysis varies within very narrow ranges. The major variable cost component is data collection. Therefore, major cost savings can be expected from the data collection stage and not from cutting corners at the design and analysis stages' [40].

A little bit of prudence is suggested for a correct assessment of the expected value deriving from the segmentation analysis and possible alternatives, should it be needed. The costs potentially deriving from the implementation of different segmentation strategies should be considered. The overall cost drops continuously with increasing levels of technology.

Another practical aspect worth mentioning is related to the reliability of the data when looking at social and educational status in consumers: 'Self-administered questionnaires, for example, were found to be better when the information was available in records or possessed by other members of the respondent family. They were also better with highly educated and high-income respondents' [40].

Furthermore, due to commercial secrecy and competition, firms do not often communicate the details of the methodology used to build their classifications [27]. Hence, most of the time, the problem is that geodemographics are seen as empiricists' classifications, of little use in explaining contemporary social dynamics by social scientists. Thus, a small amount of literature deals with technical and methodological aspects of classifications [7].

8.6 Targeting and positioning

Segmentation is the base of targeting. In marketing, the word 'targeting'means the marketing effort made to serve specific customer segments. Provided that we can group the market into different homogeneous subsamples of the population, i.e., our segments, we do not necessarily want to (nor can we) satisfy them all with the same value proposition. We might also observe that different segments' have different perceptions about our products.

8.6.1 Targeting

Targeting is necessary for different reasons. For instance some market segments might not be remunerative enough. Others might show very little appeal for our products. Other segments might have too few members, so we could be in the position of not being interested in serving all segments. Furthermore, in the case of SMEs, we have to consider that resources are limited, so it is critical to target the right consumers in order not to dissipate resources that are already scarce. SMEs cannot afford to 'hit and hope', trying to offer their propositions randomly to different segments, as consumers might not respond, and this would generate a loss of resources. They must target their value propositions to specific audiences. Fundamental questions to ask are, 'Who should firms target? Are they targeting the right consumers?

There are basically two options firms could develop their targeting around; both require an analysis of the segments to be operated in at two levels. First, is the segment made of people to whom existing products appeal – 'buyers' – or are they 'non-buyers'? It should be noted that, for the purpose of this section on targeting, we define buyers as people who already show an appeal for a specific product, although the word is generally used in marketing and supply chain management to designate the person in the firm who deals with procurement. The second level of segmentation analysis looks at specific characteristics of the segments themselves.

Buyers are open to trying new versions of the product because it already appeals to them, so it is fairly easy to convince them to try and buy a product. Therefore, the marketing effort is not big, and chances of successful sales are very high. Targeting these consumers is a bit like pushing at an open door, as the risk that they might not like the product is generally low. Nevertheless, this type of consumer is also happy to try competitors' products and is inclined to brand and product switching, which might result in difficulties retaining the customer base, which needs continuous incentives not to switch to competitors, and might generate lower returns due to their mobility across brands.

The second type of consumers is non-buyers: people to whom existing products do not appeal. They are not really open to trying or buying new products, and it is really difficult to convince them to, so marketing effort is quite big. The chances of sales success are not very high with non-buyers. Targeting them is a bit like cracking a tough nut, as the risk that they might not like the product is quite high. Nevertheless, should they start liking a specific product or brand, this type of consumer is inclined to brand and product loyalty, so it might result in the advantage of retaining the customer base, which needs only a consistent delivery of the promise to continue to perceive value, and potentially might generate higher returns due to their low mobility across brands. However, it is really difficult to attract non-buyers, and it can be is risky if the SME does not want to incur high stock levels and low market penetration.

At the second level of targeting, the SME should look at the specific characteristics of the different segments to determine the target market. Not all of them are necessarily good targets for the SME; likewise, there could be a portfolio of segments that could be targeted with one or more value propositions, depending on the firm's strategy.

SMEs are also able to create their own segments specific to their local markets, if they wish to do so. Let us look at some common segments, divided by segmentation typology:

- **Geodemographics**
  - **Life stage segments**
    - Young adults
    - Older adults
    - Young families
    - Older families
    - Pensioners
  - **Socioeconomic segments**
    - Upmarket
    - Midmarket
    - Low market
  - **Socio-geo-demographic (CAMEO) segments**
    - Young and affluent singles

- Affluent home owners
- Comfortable mixed neighbourhoods
- Wealthy retired neighbourhoods
- Smaller private family homes
- Less affluent singles and students
- Less affluent families
- Poorer family and single parent households
- Poorer white and blue collar workers
- Poorer council tenants – many single parents
- **Geographic segmentation (for England); NUTS codes in brackets**
  - North East (UKC)
  - North West (UKD)
  - Yorkshire and the Humber (UKE)
  - East Midlands (UKF)
  - West Midlands (UKG)
  - East of England (UKH)
  - London (UKI)
  - South East (UKJ)
  - South West (UKK)
- **Psychographics**
  - **Lifestyle segments**
    - Premium shopper
    - Price sensitive
    - Convenience shopper
    - Traditionalist
    - Health conscious
    - Mainstream brands shopper

For the purpose of this book we will not describe each segment in detail because this is only an example of market segments that can be used as basis for targeting. However, what we describe is the targeting mechanism, in light of consumers' preferences.

As noted previously, in order to target, we should identify targeting opportunities among buyers or non-buyers, taking into account the characteristics of the different market segments. Let us say, for example, that we are selling a product that appears particularly appeal to elderly people. We already know that the buyers are elderly, so from a geodemographic point of view, older adults and pensioners should be the groups who express major interest in the product. Therefore, our buyers are elderly people.

Now a new question arises: What is the purchasing power of this group of people who appear to like the product very much? A look at the segments in detail could show that the product is also popular with those elderly people who have high purchasing power; therefore, they are not really price-sensitive (psychographics). We can now see that a combination of geodemographics and psychographics – rather than trial and error attempts – helps us to focus better on identifying the target segment.

Continuing with this example, if elderly people with high purchasing power favour the SME's product, then all of the communication strategy and marketing mix should be aimed at this specific category. This also means that if elderly people express some preferences for the product, the SME should really try to modify the marketing mix to be able to capitalise on other factors, such as fame, customer satisfaction with the product, usability, colour preferences, and so on. By modifying the value proposition to tailor it to specific target segments' preferences, the firm could improve its brand or positioning.

Positioning

We have already encountered the concept of positioning in the chapter on branding, as these two elements are linked. The concept of positioning was introduced in the 1960s by researchers [30] who found that when consumers are exposed to a great deal of information (like in the case of excessive advertising), their minds automatically start discarding some of the information by blocking messages, while increasing the focus on a very little quantity of information. These bits of information that the mind focuses on often relate to the solution of a problem, like the purchase of a certain product on a specific shopping mission.

Positioning is 'an organized system for finding a window in the mind. It is based on the concept that communication can only take place at the right time and under the right circumstances' [30]. Therefore, positioning is about trying to craft a message that finds a 'position' in the mind of the consumer with respect to the messages of competing firms, so an essential tool is the creation of effective messages to be communicated to consumers, to reduce the noise created by excessive information.

Positioning is referred to products, firms and brands. It aims to create a place for a brand in consumers' minds, positioning it with respect to other brands. Kitkat, for the food and drink industry, and Ryanair, for airliners, offer examples of successful positioning. A Kitkat bar is a chocolate-coated wafer biscuit created by Rowntree's, a UK firm. The snack is now produced by world-renowned chocolate maker Nestlé. The candy is made of 2 or 4 bars of chocolate, each of which can be broken off of the others . In the 1960s, the brand was positioned as a snack by the clear message. 'Have a break...have a Kit Kat', which positioned the well-known chocolate bar against competitors.

The second example of positioning is the no-frills airline Ryanair. This low-cost Irish airline has become synonymous with cheap flights that offer little service. Businessmen Christopher Ryan, Liam Lonergan and Tony Ryan founded it in 1985. Later on, Michael O'Leary improved the firm's profitability by identifying as its core business the no frills, low cost, no business class service operated with a fleet made of only one type of airplane (Boeing 737–800 aircrafts). Ryanair positions itself as a no frills airliner, a 'point A to point B' carrier. They have positioned themselves so well that they were also recognised by *The Economist* [1] for becoming 'a byword for appalling customer service...and jeering rudeness towards anyone or anything that gets in its way'. Therefore, to Ryanair's customers the message is clear: you cannot find a cheaper airline, but you should not expect anything more than to be carried from one airport to another.

Positioning could also be visualised through the help of graphs by adapting the technique explained in Chapter 5: perceptual maps. SMEs could find a way to position their brands or products by asking their consumers to rate also competitors' products the same way they rated the SME's products. Then, by following the instructions described in the chapter, it is possible to create some perceptual maps of the SME's products with respect to competing products, measured against the attributes that consumers rated. Once the position of the SME's products with respect to competing products it is known, then the firm could see whether there are some elements of the value proposition that could be improved. Also, by knowing how consumers' compare the SME's products with competing brands, it is possible to modify the relevant aspects of the product design or concept. In what follows, we will look at the product design process, thinking about what type of manipulations SMEs can operate on (if any should be done at all). We will also provide an overview of the classifications of the different types of products usually found in marketing, highlighting that not all products have the same functions.

8.7 Product concept design

In light of what has be said so far about segmenting and targeting, another important element of the value proposition is the type of manipulations of the product in order to increase its consumer appeal. Several questions are related to the product concept. Fundamentally, once the SME has investigated the market and understood what segments they might concentrate on, and they have acquired enough knowledge about the preferences and characteristics of those segments, the next important questions includes, What should be changed in the product concept? Are there some products characteristics that need to be modified? Does the packaging convey the right message for the target market?

These are all important questions in order to address potential product modifications in the new product development (NPD) process that might lead to either a physical or conceptual change in the product. These are two distinct things. The first refers to a modification of the physical characteristics of the product, such as a change in colour or size, which takes place when consumer insight highlights the need for some aesthetic changes in the product in light of different consumers' preferences.

Conceptual change is more radical, and it implies a serious engagement with the NPD process so to rethink and redesign the product in light of consumers' preferences. Often, the reengineering process of a product requires a total rethinking of the whole product concept, and the changes are more substantial. Let us see in the next section what types of manipulations can take place when designing the product concept.

8.7.1 Levels of product manipulation

The product concept is a bit like an onion: There are different layers. It can fundamentally be manipulated at three different levels [34]: core, actual, and augmented

The core level provides the basic benefits of the product. It is the main function the product is purchased for. Let us make an example: in the case of the purchase of a car, the core benefit consists of the 'transportation' function. You can travel from one place to another, or you can use it to transport anything else other than yourself. You can transport your family (provided they wear seatbelts), as well as your favourite pet (provided you comply with health and safety rules). You can also carry...a nice warm pizza that you are going to share with your friends. However, a car not only carries you and your belongings from one place to another: sometimes it also functions as an image enhancer. This is the reason why some of your friends screwed some blue lights under the car...to impress.

The main concept embodied by the product at the core level is the fundamental function for which somebody buys it. Modifications that take place at this level are not easy to implement, and often, modifying the product at the core also means modifying completely the concept of the product itself: its essence. A historic example is the invention of a flying machine by the Wright brothers in 1903. It was able to fly for sustained periods of time, and the Wrights led a transportation revolution with the first airplane.

A second example of a manipulation of the product at its core is the invention of the world-renowned electronic game, Tamagotchi, which features a digital pet whose life you were responsible for. It was developed by Akihiro Yokoi and Aki Maita and commercialised by Japanese firm Bandai in the1990s. The videogame developed from portable videogames, shifting the core function from a one-off game adventure to a game extended over time that requires constant attention, revolutionising the concept of gaming.

The actual level of the product concept refers to the aesthetic and physical characteristics or features of the product, including packaging, branding and appearance. In the example of the car, its engine size, the colour of its bodywork, the make and model of the car are all features manipulated at the actual level. The final stage, the augmented level, relates to the intangible (and often ancillary) elements of the product: years of warranty, the type of service available for free (e.g., oil changes), potential access to credit, and so on.

Changes to the design of the product should take place in light of the information acquired through marketing intelligence. It is important for firms, especially SMEs, to clearly evaluate the extent of the manipulations to operate in light of consumers' preference, available resources and potential financial or economic return. It should be highlighted that not all products are modifiable at their core, actual and augmented levels, as this depends on the type of product the firm is dealing with. An overview of the types of products SMEs might deal with follows.

8.7.2 Types of products

All SMEs should know exactly what type of product they deal with. Some market segments are more inclined to use different products, depending on both their personal characteristics and the product's function. Some products satisfy consumers' wants (therefore, their purchase is influenced by personal wishes, and consumers' decision-making is characterised by a less rational component, so it is also less predictable), while other products satisfy consumers' needs (therefore, their purchase is influenced by a real need to be satisfied in a timely fashion, and consumers' decision-making is more rational and perhaps predictable). We will categorise the three main typologies of products that are generally recognised in the marketing literature and will describe what types of products belong in these categories. The three main categories are convenience, shopping and industrial products.

Convenience products are products characterised by their ability to satisfy impulses, although their purchase is often motivated by the surge of a need. This category includes staple, impulse and emergency products.

Staple products are low-involvement, meaning that consumers tend not to put much effort in the transaction. These products generally require the attention of the consumer for the first transaction. However, once that takes place, subsequent purchases are generally quite automatic, and the level of loyalty is generally high. Examples of products belonging to this subcategory are toothpaste, deodorant, and shampoo. Availability is critical to the success of the continued purchase. Unless there is a lack of product available on the shelves, consumers are generally not tempted to switch brands. Therefore the substitution effect, which is often triggered by lack of stock, is a threat to the success of staples.

A second convenience products subcategory is impulse products. Impulse product purchases are rooted in consumers' wants rather than real needs. Impulse products are often purchased on an irrational basis; examples include chocolate, ice cream, and indulgence food. Exposing the consumer to the product often triggers impulse behaviour. Consumers who are exposed to the product, if they are required to make a purchase decision under stress, act impulsively and purchase it. This is particularly true when it is a low-involvement purchase because it is inexpensive. However, a major threat to this type of products is the possible emergence of cognitive dissonances in consumers.

Another subcategory of convenience products is emergency products, which are generally low involvement, and their purchase is stimulated by an immediate need. Examples are umbrellas on rainy days or bottles of water on the top of a mountain. The sales of these products capitalise on stock availability; therefore, SMEs dealing with this type of products should make sure they always stock some minimum quantities to front sudden increased demand, or they might lose business. Furthermore, these products are often characterised by a strong and sudden need, so price sensitivity decreases, and consumers might be (unhappily) ready to pay a higher price.

Shopping products are different from convenience products. They are characterised by medium to high involvement and more rational choices are made for the products in this category. These products are split into further subcategories: homogeneous, heterogeneous, specialty, and unsought products.

Homogeneous products have very low differentiation features between brands. Although in recent years there are some exceptions, generally, these are commodities, such as eggs, chicken or beef. Each brand's chicken breasts look the same, some might argue. The sale of this type of products is leveraged on consumers' perceptions of quality. Purchase decisions take place under the condition that it is often very difficult to distinguish one brand from the other because the product is fundamentally perceived as being the same. The purchase involvement of these products is often low; therefore, consumers often purchase the product based on the visual information they receive from packaging and labelling. SMEs dealing with these products should try to differentiate the product by capitalising on product concept manipulations at both the actual and augmented level.

A quite different subcategory is heterogeneous products. While homogeneous products all look alike, heterogeneous products are all different from one another. Although the core level of the product concept is often identical for all heterogeneous products, consumers' choices are often influenced by their aesthetic characteristics. One example is clothing. There are many different types of pullovers in clothing shops, and they come in different shapes, colours, sizes, patterns and fabric. The purchase is often high involvement, as consumers often need time to reflect on what to choose amongst a great deal of offered items. Therefore, firms dealing with these products should capitalise on the aesthetics of the product and, where possible, add value through a modification of the design at core level (e.g., a warmer-than-average pullover) or by manipulating the product at augmented level (e.g., including sartorial modifications in the purchase price).

Another subcategory is specialty products, which feature really high involvement, meaning that consumers pay really close attention to the characteristics and price. These products are often expensive and cannot be found everywhere; they must be purchased in specialised shops. These products are often bought infrequently and sometimes even just once or twice in a lifetime. Examples of these products are musical instruments, like pianos, and jewels. Consumers who purchase these look at all aspects of the product concept and are often pushed by the feeling of exclusivity in the purchase experience. SMEs that sell this type of product should make sure they match consumers' preferences, both at the core and actual product levels, and on top of that, they should also capitalise on the post-sale service.

Finally, there are unsought products. These products are often high-involvement, and consumers find themselves suddenly needing to purchase something they never thought about before they needed it. Examples of products in this subcategory are medicines or coffins. Consumers purchasing these products are often ready to pay a higher price because of the need for a solution to an unusual or awkward problem, like a headache.

The last category consists of industrial products: equipment (i.e., machinery), installations (e.g., production lines), spare parts (e.g., bolts to use in machinery), or raw materials, as well as semi-worked materials (e.g., hardware components for a computer manufacturer), and the supply of services (e.g., shipments). These products are often used in a B2B context and might be high-involvement products (like equipment or installations) or low-involvement products (like spare parts or semi-worked materials). Consumers, which are generally firms, that purchase these types of products need a guarantee of the quality of what they purchase. SMEs dealing with this type of products might need to manipulate the product concept both at the core level (whenever possible, perhaps by a modification of the basic function of machinery to be supplied to a firm) or at the augmented level (e.g., post-sale service). Consumers purchasing these products are less interested in modifications at the actual level, which are mainly aesthetical.

References

[1] The Economist. All the way to the bank.. 23 August 2007.
[2] Anderson WT, Golden LL. Lifestyle and psychographics: a critical review and recommendation. Advances in Consumer Research. 1984; 11(1): 405–11.
[3] Assael H, Roscoe J, Marvin A. Approaches to market segmentation analysis. Journal of Marketing. 1976; 40(4): 67–76.
[4] Barnes C, Blake H, Pinder D. Creating and Delivering Your Value Proposition: Managing Customer Experience for Profit. Kogan Page Publishers; 2009.
[5] Birkin M, Clarke G. GIS, Geodemographics, and Spatial Modeling in the U.K. Financial Service Industry. Journal of Housing Research. 1998; 9(1): 87–98.
[6] Bonney L, Clark R, Collins R, Fearne, A. From serendipity to sustainable competitive advantage: insights from Houston's Farm and their journey of co-innovation. [Case Study]. Supply Chain Management: An International Journal. 2007; Vol. 12 (No. 6): pp. 395–9.
[7] Burrows R, Gane N. Geodemographics, software and class. Sociology. 2006; 40 (5): 793–812.
[8] Buttle F. Customer relationship management. Routledge; 2012.

[9] Callingham M, Baker T. We know what they think, but do we know what they do? International Journal of Market Research. 2002; 44 (3 [Quarter 3]): p. 299.
[10] Charlton M, Openshaw S, Wymer C. A poor man's ACORN. Journal of Economic & Social Measurement. 1985; 13(1): pp. 69–96.
[11] Christopher M. Logistics and Supply Chain Management: Creating Value-Added Networks. Harlow: Prentice Halls Financial Times; 2005.
[12] Croxton KL, Garcia-Dastugue, SJ, Lambert, DM, Rogers, DS The supply chain management processes. The International Journal of Logistics Management. 2001; Vol. 12 (No. 2): pp. 13–36.
[13] Debenham JC, G. Stillwell, J. Extending geodemographic classification: a new regional prototype Environment and Planning A. 2003; 35 (6): 1025–50
[14] Fearne A. Sustainable Food and Wine Value Chains. Adelaide: Government of South Australia; 2009. pp. 1–42.
[15] Goss J. "We know who you are and we know where you live": The instrumental rationality of geodemographic. Economic Geography. 1995; 71 (2): p. 171.
[16] Harris R, Sleight, P, Webber, R. Geodemographics: neighbourhood targeting and GIS. Chichester: Wiley; 2005.
[17] Hoek J, Gendall P, Esslemont D. Market segmentation: a search for the Holy Grail? Journal of Marketing Practice: Applied Marketing Science. 1996; 2 (1): 25–34.
[18] Humby CR. New developments in demographic targeting – the implications of 1991. Journal of the Market Research Society. 1989; 31 (1): 53–73.
[19] Kaplan RS. Strategy maps: Converting intangible assets into tangible outcomes: Harvard Business Press; 2004.
[20] Ketchen Jr DJ, Hult GTM. Bridging organization theory and supply chain management: the case of best value supply chains. Journal of Operations Management. 2007; 25 (2): 573–80.
[21] Kotler PH. Marketing Management: Analysis, Planning, and Control. 7th ed. Englewood Cliffs, NJ: Prentice-Hall; 1991.
[22] Lin CF. Segmenting customer brand preference: demographic or psychographic. Journal of Product & Brand Management. 2002; 11 (5): 249.
[23] Longley P. Geographical Information Systems: a renaissance of geodemographics for public service delivery. Progress in Human Geography. 1 February 2005 ; 29 (1): 57–63.
[24] Martin RL, Osberg S. Social entrepreneurship: the case for definition. Stanford Social Innovation Review. 2007; 5 (2): 27–39.
[25] Mitchell V-W, McGoldrick PJ. The role of geodemographics in segmenting and targeting consumer markets: A Delphi study. European Journal of Marketing. 1994; 28 (5): 54–72.
[26] O'Malley L, Patterson M. Retailer use of geodemographic and other data sources: an empirical investigation. International Journal of Retail & Distribution Management. 1997; 25 (6/7): 188.
[27] Openshaw S. Making geodemographics more sophisticated. Journal of the Market Research Society. 1989; 31 (1): 111–31.
[28] Payne A, Frow P. Customer relationship management: from strategy to implementation. Journal of Marketing Management. 2006; 22 (1–2): 135–68.

[29] Porter M. Competitive Advantage – Creating and Sustaining Superior Performance. 2nd ed. ed. New York: The Free Press; 1985. pp. 59.
[30] Ries A, Trout J. Positioning, the Battle for Your Mind. New York: McGraw-Hill; 2001.
[31] Robinson J. The Economics of Imperfect Competition. London: McMillan; 1938.
[32] Segal MN, Giacobbe RW. Market segmentation and competitive analysis for supermarket retailing. International Journal of Retail & Distribution Management. 1994; 22 (1): 38–48.
[33] Sleight P. Targeting Customers: How to Use Geodemographic and Lifestyle Data in Your Business. 2nd ed.1997.
[34] Solomon MR, Marshall GW, Stuart EW, Barnes B, Mitchell V-W. Marketing: Real People, Real Decisions. London: FT Prentice Hall; 2009.
[35] Tonks D. Pinning down geodemographics. Marketing Intelligence & Planning. 1990; 8 (2): 4–10.
[36] Ulaga W, Reinartz WJ. Hybrid Offerings: How Manufacturing Firms Combine Goods and Services Successfully. Journal of Marketing. 2011;75 (6): 5–23.
[37] Vickers D. Creating the national classification of census output areas: data, methods,and results. Leeds: School of Geography, University of Leeds; 2005.
[38] Voas D, Williamson P. The diversity of diversity: a critique of geodemographic classification. Area. 2001; 33 (1): 63–76.
[39] Wells WD. Psychographics: a critical review. Journal of Marketing Research. 1975; 12 (2): 196–213.
[40] Wind Y. Issues and advances in segmentation research. Journal of Marketing Research. 1978; 15 (3): 317–37.
[41] Young S, Ott L, Feigin B. Some practical considerations in market segmentation. Journal of Marketing Research. 1978; 405–12.
[42] Zeithaml VA. Consumer perceptions of price, quality, and value: a means-end model and synthesis of evidence. Journal of Marketing. 1988; 52 (3): 2–22.

9
Pricing and Distribution Decisions in a Context of Low Distribution Capacity

SMEs often have to deal with the problems related to low profitability and low liquidity. Low profitability might also be affected by slow business growth and gives an indication of the lack of efficiency within an SME, whereas lack of business growth might indicate difficulties in the existing market, other than with the firm itself. Low market growth and low profitability cause problems in terms of liquidity, because undercapitalised SMEs do not have the necessary working capital – i.e., the capital used to cover liabilities with current assets – and therefore are subject to debt when assets cannot be turned quickly into cash.

You can imagine the difficulties in dealing with lack of liquidity. It means firms might not be able to pay their suppliers, or might find themselves in difficulties at providing different bits and pieces of their service, therefore limiting the distribution of their products to consumers. The decrease in distribution capacity causes loss of business. An example you might be familiar with is when you go to a small, undercapitalised café, and you struggle to order food because of a lack of product availability. Although they might have an extensive menu printed on paper, in fact, the available options are very limited. This is often caused by a lack of liquidity and the café's inability to purchase all the ingredients for all the options on their menu. Given a lack of liquidity, firms start cutting on costs, and unfortunately, they often find they need to cut down on essential things that eventually will negatively affect their performance with consumers.

In order to avoid ending up with problems related to working capital, SMEs should ask themselves two important questions: "Are my products' prices appropriate for my target market?" and "Where do my consumers live?"

These two questions are critical in order to limit potential problems deriving from little liquidity. In order to improve the effectiveness of their marketing, SMEs should first of all understand whether they erode value by pricing the product incorrectly, with respect to the target segments' purchasing willingness. Likewise, SMEs should also try to understand whether the channel of distribution they use and the geographical location they cover are appropriate to match their products to their target segments.

9.1 Pricing strategies

Pricing strategies in SMEs are not very different from classical strategies used by larger organisations. There are, of course, some differences in the way promotions are designed and run. However, the pricing strategies you may have learnt in previous university modules like Introduction to Marketing and Marketing Strategy can apply to SMEs. Therefore, we would recommend revising existing pricing strategies used in classical marketing textbooks [1, 3–9].

For SMEs, it is important to pitch the price at the right level. Quite often, SMEs are unable to price their products according to their specific target market. It becomes, therefore, very important to be able to see the price as an element of the value proposition, rather than as a separate and detached attribute of the product. In previous chapters, we indicated how important it is for SMEs to think in terms of value propositions, in order to segment and target specific consumer groups. However, many SMEs find it difficult to pitch the price at the right level.

SMEs do not have access to marketing information to let them know the price preferences of specific target segments, nor do have they information about the performance of a specific channel of distribution. Nevertheless, SMEs can find ways to collect and analyse information that help them to support marketing decision-making in terms of pricing and distribution strategies.

In order to answer the previous question, 'Are my products' prices appropriate for my target market?' we should look in more detail at the price-sensitivity of consumers. In the segmentation chapter, we classified consumers according to different geographical, social, economic and psychographic characteristics. Nevertheless, we also often grouped consumers within those classifications by indicating their level of price sensitivity. In order to understand the concept, we have to look into the value continuum, as consumers tend to swing either towards high quality and higher price or lower quality and lower price [10].

Furthermore, 'successful retailers increasingly target their offers towards two consumer categories: those with an emphasis on value and those for whom time pressure is the key' [2].

We can build a value continuum for every single product, and the product will have stronger or weaker appeal to different target segments depending on the position of the product on the value continuum. Let us take a simple example from the food and drink industry, and try to position white bread on the value continuum. White bread is a commodity whose sales are – at least in the UK – associated with the lower classes, i.e., white bread is not as healthy as brown bread, is much cheaper, and is widely available in big pack sizes, unlike brown bread. However, it is possible to differentiate a commodity such as white bread by improving its taste and texture, creating specialty bread. Let us look at the profile of supermarket shoppers who purchase 'crusty white bread' (baked in-store) versus the profile of those shoppers who purchase 'specialty breads' (always baked in-store).

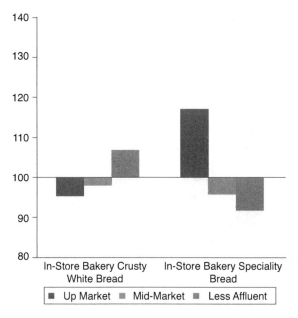

Figure 9.1 White bread shoppers' profiles. (Data for a major UK supermarket for 52 weeks from 29 September 2008 to 27 September 2009)

Source: Author's own (data source: © dunnhumby 2009).

Pricing and Distribution Decisions in a Context of Low Distribution Capacity 153

In the graph, coloured rectangles represent shoppers: purple for up-market shoppers (They have sophisticated tastes and high purchasing power), dark yellow for mid-market shoppers (They have high available income, although it is lower than the up-market shoppers'; they prefer well-known brands), and finally, light brown represents less affluent shoppers (They have little available income, and their taste if often unsophisticated). The reference line to compare those groups is the line with base value set on 100 (This is an index, created to simplify calculations), and our value of 100 indicates this is the average value of reference in terms of consumers' preferences. Those rectangles that are above the 100 base line indicate a strong appeal for the product, whereas those rectangles that extend under the 100 base line indicate a lack of appeal. The further they are from the 100 base value, the stronger or weaker the appeal.

As it can be seen by the graph, simple white bread appeals more to less affluent shoppers, as it is a bit cheaper than other types of bread, and it is also very simple. Nevertheless, specialty bread has a stronger appeal with up-market shoppers who are willing to pay for a higher price to satisfy their taste, which is more sophisticated. Therefore, we can draw a continuum from our bread example, which could apply to many other products or services.

The continuum goes from a cheaper, or more basic, option to a more expensive or premium option. A basic product is simple, often undifferentiated, and consumers' drive to purchase is mainly the price. Price, along with low purchase involvement, makes a success of products belonging to the basic type. Basic products are often associated with lower quality and have a very cheap price. On the other side of the spectrum, there are premium products, which are characterised by high differentiation.

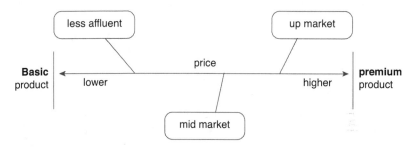

Figure 9.2 Value continuum
Source: Author's own.

These products are often associated with very high quality and higher price; therefore, the level of involvement during the phase of purchase is higher than basic products. Depending on the products' characteristics, the target market's personal characteristics, and finally the price, the offered products will be more or less strongly appeal to the SME's target segment .

Another important aspect to take into consideration, as part of the sales' strategy, along with pricing, is the type of distribution the SME chooses for reaching its consumers with its value propositions. Distribution will be dealt with in the next section.

9.2 Distribution strategies

SMEs, like larger organisations, can capitalise on different channels of distribution. The choice of the channel of distribution should be thought of as a strategic choice for the firm because it will determine the success or failure of the distribution of the firm's products. Different channels of distribution exist, and, again, this is a topic largely discussed in fundamental modules of marketing in most universities; therefore, we would – once more – refer to traditional marketing books [1, 3–9] for the theory on distribution.

Nevertheless, there are some important considerations for SMEs' distribution strategies. First for all, we have to say that consumer segments live, work and shop in different geographical areas. So the very first consideration is related to where the target consumers live. SMEs often do not have access to formal market research, and therefore, it is difficult for firms to identify what is the most effective channel of distribution. Depending on the sector and industry the SME operates in, it might be possible to collect information about consumers and perhaps determine the geographical location of a little sample of consumers, to have an idea of where consumers live and work.

Offers could be better targeted according to the geographical distribution of the consumers in the territory. Some consumer segments have a stronger preference for specific channels of distribution than others. For instance, some shoppers prefer purchasing products online, and others prefer accessing products in a shop. Some might have a preference for home delivery or catalogue sales, and so on. Therefore, identifying consumers' preferences in terms of channel of distribution is beneficial to the construction of the firm's distribution strategy. Often, firms choose a specific way of distributing their products only based on the firm's convenience. Nevertheless, the distribution strategy should be consumer-lead. By gaining a better understanding of consumers' purchasing venues preferences, SMEs make sure they can reach consumers in a timely, smooth manner, which would be ignored if we distributed them through the wrong channels.

The second consideration to look at consists of the level of customer penetration that firms can find in different geographical areas. Different segments that concentrate in different geographical areas prefer different channels of distribution. By looking at the level of customer penetration for a specific product from a specific geographical area, SMEs could determine the level of preference or consumers' willingness to purchase their products. An example could be the purchase of homemade jam, which an SME might sell over the Internet. By collecting information about the geographical location of their consumers, the SME could determine the level of customer penetration for their homemade jam within specific geographical boundaries, thereby knowing the destination of their purchases and the willingness to purchase.

The determination of the right combination of distribution channels is not easy to discuss in general terms, as each firm is different, and some channels of distribution are industry-specific. Therefore, in this venue, it is not possible to discuss all the possibilities for a successful distribution strategy. Nevertheless, this type of knowledge might enable SMEs to know how to improve sales by targeting their marketing communication efforts to those geographical areas whose appeal for the product over- or underperforms with respect to all the geographical areas taken into consideration by the firm. Likewise, SMEs could also use this type of information to develop underdeveloped channels or locations with different offers, as well as to increase repeat purchase and purchase frequency in those areas with a stronger appeal than the average.

References

[1] Berkowitz EN, Kering RA, Hartley SW, Rudelius W. Marketing. 4th ed. Homewood, IL: Irwin; 1994.
[2] Burden S. Current trends and issues in the retail sector. European Venture Capital Journal. 1998; 1(November): 1–5.
[3] Dibb S, Sinkin L, Pride WM, Ferrell OC. Marketing: Concepts and Strategies. 3rd European ed. Boston, MA: Houghton Mifflin; 1997.
[4] Hollensen S. Global Marketing: A Decision-Oriented Approach. Madrid, Spain: FT Prentice Hall; 2010.
[5] Jobber D. Principles and Practice of Marketing. 4th ed: McGraw Hill Ed; 2004.
[6] Kotler P. Marketing Management. Upper Saddle River, New Jersey: Prentice-Hall; 2000.

[7] Kotler PH. Marketing Management: Analysis, Planning, and Control. 7th ed. Englewood Cliffs, NJ: Prentice-Hall; 1991.
[8] Saren M. Marketing Theory: A Student Text. London: Cengage Learning; 2000.
[9] Solomon MR, Marshall GW, Stuart EW, Barnes B, Mitchell V-W. Marketing: Real People, Real Decisions. London: FT Prentice Hall; 2009.
[10] Sweeney JC, Soutar GN. Consumer perceived value: The development of a multiple item scale. Journal of Retailing. 2001; 77(2): 203–20.

10
Building Brands in SMEs

Brands are nowadays paramount to the success of an organisation. We live in a branded world. If you look around, everything you use in your life, be it clothes or electrical appliances, books or pens, means of transport or a take-away meal, you cannot avoid encountering brands.

Brands play a crucial role in helping organisations that use them to gain consumers' attention. Brands are not only a distinctive logo or sign to differentiate the product from a competitor. They are a powerful means of communication that organisations can use to build a relationship with their consumers. Brands can be used to communicate the quality of the product to consumers in a first instance, but they can also help the company to communicate what the company stands for. They can communicate the philosophy, mission and vision of the organisation that uses them.

Brands have always been important to differentiate a product sold in competitive markets, but, nowadays, branding is an essential tool to support organisational identity and reputation[38]. By aligning brands, organisational identity and reputation has proven to be a very powerful marketing tool for larger organisations; however, in time, SMEs also started approaching the concept of branding[2].

This chapter provides information about the function of brands and branding activity in SMEs. In this chapter, you can also find a description of those factors that are important for brands' success, and learn how brands link with the mission and vision of an organisation.

10.1 Brands functionality and the branding activity

All the definitions of brand tend to highlight two functions: first, a competitive function – i.e., brands exist to differentiate a product, service or company from the competitors[13] – and second, the relational function – i.e., brands communicate to the consumer what the organisation stands for[1, 13].

One way to discuss the different definitions of brand is according to their focus. There are three groups: functional definitions (focusing on the physical features of the product) developed between the 1960s until the late 1980s; customer-oriented definitions (whose focus is on the customer as the centre of the branding activity) developed in the 1990s; and relational definitions (focusing on the brand as a relationship between the consumers and the company) developed in the last decade or so and strictly connected to the concept of value proposition.[1]

10.1.1 Differentiating function

The seminal definition of brand focuses mainly on the functional and physical elements of differentiation (e.g., logotype, name, font, colour, shape, etc.). 'A brand is a name, term, design, symbol or any other feature that identifies one seller's goods or service as distinct from those of other sellers'. Several authors share the same definition[8, 14, 28, 33], focusing on the physical attributes or features of the design aimed to obtain a competitive advantage because these physical features are more straightforward to people's perceptions and understanding.

Considering the physically related definition of brand, which is associated with the physical features (e.g., name, sign, symbol), there is a strong tendency among practitioners to combine marketing and design. Design allows the company to express its personality through the product or service. When customers engage with the company through the tangible, physical, aesthetical characteristics of the product, the brand receives a personality and creates a meaning in the customers' minds, in which the product or service is just one expression of this same meaning.

For example, the iPad represents high technology and entertainment in a young, active, cool and fashionable device. Similarly, the dancing Chinese character 'Jing',[2] presented in a white and red calligraphic stone carving, represented activity, vibrant and energetic movement, noble sentiments in sport, tradition, and modernity for the Olympics in Beijing in 2008.

10.1.2 Communication function

An overly strong focus on the physical aspects of the brand might create confusion about what a brand really is, if it is only about the logo type, colour and functional features. This gave rise to criticism in the 1990s that called for a refocus on customers or consumers – the ultimate targets of the brands – whose views, attitudes and perceptions are critical to the development of brand awareness and brand loyalty.

Wood[41] comments on the seminal definition of brand, stating that the key aspects of the definition are the words 'any other feature', as this allows for intangibles, such as image, to be the point of differentiation. The particular value of this definition is that it focuses on a fundamental brand purpose, which is differentiation[41]. These intangibles allow the definition of brand to shift over time from a functional definition toward a customer-oriented definition.

Ambler[4] considers the brand to be 'the promise of the bundles of attributes that someone buys and provides satisfaction'. The attributes Ambler[4] refers to can be tangible or invisible, rational or emotional, and real or illusory. Thus, the focus of this definition shifts from the physical aspects of the brand proposition to the perceptions of customers and/or consumers. It focuses on the implicit fact that it is customers who buy the brand, and they should be satisfied through the promises made by the company, which are stated by the brand.

In a later work, Ambler and Styles[5] revised the brand development process and, consequently, they now define brands according to two different approaches: 'product plus' and 'holistic'. The product plus approach does not differ from the previous definitions, as it sees the brand as a distinctive element of the product line, identifying the product or company. However, by the holistic point of view, 'the brand is considered to be the sum of all elements of the marketing mix: product is just one element, alongside price, promotion and distribution'[5], seeing the brand in all its extensions. The major contribution of this perspective is the inclusion of the marketing mix, so that brand is no longer just the name or logotype, but also encompasses the distribution channel, the price dimension and the way the message is communicated.

The functional and the physical elements of the brand provide a vehicle for physical differentiation (e.g., appearance of the product, packaging, labelling, etc.), whereas the customer- and consumer-centric definition of Ambler and Styles[5] emphasises the deeper (emotional) relational function of branding.

10.1.3 Relational function

The definition of brand has shifted over time – from the customer-related definition towards the relational definition – as brands create relationships with the consumers or customers. Brands should differentiate while communicating to the customers and consumers with whom they are seeking to build a relationship[1, 12, 27].

Brown[9] proposes that a brand is all the mental connections that people have around it, so every time a customer or consumer thinks of or encounters a brand, some mental connections are generated, creating a relationship with the brand through recognition.

De Chernatony and McDonald[13] see brands as a 'relationship' with the customer:

> This relationship is personified either by the organization's name, or by the brand name on the product itself. ... When we refer to the term "brand" ... we use it to encompass not only consumer products, but a whole host of offerings, which include people (such as politicians and pop stars), places (such as Bangkok), ships (such as the QEII), companies, industrial products, service products, and so on[13].

Therefore, a brand is more than just the sum of its component parts. 'It embodies, for the purchaser or user, additional attributes which, whilst they might be considered by some to be "intangible", are still very real' [13]. In this last statement, de Chernatony and McDonald[13] build a more complete definition:

> A successful brand is an identifiable product, service, person or place, augmented in such a way that the buyer or user perceives relevant, unique added values which match their needs most closely. Furthermore, its success results from being able to sustain these added values in the face of competition[13].

An extended definition of brand – categorised as relational – is provided by Aacker[1], who states that a brand is more than a product. The latter is characterised by its scope, attributes, quality/value and uses³, whereas a brand has additional elements⁴. For example, brand users (the Charlie woman), country of origin (Audi has German craftsmanship), organisational associations (3M is an innovative company), brand personality (Bath and Body Works is a retail brand with energy and vitality), symbols (the stagecoach represents Wells Fargo Bank), brand-customer relationship (Gateway is a friend), emotional benefits (Saturn owners feel pride about driving an American car) and self-expressive benefits (a Hobart customer uses only the best), can all be categorised as relational because of the different relational elements entering the definition, i.e., all those elements that contribute to create a relationship, or bond, with the customer or consumer.

10.1.4 The 'value' element of branding

In addition to the introduction of the concept of relationship in the definition, the major contribution of these authors to the definition consists in the insertion of the value element when stating that the buyer or user perceives relevant, unique added values matching their needs. This definition encompasses both the functional and the customer-oriented definitions, adding the value perception dimension, which is most relevant to the completion of the transaction – the purchase. The reference to uniqueness brings us back to the concept of competition, because a company that has a unique (added) value proposition which matches most closely what its customers wants is more likely to succeed. Once more, it is underlined that the core function of a brand is to differentiate. However, the issue of value receives particular attention in the relational definitions.

Value is perceived when the advantage or benefit gained by the customer or consumer is higher than the costs (monetary costs, opportunity costs and risk) involved in acquiring this advantage. According to Monroe[32], it is the ratio of the perceived benefits and perceived sacrifice. Value is the basic foundation of everything that is done in marketing[21], and it is recognised that customers' satisfaction depends on value[22, 29].

The competitiveness of a brand, though, can be based on only two strategies[13]: the first is cost driven – which is based on the ability to sell at a lower price due to lower costs – and the second is value added – which is based on the creation of value. This is the element that proves the effectiveness of the brand, because customers' purchases take place when they perceive genuine value: because of low price (value for money) or enhanced benefits (emotional value).

According to the relational definitions, brands have to create a relationship with consumers or customers by delivering value. It is important for companies to pursue a relationship marketing strategy because it creates more value for its customers than companies that focus on the product only through stronger ties – related to technology, information and knowledge[19]. Value is delivered through value propositions, i.e., a valuable offer (everything that is offered to the customer against his/her price). The value proposition describes the unique product and service mix, customer relations, and corporate image that are offered by the company[25].

By following a cost-driven strategy, the value proposition finds its essence or value in the lower price, due to its ability to lower cost production, whereas a value-added value proposition finds its essence in the perceived higher benefits deriving from the purchase. The introduction of product or service features that are not driven by the actual customers' needs can be nothing more than a short-term solution[20].

10.2 Mission statements and consumers' experience

Mission statements are specific messages or mottos a firm uses to channel the ethos of the company. There are different types of mission statements, depending on the purpose for which they have been created by the firm[10]. Some mission statements express in one sentence (or a few) the overall vision of the firm (what it desires to be in the very long term) or the strategy the firm is pursuing: that is, what the company aims to achieve with their activities. Mission statements are very helpful to determine a very clear direction to the employees of the firm and are the flagship of the company, so they indicate the type of culture shared within the organisation.

However, in some cases, mission statements can also be constraining if they are not created properly. They are often public, and both customers and consumers can access them. In some cases, mission statements become part of the brand or are strongly associated with it, so they can contribute to the overall customer experience. Firms with clear mission statements are more likely to monitor the success of their mission statements and are more likely to survey their customers, therefore finding ways to improve customers' experiences[17] with their products or brands. So, overall, clear mission statements can speak to a firm's stakeholders (including employees and customers) about what the firm stands for. The mission statement reinforces the brand, and the brand reinforces the mission statement.

10.3 The importance of branding and branding success factors

Marketing information contributes to brand equity, and, according to Keller[26], the main motivations to pay attention to a company's brand equity can be found in the financial need to estimate the value of a brand (in terms of asset valuation, i.e., for merger, acquisitions or divestiture) and in the need to improve marketing productivity. Therefore, branding is an important tool firms can capitalise on. However, there are some specific factors that affect the success of brands.

10.3.1 Why branding is important

Branding is a vital activity for companies, and several reasons have been given in the literature to support the importance of branding for businesses. First, they differentiate one company's products or offer to the customer from another[3, 8, 13-14, 28, 33].

A second reason sees brands expressing the uniqueness of a company's value proposition, creating a relationship with the customer or consumer [1, 12-13, 25, 27]. Brands help companies to position their products or services, and therefore, they become a strategic asset through the creation of brand awareness and recognition, better relationships and higher loyalty, which can potentially generate overall future income (brand equity). Brands can create a mental connection with the customer[9], in fact:

'A brand is a strategic asset that is key to long-term performance and should be so managed' [1]. There is evidence that brands contribute to the creation of relationships with the customer or consumer. De Chernatony and McDonald support the relationship function of brands [13]: 'Brands can develop different relationships with customers...and a successful brand aims to develop a high-quality relationship, in which customers feel a sense of commitment and belonging', they maintain, adding that 'relationship marketing aims to develop long-term loyal customers'.

However, the importance of branding is dependent on the role of the brand as perceived by the brand owner. For example, some practitioners (especially in SMEs) might perceive the brand as nothing more than a name on a package, whereas others might perceive the brand as a promise to deliver what the customer wants, and still others may view the brand as a vehicle for communicating the core values of the business.

To companies dealing with commodities, the functional element of the brand might be more prominent than the emotional aspects, whereas in other sectors, the emotional element might be more relevant. Therefore, the orientation to branding might affect the company in the perception of the importance of the brand.

A third reason for branding's importance can be found in the ability of brands to create recognition[31, 39], and consequently, the success of a brand can be defined as the degree of brand recognition. Brand recognition occurs when customers or consumers know the brand and its qualities,[39] and consumers tend to recall those with high recognition more easily[31].

As a fourth reason, brands can generate and increase trust and decrease the perception of risk related to potential cognitive dissonances. Brands can do this because, generally speaking, people fear the unknown, and there is a higher tendency to be loyal to or to trust brands that are well known, long established and already 'run-in'[6, 15]. Familiarity generates higher trust, and more information about the brand means the customer is better positioned to make the right decision and reduce risk[24]. The more people know about a brand, the easier it is to trust it, simply because the risk is lower; branding reduces uncertainty[7, 11, 23, 36].

Brands with high recognition are undeniably valuable because they guarantee future income streams. Companies know that loyal customers will repeatedly buy their brands and are also more willing to support them during a crises[13].

A fifth reason branding is important is found in brands' ability to deliver satisfaction through a promise of performance [4] and to encompass all the elements of the marketing mix[5].

A sixth reason for the importance of branding is the creation of value[1, 30]. Brands can compete when they are able to deliver a value to the consumer, i.e., when the benefit they deliver is greater than the cost (financial and non-financial) and the risk involved in the transaction.

In light of the literature, it can be concluded that brands are important tools to compete on the market because of the potential differentiation they can express. This differentiation can be expressed through brands that are able to create relationships with the customers or consumers. However, the relationships are built on the messages the brand manages to communicate through its identity, i.e., it depends on how it manages to position itself in people's perceptions. The identity of a brand should be clear, so it is reflected in the value proposition and conveys the functional and emotional meanings to the customers or consumers. However, the ability to convey the meanings depends on the level of understanding of the brand by the practitioner. It differs from one company to another because the business world is heterogeneous with companies of all sizes and resources operating in different markets.

10.3.2 Success factors in branding

The literature points out eight main factors of success in brand building. First, it appears that a clear statement of intent about what the brand stands for is an essential ingredient in branding[1, 13], contributing to a crystal-clear brand identity by capitalising on a strong value proposition.

Second, culture is another success factor, alongside customer focus. The most relevant success factor is the acquisition, analysis and use of marketing information, on the grounds that no effective and efficient decision-making can take place without a sound knowledge of the market, thereby disabling the competitiveness of the company operating in blindness on the market. From the literature, it emerges that the lack of marketing information is a barrier to the brand development process.

The cultural element and the quality of the leadership are important aspects of the potential success of branding because what brands communicate is captured by people's perceptions and translated into a positioning in customers' minds. Customers then match their perceptions of value to the value proposition positioned in their minds[35].

Aacker [1] agrees that 'brands are the basis for sustainable advantage for most organisations. However, strong brands do not just happen. Rather, they result from the creation of winning brand strategies and brilliant executions from committed, disciplined organizations'[1].

A third factor of success is the fact that committed organisations are probably more likely to build strategies on the basis of the information collected from the market. Therefore, marketing intelligence plays a fundamental role because, through the collection of data, there is a higher probability that a business will gain a deeper understanding of the information necessary to develop a brand[18].

And fourth, positioning and image creation are other factors of success in brand development, along with the creation of an image [13, 34, 40].

Ries and Trout[34] make the point that creating positioning in customers' minds is of utmost importance as, in today's marketplace, the strategies that worked in the past do not work anymore, because there is an overload of offers in terms of products and brands, and the only way to create a successful brand[5] is, according to the authors, to keep it simple and deliver straightforward messages. They suggest touching base with reality, and the only reality worth considering is the one lived by the consumers or customers.

They maintain that creating something new is almost impossible nowadays, so a better tactic is to reposition what already exists.

Differentiation is the core of branding; however, it is often difficult to find the right way to generate something different. This is especially true in sophisticated and fast-moving markets. Different levels of sophistication correspond to some behavioural tendencies, so where there is low sophistication, brands stress product features. However, when there is high sophistication, and with the increase in the competition, product features are a given, the stress shifts to the emotional and rational components of value perception.

A fifth factor is brand identity, along with coherence of thought and action[1, 13, 37]. It is important because it attracts customers' interest and possibly builds loyalty. The basic step is to have a clear specification of brand identity and position – where the brand stands – in order to provide value[1, 12–13].

Strong coherence of thought and action should be shown in order to contribute to a clear identity that will be expressed in brand recognition through the image positioned. Among the examples that can be found to support this assertion is the case of Innocent Drinks' smoothies. They attribute most of their success to the image created through an integration of good graphic design, product characteristics and corporate culture.

Coherence of thought and action can result in the creation of added value and stronger brand identity for the firm. Furthermore, it contributes to an appropriate structure in the organisational assets of the corporate management and professional groups, as Schroeder and Salzer-Möling[37] suggested; de Chernatony and McDonald[13] supported the notion: 'Everyone should be aware of what the brand stands for and they all need to be committed to contributing to its success'.

Coherence of thought and action leading to consistency over time can be achieved with a continuous effort to position the brand. Positioning can be effective through the action of leadership, which is able to serve the need of coherence between what the brand communicates and the company values. It is business culture that determines the clarity of the value proposition. In other words, when the leadership is able to define clearly what the brand represents, it is more likely that other people within the business will be able to do so. More importantly, vision, corporate culture, and brand identity and image on their own are not very useful; it is the relationship among them that determines success, as Vallaster and de Chernatony[40] proposed.

Aacker considers brand identity to be one of the four main dimensions of brand equity,, as well as the heart and soul of the brand. In order to create a successful brand, it must be provided with a soul. There is the need to focus on the creation of a strong and coherent brand identity in order to maximise the strength of the brand.

Aacker warns of four main traps that firms fall into, in the context of brand identity[6], ending in dysfunctional brand strategies or an excessively narrow tactical focus: brand image trap, brand position trap, external perspective trap, and product-attribute fixation trap.

Brand image, i.e., how customers perceive the brand, is important to brand identity, but the main trap is making the mistake of identifying the brand image with the brand identity when image is just an aspect of identity. Falling into this trap shows when there are some image inadequacies caused by consumers' past experiences, or by changes in their needs, so the image no longer transmits or communicates its identity statement[1].

Brand position is defined by Aacker[4] as the 'part of the brand identity and value proposition that is to be actively communicated to the target audience and that demonstrates an advantage over competing brands'. It is related to the communicative aspects of the identity to the customers and to the statement related to the brand. The second trap consists of considering the brand position as the main brand identity, eliminating all those aspects that are not considered worth communicating. When communicating the brand position, if it is believed to be the brand identity, there is a tendency to stress the product attributes, while forgetting to show the personality of the brand, the symbols connected to it, or the associations with the company's values and vision.

The third trap consists of the lack of understanding of the importance of the role of brand identity.

> [The] external perspective trap takes place when the company does not manage to understand the basic values and purpose of identity of a brand. The trap consists in the lack of coherence between creating an image and not believing in the values. If the company is not able to communicate what the brand stands for or what it is about by specifying the strengths, values and vision based on disciplined efforts, it is hard to expect employees to make a vision happen if they do not understand and buy into that vision[1].

In order to have the values of the brand exposed outside or externalised – giving strength to the brand itself – employees' responses and buy-ins should be inspired by a strong brand identity.

The last trap is the product-attribute fixation. This means that the company focuses exclusively on the product's attributes, erroneously assuming that they are the only elements in the decision-making process of the consumer or customer.

This trap occurs when consumer insight is focused on the attributes of the product. According to Aacker[1], this kind of market research is conducted in such a way that marketing information is 1) often effective, as the attributes are important to purchasing choices; 2) easy, as customers have to talk about something tangible (the physical attributes of the product) and do not end up in irrationality; and 3) a reassurance for managers, since customers use a logical model to evaluate brands, so decisions are easier to understand and behaviours can be predicted (even if most of the choices are irrational or governed by many variables, rational and emotional).

A sixth factor of brand successs consists of the way a brand communicates. Aacker [1] maintains that a brand, in order to be successful, should be able to express its identity through the consideration of the brand as a product, an organisation, a person and a symbol.

The goal for these levels of consideration is justified by helping 'the strategist consider different brand elements and patterns that can help clarify, enrich, and differentiate an identity', but 'not every brand identity needs to employ all or even several of these perspectives. For some brands, only one will be viable and appropriate'[1]. The important point is that companies try to articulate what the brand should stand for in the minds and perceptions of the customers or consumers.

The seventh and eighth factors are connected to the creation of value and creativity[13, 16].

According to de Chernatony and McDonald [13], there are four main characteristics companies should take into consideration when developing brands, to show how a product can be augmented by adding value in increasing levels of sophistication. These characteristics are expressed in levels – generic, expected, augmented and potential.

The generic level consists of the fundamental form of commodity, in which the product satisfies the basic needs of the customer. This level might be, according to de Chernatony and McDonald, easy prey for competitors, as it is not difficult to copy.

Successful brands are supposed to be at a higher level, on a scale made of generic, expected, augmented and potential levels. The 'expected' level, where the 'commodity is value engineered to satisfy a specific target's minimum purchase conditions, such as functional capabilities, availability, pricing, etc.'[13]. There, repeat purchases result from a higher level of customer orientation in the firm.

The augmented level comes next, as customer sophistication increases. This level is more refined than the previous ones, and the added value can be found in non-functional elements (e.g., emotional). At this level, the product might satisfy needs such as social standing or status by ownership of it.

With regards to the potential level, according to the authors, the only limit is the limit of creativity. For example, Nestlé pushed the brand to the potential level through the development of software, so retailers could manage shelf space, thereby maximising their profits by helping their customers to maximise theirs. At this level, the company focuses on diversifying in order to avoid stepping back to the expected level of competing on price.

Creativity is always a significant element in the brand-building process, besides the characteristics related to the level of sophistication of the market. The need for creativity is sustained by Frank and Krake's[16] argument:

> Set the building and management of your brand high on your list of priorities. Make time available for this. A strong brand is an excellent way to distinguish yourself from your competition and, if properly applied, emphasise the quality of your product. ... Highlight one or two specific distinguishing product features and associate them with your brand. ... So be creative. And if you cannot be creative, hire someone who is [16].

However, it is not clear if highlighting one or two specific distinguishing product features is enough to lead to success. This might be true in a commodity market, but it contradicts de Chernatony and McDonald (2001) if it is extended to all markets, because an increase corresponds with a shift in the drivers to the purchase of the brand from product features to emotional elements.

De Chernatony and McDonald[13] promote the idea that

> to succeed in the long run, a brand must offer added values over and above the basic product characteristics, if for no other reason than that functional characteristics are so easy for competitors to copy. ... It is most important to realize that the added values must be relevant to the customer and not just to the manufacturer or distributor.

'Buyers perceive added value in a brand', de Chernatony and McDonald add, 'because they recognize certain clues which give signals about the offer'.

As indicated by the body of literature described in these sections, branding is an essential element in firms' marketing. Scholarship depicts branding in companies as a powerful marketing tool they can use to communicate the value they offer to consumers. Brands may have an impact on growth, due to their communication role.

This chapter described branding for SMEs. Although branding is a marketing activity typical of larger organisations, more and more SMEs create brands. Section 9.1 dealt with brands' functionality and the branding activity per se, looking at different definitions of branding depending of the many branding functions that there are. The element of 'value', paramount to the understanding of branding, is highlighted. Section 9.2 described the reason for having a specific mission statement to give direction to the organisation, but also to position the idea of what the company stands for clearly in the mind of customers and consumers. The last section described the importance of branding for firms and the factors to consider for successful branding activity.

References

[1] Aacker DA. Building Strong Brands. Bath: The Bath Press; 2002.
[2] Abimbola T, Vallaster C. Brand, organisational identity and reputation in SMEs: an overview. Qualitative Market Research: An International Journal. 2007; Vol. 10 (No. 4): 341–8.
[3] AMA. Marketing Definition: A Glossary of Marketing Terms. Chicago, IL: American Marketing Association; 1960.
[4] Ambler T. Need-To-Know Marketing. London: Century Business; 1992.
[5] Ambler T, Styles C. Brand development versus new product development: towards a process model of extension decisions. Marketing Intelligence & Planning. 1996; Vol. 14 (No. 7): pp. 10–19.
[6] Arrow K. The Limits of Organization. New York: W.W. Norton & Company; 1974.
[7] Bauer RA. Consumer Behaviour as Risk-taking. Dynamic Marketing for a Changing World. Chicago, IL: American Marketing Association; 1960.
[8] Bennett PD, Anderson PF. Dictionary of Marketing Terms. Chicago, IL: The American Marketing Association; 1988.
[9] Brown G. People, Brands and Advertising. New York, NY: Millward Brown International; 1992.
[10] Campbell A. Mission statements. Long Range Planning. 1997; Vol. 30 (No. 6): pp. 931–2.
[11] Cunningham RM. Brand loyalty what, where, how much? Harvard Business Review. 1956; Vol. 34: pp. 116–28.
[12] de Chernatony L. Creating Powerful Brands. Oxford: Butterworth-Heinemann; 1992.
[13] de Chernatony L, McDonald M. Creating Powerful Brands in Consumer, Service and Industrial Markets. 2nd ed. Oxford: Butterworth-Heinemann; 2001.
[14] Dibb S, Sinkin L, Pride WM, Ferrell OC. Marketing: Concepts and Strategies. 3rd European ed. Boston, MA: Houghton Mifflin; 1997.
[15] Dierickx I, Cool K. Asset Stock Accumulation and Sustainability of Competitive Advantage. Management Science. 1989; Vol. 35 (No. 12): pp. 1504–11.
[16] Frank BG, Krake JM. Successful brand management in SMEs: a new theory and practical hints. Journal of Product & Brand Management. 2005; Vol. 14 (No. 4): pp. 228–38.

[17] Germain R, Cooper MB. How a customer mission statement affects company performance. Industrial Marketing Management. 1990; Vol. 19 (No. 1): pp. 47–54.
[18] Gregory J, Sellers LJ. Building corporate brands. Pharmaceutical Executive. 2002; (January): pp. 38–44.
[19] Grönroos C. From marketing mix to relationship marketing: towards a paradigm shift in marketing. Management Decision. 1994; Vol. 32 (No. 2): pp. 4–20.
[20] Grönroos C, Ravald A. The value concept and relationship marketing. European Journal of Marketing. 1996; Vol. 30 (No. 2): pp. 19–30.
[21] Holbrook MB. Customer value and autoethnography: subjective personal introspection and the meanings of a photograph collection. Journal of Business Research. 2004; Vol. 58 (No. 1): pp. 45–61.
[22] Howard JA, Sheth JN. The Theory of Buyer Behavior. New York, NY: John Wiley and Sons; 1969.
[23] Javalgi RG, Moberg CR. Service loyalty: implications for service providers. The Journal of Services Marketing. 1997; Vol. 11 (No. 3): pp. 165–79.
[24] Kania D. Branding.com. New York: USA: McGraw-Hill; 2001.
[25] Kaplan RS and Norton DP. (2000) Having trouble with your strategy? Then map it. *Harvard Business Review* (September-October), 3–11
[26] Keller KL. Conceptualizing, Measuring, Managing Customer-Based Brand Equity. Journal of Marketing. 1993; Vol. 57 (No. 1): pp. 1–22.
[27] Keller KL. Strategic Brand Management: Building, Measuring and Managing Brand Equity. Englewood Cliffs, NJ: Prentice-Hall; 2003.
[28] Kotler PH. Marketing Management: Analysis, Planning, and Control. 7th ed. Englewood Cliffs, NJ: Prentice-Hall; 1991.
[29] Kotler PH, Levy SJ. Broadening the concept of marketing. Journal of Marketing. 1969; Vol. 33 (February): pp. 10–15.
[30] Mankelow G, Merrilees B. Towards a Model of Entrepreneurial Marketing for Rural Women: A Case Study Approach. Journal of Development Entrepreneurship. 2001; Vol. 6 (No. 3 [Dec]): pp. 221–35.
[31] Mead M. Cultural Patterns and Technical Change (A manual prepared by the World Federation for Mental Health). Paris: UNESCO; 1953.
[32] Monroe KB. Pricing – Making Profitable Decisions. New York, NY: McGraw-Hill; 1991.
[33] University of Oxford, 2006,; A Dictionary of Business and Management, J Law eds, 4th ed, Oxford: Oxford University Press
[34] Ries A, Trout J. Positioning, the Battle for Your Mind. New York: McGraw-Hill; 2001.
[35] Rositer J, Percy L. Advertising Communications and Promotion Management. New York, NY: McGraw-Hill; 1996.
[36] Sappington DEM, Wernerfelt B. To brand or not to brand? A theoretical and empirical question. The Journal of Business. 1985; Vol. 58 (No. 3 [July]): pp. 279–93.
[37] Schroeder JE, Salzer-Möling M. Brand Culture. Routledge Taylor and Francis Group; 2006.

[38] Shultz M, Hatch MJ, Larsen MH. The Expressive Organisation: Linking Identity, Reputation and the Corporate Brand. Oxford: Oxford University Press; 2000.
[39] Simeon R. A conceptual model linking brand building strategies and Japanese popular culture. Marketing Intelligence & Planning. 2006; Vol. 24 (No. 5): pp. 463–76.
[40] Vallaster C, De Chernatony L. Internal brand building and structuration: the role of leadership. European Journal of Marketing. 2006; Vol. 40 (No. 7/8): pp. 761–84.
[41] Wood L. Brands and brand equity: definition and management. Management Decision. 2000; Vol. 38 (No. 9): pp. 662–9.

11
Supply Chain Relationships Management: SMEs' Partners

In the past two decades, the disciplines of marketing and supply chain management got closer and closer, to the point where now parts of supply chain management have merged with marketing, and in the most recent publications and textbooks about marketing, we can find chapters on supply chain management. But why is it so important to marketing?

We live in a dynamic world, and 30 years of globalisation increased the importance of supply chain management. Firms produce products aimed at different consumers. The market demands that SMEs innovate and differentiate because over time, consumers have become more and more demanding about the types of products they want to purchase. This increase in the sophistication of consumer demand was also enhanced by increased competition. Globalisation gave firms more opportunities to reach audiences and customer bases they were not able to reach before, but it also meant increased competition, as non-local firms managed competed with local firms in local markets.

Supply chain management became essential in an increasingly complex world, where firms have opportunities for convenient procurement and sale, but supply chains more frequently become longer and more complex.

There are two strategies for competition in almost all the countries of the world: a firm either has a competitive advantage in terms of cost-leadership or differentiation leadership, so it is able to produce and sell at the cheapest price, or it can provide the highest possible quality. In order to achieve competitive advantage, the firm has to manage its resources and coordinate its functions (marketing, sales, finance, production, procurement and so on). However, SMEs often do not have formalised functions like larger organisations do, so the decision-making burden is all on the small business owner.

Nevertheless, SMEs do need to engage the stakeholders in their supply chain, of which all SMEs are necessarily a part SMEs benefit from a better understanding of their supply chain and from an improvement in their relationships with their stakeholders. In what follows, we will see what a simple supply chain structure looks like, and what flows we can find within it. We will also look at how SMEs can capitalise on the relationships with their stakeholders to create value.

11.1 Different partners... different audiences

Many supply chains are composed of SMEs that provide a product or a service at some stage, either upstream (towards the producers) or downstream (towards the customers).

A supply chain consists of all parties involved, directly or indirectly, in fulfilling a customer request. The supply chain includes not only the manufacturer and suppliers, but also transporters, warehouses, retailers, and even customers themselves... A supply chain is dynamic and involves the constant flow of information, product, and funds between different stages... The objective of every supply chain should be to maximize the overall value generated. [8]

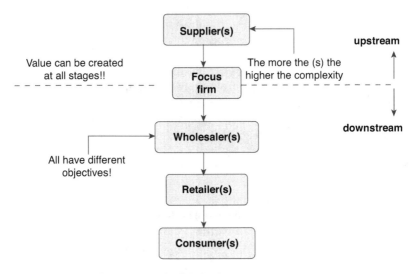

Figure 11.1   Simple structure of a supply chain
Source: Author's own.

The definition of supply chain implies the integration of processes to 'involve all parties', but it also highlights that supply chains are 'dynamic', and there is 'constant flow' of information, materials and money. The management of these flows requires efficiency. When the supply chain is properly managed, we can create and maximise value for all the different stakeholders involved with the focus firm.

Upstream (on the top) are the suppliers of a product. They can either be primary or secondary producers – primary produce from raw materials, whereas secondary process materials that are produced by somebody else – or they can be intermediaries who purchase a product from a producer and resell it to other firms, such as importers, exporters, resellers and so on. The next step of the supply chain is the focus company, which is the firm generally considered to be the main subject of the supply chain. In this context, it could be an SME who needs to understand how to capitalise on the relationships with all the other stakeholders.

Downstream (towards the bottom) are wholesalers – firms (perhaps other SMEs) that purchase from the focus company and resell to other firms – the retailers – which then sell to the final consumer.

As you can easily observe from the structure represented in the picture, the focus company has different stakeholders within the supply chain. There are several suppliers upstream, whereas downstream there are wholesalers, retailers and consumers. As indicated by the arrows out of the supply chain, all these stakeholders have different (and sometimes diverging) interests; the firm has to communicate with these different audiences and learn how to manage relationships with all stakeholders.

One of the major problems many SMEs (and, to a certain extent, larger organisations, too) have is a lack of knowledge about the consumers of their products. There are heaps of focus companies that limit their understanding of the market to the elements of the chain that are closest to them: suppliers and customers (i.e., wholesalers or retailers). Therefore, it is very important for firms to understand the difference between customers, who purchase the product, and consumers, who are the destination of the product, as the needs, wants and behaviours of these two actors on the supply chain are often different and sometime contrasting. For instance, customers might be more interested in stocking and selling products from the focus firm that provides wholesalers and retailers with the highest margin, whereas consumers may have a preference for the products from the firm that provides *them* with more benefits.

What is supply chain management per se? Different authors define what it consists of, and all definitions stress the importance of creating value, possibly through an improvement of the efficiency and effectiveness of both business processes and relationships:

> Supply chain management is a set of approaches utilized to efficiently integrate suppliers, manufacturers, warehouses, and stores, so that merchandise is produced and distributed at the right quantities, to the right locations, and at the right time, in order to minimize system wide costs while satisfying service level requirements. [30]

The definition of supply chain management focuses on efficiently integrating processes in order to minimise costs and satisfy service levels in order to create value. For SMEs to fully understand their supply chain and how to identify needs amongst actors and handle relationships in such a way to create value along the whole chain, they should have clear ideas about the existing supply chains flows to be managed. In what follows we will describe what supply chain flows are and how a better understanding of them can help firms to improve their marketing activities, add value, and gain competitive advantage.

11.2 Supply chain flows

There are several types of flows along the supply chain, moving from upstream to downstream and the other way around. However, the flows are classified in three main categories: materials, information and money. Materials refers to a very general category that includes raw and semi-worked materials (for industrial manufacturing) or produce and products (for industrial processing), mechanical and electronic parts and components, as well as services. These flow both up- and downstream, depending on the firm's needs, as shown in the figure that follows.

The second type of flow is money. Money generally flows from downstream up (a bit like salmon!), unless a firm has to refund money to a customer for whatever reason. Generally, each stage of the supply chain is the supplier of the actor that follows; therefore, the consumer transfers money to the retailer, perhaps through payment for goods purchased, and the retailer will pay the distributor or wholesaler for goods purchased, and so on, .

The third type of flow is information of different types (e.g., about consumers' preferences), among them 'demand', which is information about the quantities of product needed at different stages of the supply chain, and 'forecasts', which help to try to guess future needs in terms of stock.

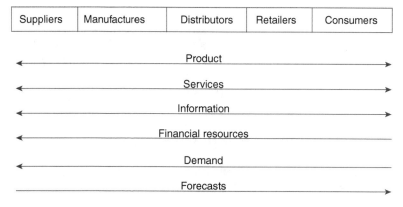

Figure 11.2 Diagram of supply chain flows, adapted from Mentzer [25]
Source: Author's own.

Mentzer [25] gives a good example of the importance of correct management of all flows within a supply chain:

> Product flows from suppliers through manufacturers, through distributors, through retailers, to final customers. The product arrow [in the previous figure] flows both ways because many supply chains (soft drink bottlers, for example) must manage the flow of the remains of the consumption (empty bottles) back up the supply chain. In the 1970s, when Michigan passed a "bottle ban" law, which required all plastic, metal, and glass containers to have a deposit, the supply chain was not ready for the volume of product flow back up the supply chain that resulted. The supply chains for these products were primarily focused on getting the product to the retailer, not taking the empties back to the manufacturer. The results for several months were huge piles of empties in the parking lots outside the retailers (often piles larger than the actual store), until the supply chains were reconfigured to not only deliver product to the retailer but to also take the empties away from the retailer.

All three types of flow are important, because products must be delivered when requested, and in order to do so, they must be produced and stocked. In order to produce them, there is the need for the right amount of material and so on. However, among the three types of flows, a very critical one is the flow of information, which is very well described in a recent research paper [29], as the information that flows from downstream feeds into business decision-making at different levels of the supply chain. For instance, at the retail and wholesale levels, there is the need to forecast demand so that the right stock is kept available in retail businesses in order to be ready to be supplied to consumers, and for wholesalers, there is the need to order the right quantities of stock to supply retailers.

Likewise, information about demand and stock at retail and wholesale levels is helpful for the focus firm to plan production and manufacturing/processing, depending on the forecast demand. At focus firm level, this type of information is also helpful to make decisions related to procurement, as the focus firm needs to know what to order from their suppliers in order to produce their products [29].

In the same way, information about the quantities of material needed by the focus firm is valuable to their suppliers to know how much to produce and stock. Eventually, some of the information moving upstream will also give direction on the types of modifications to be implemented in the products' specifications in order to satisfy consumers' demand. This might generate the need for the production of a new product. In any case, it will inform the supply chain at different stages on potential modifications to the product in order to improve its appeal to consumers.

11.3   Creating value through relationships

Managing flows along the supply chain and resources within the firm is a remarkable activity for most SMEs, who sometimes tend to operate in a vacuum, without taking the external environment too much into consideration [7]. However, value creation at the supply chain level takes place through a better knowledge of the firm's stakeholders. This means better familiarity with their vision and mission in business, their processes, and their needs [8]. Sometimes stakeholders are also ready to share their strategy if this can bring them some advantages in terms of collaboration [25].

But how do we know on what to collaborate with our stakeholders? There are some activities that are common to all firms, more or less. For instance, most firms do design their own products. Many physically make their own products. Some create brands, and others do not; they produce on the specifications of a brand owner, so these firms only act as brand manufacturers. All firms have to set prices, and some also engage with promotion. All firms buy and sell something, be it raw materials, final products or services. Most firms do have to deal with stock, warehousing and inventory, and most firms somehow display their products (either physically – in a shop – or online). All firms deliver goods or services, and all firms deal, to some extent, with the management of their finances.

Fundamentally, all firms engage with these activities but do not necessarily have to deal with all of these activities on their own, as they can opt to outsource some of them. Some activities are core activities, and some activities are simply...accessories. For instance, for a baker, the core activity is to make good bread;, advertising his bakery is not his core activity. This means that, although advertising the bakery is really important, if s/he starts spending time to plan a communication strategy to convert into a piece of advertisement, s/he will waste time that should be dedicated to bread production. Therefore, firms can decide to focus on their core activities while leaving others to deal with their non-core activities.

Collaboration can take place on two different grounds: core competencies or non-core competencies. Core competencies are those activities that we do well and that give us a competitive advantage in the marketplace, whereas non-core competencies are those activities that someone can delegate to others (outsource), while we concentrate on the core activities. (Yes! This also explains why many graduate students are often offered extra cash to do data input for their professors. Data input is not professors' core activity. It's as simple as that!)

Mentzer [25] described the case of Ford, the American automotive firm that at the beginning had full control over all the activities that were related to the production of their cars. Ford owned the very same iron ore they were using to make cars with. They also owned the fleet of ships on which iron was loaded to be sent to the plant. Obviously, they owned the plant where iron was melted, and once the iron was ready, it was sent to the Ford factory to be turned into a Ford vehicle. The cars that were produced were shipped to and sold in Ford-owned shops.

However, full control over the whole supply chain came at a dear price:

> It was not long before Henry Ford and the directors of the company realized that too much capital was required for Ford to have the luxury of controlling the entire supply chain. What evolved then is what has evolved in many modern supply chains: a struggle to balance the need to control operations with the need to manage risk. Companies are constantly evaluating the question, "What should we do ourselves, and what should we allow someone else to do for

us?" The answer to that question is often, "Can we do it cheaper than someone else?" If the answer is no, we must ask ourselves if the function is a core competency.... Not everything we do well is a core competency. For functions that are core competencies, however, even though they may cost us more money to do them ourselves, we still should keep control over them. [25].

SMEs can also improve their efficiency and effectiveness by focusing on their core competencies and by outsourcing those activities that are not core to their businesses to be delegated to other firms. Among the activities that SMEs should not delegate, however, are strategic activities – for example, the procurement of raw materials – if it is critical to the production of their products. An effective way to outsource non-core activities is to collaborate closely with stakeholders. If collaboration is possible because both firms have a common interest in collaborating, and if relationships are managed effectively, this creates value for both the focus firm and the stakeholders.

Creating value along the supply chain often means being able to cooperate with your stakeholders' activities, considering them truly business partners, and working together towards reciprocal understanding and the achievement of common aims and objectives. However, Mentzer indicated some antecedents to cooperation [25]: trust, commitment, cooperative norms, interdependence, organisational compatibility, environmental uncertainty perception, and relationship extendedness

First trust and commitment are essential ingredients for successful cooperation. Trust is a construct made by two main elements, which are honesty and benevolence [24]. The first one refers to the ability to believe people will do what they say they will do, and the latter is about having a sincere interest in the harmony of the collaboration, even though sometimes something has to be compromised. The basis of trust lies in the belief that none of the partners will behave unexpectedly in a damaging way towards the collaboration and the other partners [3], whereas commitment is about putting effort into the success of the collaboration.

Trust and commitment are important aspects of a collaboration, without which an effective partnership is not possible. They balance out the distribution and struggle for power amongst partners [16, 32] and stimulate communication [1, 28]. Granovetter [17] also identified trust and commitment as reducing opportunistic behaviours and the consequent softening of social structures of control [18].

However, for commitment to be strong in a relationship, the partners must follow specific cooperative norms, which are defined [4] as 'the perception of the joint efforts of both the supplier and distributor to achieve mutual and individual goals successfully, while refraining from opportunistic actions'. They are unspoken norms, rooted in the belief that all partners have to commit with sincerity and must put effort in the collaboration to achieve success [4, 6].

Firms' commitment is generally stronger when there is interdependence amongst them. Firms whose success depends on each other tend to be better coordinated and highly committed because the stakes are very high [22–23]. When there is interdependence amongst firms, the outcomes obtained by the collaboration are considered highly important, and therefore partners have propensity to consider the relationship important, dedicating to it thorough attention [19–20]. However, commitment should be shown at all times by the partners, as they all contributed to the relationship with time and financial and human resources, so commitment does not fade away [2, 27].

If there is trust, commitment and interdependence, the chances for a successful collaboration might increase, as the major obstacles to success are removed. Furthermore, another aspect to include in the list of antecedents to the success of collaborations is the potential compatibility with the other firm. Organisational compatibility consists of similar business philosophies and corporate cultures, and it includes, the similarity in aims, goals and objectives in the collaborating firms [5]. In fact, organisational compatibility is a critical element to the effectiveness of the alliance [13], and those relationships whose firms have high organisational compatibility perceive the collaboration as being worthwhile, since they are often very productive in terms of goals achievement [26]. As you can imagine, it is not a simple exercise to mix the cultures, practices and routines of different firms on a common project. It is time consuming, and it leaves room for potential mistakes and misunderstandings. However, a match of practices and routines is necessary to take place for the collaboration to perform well within the chain [9–12]; therefore, a great stress has to be put on clear communication and good project management practices.

Another factor affecting the success of collaboration is the manager's perception of environmental uncertainty. The development of new ventures and other forms of alliance amongst firms has been found to be positively associated with managers' perceptions of risk [14, 31]. Although fundamentally subjective and psychological, managers were shown to be able to affect the outcome of the collaboration through their adaptive behaviour if it were influenced by preconceived notions of environmental uncertainty. Managers perceived environmental uncertainty as a multidimensional construct composed of the perception of general uncertainty, which often was found to be quite high, the perception of technological volatility and volatility of consumers' demand, low predictability of competition, and the pressure deriving from requests for internationalisation of the operations by the partners. When managers perceive high environmental uncertainty, they develop opportunistic behaviours that are detrimental to the collaboration [15].

The last element affecting the outcome of collaboration is the extension of the relationship. This was firstly defined as 'the degree to which the parties anticipate that the relationship will continue into the future with an indeterminate end point'[21]. The concept of relationship extendedness is interesting in that it assumes a non-compulsory, open-ended interaction based on consensus between the parties, and the interaction per se does not require a specific agreement of collaboration, but it makes it possible, even when none of the actors in it express feelings of altruism or interest in their partners' well-being. As indicated by Mentzer [25]

> the first implication of the iterated game framework of [Heide and Miner] is that, in a prisoner's dilemma situation, extendedness in a relationship increases the probability of a pattern of cooperation. Thus, extendedness in a relationship, or open-ended interaction, has a positive effect on the level of cooperation between two interacting firms.

All these enablers of cooperation were studied within the context of larger organisations; however, SMEs can also benefit from reflecting on these aspects when making decision about their core competencies and non-core competencies. Trust and commitment are at the base of cooperation in supply chain management; however, SMEs are part of the supply chain and should therefore act in such a manner to develop trust with their stakeholders by showing commitment.. However, there are some unspoken cooperative norms to be respected: in fact, the basic assumption in collaboration is that both parties should try their best.

Firms, by outsourcing non-core activities, engage in a collaborative relationship and might develop synergies based on reciprocal interest. In that case, they become dependent upon one another; therefore, the commitment should also increase. Opportunistic relationships with little to share make cooperation less probable. Furthermore, firms should engage and work with those organisations they feel compatible with. If companies have no common goals or too-different philosophies of business, collaboration might become fragmented and inter-firm cooperation cannot exist.

Finally, the mood and perception of uncertainty affect collaborations. Therefore, SMEs should develop a way of communicating with their stakeholders that reinforces the messages of trust and commitment. The anticipation of a continuous and permanent relationship enhances the chance for cooperation; however, these messages should be passed to the collaborating partner organisations to be effective. We conclude by saying that in a relationship, dialog and communication reign supreme.

References

[1] Andaleeb SS. An experimental investigation of satisfaction and commitment in marketing channels: the role of trust and dependence. Journal of Retailing. 1996; 72(1): 77–93.
[2] Anderson E, Weitz B. Determinants of continuity in conventional industrial channel dyads. Marketing Science. 1989 Fall; 8(4): 310.
[3] Anderson JC and Narus JA. (1990) A model of distributor firm and manufacturer firm working partnerships. *The Journal of Marketing*, 54 (January): 42–58.
[4] Baker TL, Simpson PM, Siguaw JA. The impact of suppliers' perceptions of reseller market orientation on key relationship constructs. Journal of the Academy of Marketing Science. 1999; 27(1): 50–7.
[5] Bucklin LP, Sengupta S. Organizing successful co-marketing alliances. The Journal of Marketing. 1993: 57(2): 32–46.
[6] Cannon T. Enterprise: Creation, Development and Growth. Oxford: Butterworth-Heinemann; 1991.
[7] Carson DJ. The evolution of marketing in small firms. European Journal of Marketing. 1985; 19 (5): 7–16.
[8] Chopra S, Meindl S. Supply chain management: strategy, planning and operation. 5th ed. London: Pearson; 2012.
[9] Cooper. Challenges in predicting new firm performance. Journal of Business Venturing. 1993; 8: 241–53.
[10] Cooper, Gimeno-Gascon, Woo. Initial human and financial capital as predictors of new venture performance. Journal of Business Venturing. 1994; 9: 371–95.
[11] Cordes C, Richerson PJ, Schwesinger G. How corporate cultures coevolve with the business environment: The case of firm growth crises and industry evolution. Journal of Economic Behavior & Organization. 2010; 76(3): 465–80.
[12] Dahlqvist J, Davidsson P, Wiklund J. Initial conditions as predictors of new venture performance: A replication and extension of the Cooper et al. study. Enterprise and Innovation Management Studies. 2000; 1(1): 1–17.
[13] Das S, Sen PK, Sengupta S. Impact of strategic alliances on firm valuation. Academy of Management Journal. 1998; 41(1): 27–41.
[14] Dickson PH, Weaver KM. Environmental determinants and individual-level moderators of alliance use. Academy of Management Journal. 1997; 40(2): 404–25.

[15] Dickson PH, Weaver KM, Hoy F. Opportunism in the R&D alliances of SMES: The roles of the institutional environment and SME size. Journal of Business Venturing. 2006; 21(4): 487–513.
[16] Dwyer FR, Schurr PH, Oh S. Developing buyer-seller relationships. The Journal of Marketing. 1987: 51(2)11–27.
[17] Granovetter MM. The strength of weak ties. American Journal of Sociology. 1978; 78(6): 1360–80.
[18] Granovetter MM. The Sociology of Economic Life: Westview Press; 2001.
[19] Heide JB, John G. The role of dependence balancing in safeguarding transaction-specific assets in conventional channels. The Journal of Marketing. 1988: 52(1):20–35.
[20] Heide JB, John G. Alliances in industrial purchasing: the determinants of joint action in buyer-supplier relationships. Journal of Marketing Research. 1990:27(February): 24–36.
[21] Heide JB, Miner AS. The shadow of the future: Effects of anticipated interaction and frequency of contact on buyer-seller cooperation. Academy of Management Journal. 1992; 35(2): 265–91.
[22] Kim SK, Hsieh P-H. Interdependence and its consequences in distributor-supplier relationships: a distributor perspective through response surface approach. Journal of Marketing Research. 2003: 40(1)101–12.
[23] Kumar N, Scheer LK, Steenkamp J-BE. The effects of perceived interdependence on dealer attitudes. Journal of Marketing Research. 1995: 32(3) 348–56.
[24] Kumar N, Scheer LK, Steenkamp J-BE. The effects of supplier fairness on vulnerable resellers. Journal of Marketing Research. 1995: 32(1) 54–65.
[25] Mentzer JT. Fundamentals of Supply Chain Management: Twelve Drivers of Competitive Advantage. London, Sage; 2004.
[26] Perry ML, Sengupta S, Krapfel R. Effectiveness of horizontal strategic alliances in technologically uncertain environments: are trust and commitment enough? Journal of Business Research. 2004; 57(9): 951–6.
[27] Ross WT, Anderson E, Weitz B. Performance in principal-agent dyads: the causes and consequences of perceived asymmetry of commitment to the relationship. Management Science. 1997; 43(5): 680–704.
[28] Schurr PH, Ozanne JL. Influences on exchange processes: buyers' preconceptions of a seller's trustworthiness and bargaining toughness. Journal of Consumer Research. 1985: 939–53.
[29] Sherer SA. From supply-chain management to value network advocacy: implications for e-supply chains. Supply Chain Management: An International Journal. 2005; 10(2): 77–83.
[30] Simchi-Levi D, Kaminsky P, Simchi-Levi, E. Designing and Managing the Supply Chain: Concepts, Strategies and Case Studies. 3rd int. ed. New York: McGraw Hill; 2009.
[31] Weaver KM, Dickson PH. Outcome quality of small-to medium-sized enterprise–based alliances: The role of perceived partner behaviors. Journal of Business Venturing. 1998; 13(6): 505–22.
[32] Wilson DT. An integrated model of buyer-seller relationships. Journal of the Academy of Marketing Science. 1995; 23(4): 335–45.

Notes

2 The Nature of the Small and Medium-Sized Enterprise

1. As quoted in [70], Steinhoff D. Small Business Management Fundamentals. Maidenhead: McGraw-Hill; 1978.
2. As found in the following documents: [14] Business Link. Here's how I've changed my business for the better – Case studies from businesslink.gov.uk: Department of Trade and Industry 2005, [15]Business Link. Here's how I've started my business – Case studies from businesslink.gov.uk: Department of Trade and Industry 2005, [16] Business Link. Here's how I run my business – Case studies from businesslink.gov.uk: Department of Trade and Industry 2005, [41] Hauge E, Havnes P-A. The Dynamics of SME Development – Two Case Studies of the Internationalisation Process. RENT XV Conference; Turku – Finland: Adger Research Foundation, Norway; 2001. p. pp. 14, [47] IFC. Enabling SMEs to Enter the International Supply Chain: The United Nations Trade Faciliation Network 2005, [48] IFC. Access to Finance for Small and Medium Enterprises (SMEs). Monitor – Issue No 3, June. 2006, [49] IFC. Creating Opportunities for Small Business: World Bank Group 2007, [50] IFC. Linkage Programs to Develop Small and Medium Enterprises. Monitor. 2008, [52] Joquico JP. SMEs face constraints in adopting CSR. The Business Weekly – 22 June 08. 2008, [55] Kinross. Meadowhead: Soil Association 2006, [56] Kleindl B. Competitive Dynamics and new Business Models for SMEs in the Virtual Marketplace. Journal of DEvelopmental Entrepreneurship. 2000; Vol. 5 (No. 1):pp. 73–86, [60] Lamprinopoulou C, Tregear A, Ness M. Agrifood SMEs in Greece: the role of collective action. British Food Journal. 2006; Vol. 108 (No. 8):pp. 663–76, [62] O'Rourke. SME's Biggest Barriers and Risks Identified in 'Think Big'. Sidney: RSM Bird Cameron; 2008; Available from: www.eyeswideopen.com.au, [66] SCOTENT. Farm Administration Courses – SE/1769/Apr06: Scottish Enterprise 2006, [67] SCOTENT. Food Chain Industry Exchange – SE/1770/Apr06: Scottish Enterprise 2006, [69] Sparkes A, Brychan T. The use of the Internet as a critical success factor for the marketing of Welsh agri-food SMEs in the twenty-first century. British Food Journal. 2001;Vol. 103 (No. 5):pp. 331–47.

3 Small Business Owners and Their Environment

1. Reported in Burns [8] Burns P. Entrepreneurship and Small Business. 2nd ed. China: Palgrave MacMillan; 2007. p. 10

5 Growth Strategies within an SME Context

1. These studies all refer to large industrial companies, though, and are non-SME specific.

10 Building Brands in SMEs

1. The unique product and service mix, customer relations and corporate image that is offered by the company, according to Kaplan and Norton [25] Kaplan RS, Norton DP. Having Trouble with Your Strategy? Then Map It. Harvard Business Review. 2000 (September-October). It is a concept proper of the domain of relationship marketing.
2. Simplified character: 京 pinyin: jīng
3. Scope (Crest makes dental hygiene products), attributes (Volvo is safe), quality/value (Kraft delivers a quality product) and uses (Subaru is made for the snow).[4] [1] Ibid[5] See Appendix 3: A Brand is more than a Product [1] Ibid.[6] See Appendix 4: Brand Identity Traps [1] Ibid. Aacker DA. Building Strong Brands. Bath: The Bath Press; 2002.
4. Found in Aacker [1] Ibid.

Bibliography

Aacker DA. (2002) *Building Strong Brands*, Bath: The Bath Press.
Aarstad J, Haugland SA and Greve A. (2010) Performance spillover effects in entrepreneurial networks: assessing a dyadic theory of social capital. *Entrepreneurship: Theory & Practice* 34 (5): 1003–19.
Abimbola T and Vallaster C. (2007) Brand, organisational identity and reputation in SMEs: an overview. *Qualitative Market Research: An International Journal* 10 (4): 341–8.
Acs Z. (2006) Innovation and the Small Business. In: Carter S and Jones-Evans D (eds) *Enterprise and Small Business: Principles, Practice and Policy*. London: Pearson Education.
Acs, Z. (2006). How is entrepreneurship good for economic growth?. *Innovations*, 1(1), 97–107.
Agarwal R and Audretsch DB. (2001) Does entry size matter? The impact of the life cycle and technology on firm survival. *The Journal of Industrial Economics* XLIX (1): 21–43.
Aguilar FJ. (1967) *Scanning the Business Environment*, New York: Macmillan Publishing.
Ahlstrom D and Bruton GD. (2002) An institutional perspective on the role of culture in shaping strategic actions by technology-focused entrepreneurial firms in China. *Entrepreneurship Theory and Practice* 26 (4): 53–70.
Ahlstrom D, Young MN, Chan ES and Bruton GD. (2004) Facing constraints to growth? Overseas Chinese entrepreneurs and traditional business practices in East Asia. *Asia Pacific Journal of Management* 21 (3): 263–85.
Aldrich H and Fiol CM. (1994) Fool rush in? The institutional context of industry creation. *Academy of Management Review* 19 (4): 645–70.
Allinson CW, Chell E and Hayes J. (2000) Intuition and entrepreneurial behaviour. *European Journal of Work & Organizational Psychology* 9 (1): 31–43.
Alsbury A. (2001) *Quick Answers to Small Business Questions*, London: Prentice Hall.
AMA (American Marketing Association). (1960) *Marketing Definition: A Glossary of Marketing Terms*, Chicago, IL: American Marketing Association.
Ambler T. (1992) *Need-to-Know Marketing*, London: Century Business.
Ambler T and Styles C. (1996) Brand development versus new product development: towards a process model of extension decisions. *Marketing Intelligence & Planning* 14 (7): 10–19.
Andaleeb SS. (1996) An experimental investigation of satisfaction and commitment in marketing channels: the role of trust and dependence. *Journal of Retailing* 72 (1): 77–93.
Andersen O. On the internationalization process of firms: a critical analysis. *Journal of International Business Studies*. 1993; 24(2): 209–31.
Anderson E and Weitz B. (1989) Determinants of continuity in conventional industrial channel dyads. *Marketing Science* 8 (4): 310.
Anderson J. (2005) *Local Heroes*, Glasgow: Scottish Enterprise.

Anderson JC and Narus JA. (1990) A model of distributor firm and manufacturer firm working partnerships. *The Journal of Marketing*, 54 (January): 42–58.

Anderson WT and Golden LL. (1984) Lifestyle and psychographics: a critical review and recommendation. *Advances in Consumer Research* 11 (1): 405–11.

Andersson S. (2000) The internationalization of the firm from an entrepreneurial perspective. *International Studies of Management & Organization*, 30(1): 63–92.

Andrus DD, Norvell DW, McIntyre P and Milner L. (1987) Marketing Planning in Inc., 500 Companies. In: Hills G (ed) *Research at the Marketing/Entrepreneurhsip Interface*. Chicago, IL: University of Illinois at Chicago Press, 215–31.

Archibugi D and Coco A. (2004) A new indicator of technological capabilities for developed and developing countries. *World Development* 32 (4): 629–54.

Ardichvili A, Cardozo R and Ray S. (2003) A theory of entrepreneurial opportunity identification and development. *Journal of Business Venturing* 18 (1): 105–23.

Arrow K. (1974) *The Limits of Organization*, New York: W.W. Norton & Company.

Asp EH. (1999) Factors affecting food decisions made by individual consumers. *Food Policy* 24 (2–3): pp 287–94.

Assael H, Roscoe J and Marvin A. (1976) Approaches to market segmentation analysis. *Journal of Marketing* 40 (4): 67–76.

Atkinson J and Meager N. (1994) Running to Stand Still: The Small Business in the Labour Market. In: Atkinson J and Storey DJ (eds) *Employment, The Small Firm and the Labour Market*. London: Routledge.

Avlonitis GJ and Gournaris SP. (1999) Marketing orientation and its determinants: an empirical analysis. *European Journal of Marketing* 33 (11/12): 1003–37.

Baker TL, Simpson PM and Siguaw JA. (1999) The impact of suppliers' perceptions of reseller market orientation on key relationship constructs. *Journal of the Academy of Marketing Science* 27 (1): 50–7.

Baker WE and Sinkula JM. (2009) The complementary effects of market orientation and entrepreneurial orientation on profitability in small businesses*. *Journal of Small Business Management* 47 (4): 443–64.

Barnes C, Blake H and Pinder D. (2009) *Creating and Delivering Your Value Proposition: Managing Customer Experience for Profit*, London: Kogan Page Publishers.

Barney J. (1986) Strategic Factor Markets: Expectations, Luck and Business Strategy. *Management Science* 32 (10): 1231–41.

Barney J. (1991) Firm resources and sustained competitive advantage. *Journal of Management* 17 (1): 99.

Barney J. (1997) *Gaining and Sustaining Competitive Advantage*, Reading: Addison-Wesley.

Baron O, Berman O and Wu D. (2008) Bargaining in the supply chain and its implication to coordination of supply chains in an industry. Working paper. Toronto, Canada: Joseph L. Rotman School of Management, University of Toronto.

Baron RA and Ward TB. (2004) Expanding entrepreneurial cognition's toolbox: potential contributions from the field of cognitive science. *Entrepreneurship: Theory & Practice* 28 (6): 553–73.

Barrows HS. (1986) A taxonomy of PBL methods. *Medical Education* 20: 481–6.

Barrows HS. (2000) *Problem-based Learning Applied to Medical Education*, Springfield: Southern Illinois University School of Medicine.

Bates T. (1995) A comparison of franchise and independent small business survival rates. *Small Business Economics* 7: (377–88).

Bauer RA. (1960) *Consumer Behaviour as Risk-taking. Dynamic Marketing for a Changing World*, Chicago, IL: American Marketing Association.

Baumol WJ. (1990) Entrepreneurship: productive, unproductive, and destructive. *The Journal of Political Economy* 98 (5): 893–921.

Baumol WJ. (1993) Formal entrepreneurship theory in economics: existence and bounds. *Journal of Business Ventures* 83 (197–210).

Beal RM. (2000) Competing effectively: environmental scanning, competitive strategy, and organizational performance in small manufacturing firms. *Journal of Small Business Management* 38 (1): 27–47.

Bennett PD and Anderson PF. (1988) *Dictionary of Marketing Terms*, Chicago, IL: The American Marketing Association.

Bennett RJ and Robson PJA. (1999) Intensity of interaction in supply of business advice and client impact: a comparison of consultancy, business associations and government support initiatives for SMEs. *British Journal of Management* 10 (4): 351–69.

Berkowitz EN, Kering RA, Hartley SW and Rudelius W. (1994) *Marketing*, Homewood, IL: Irwin.

Berry JW. (1997) Immigration, acculturation, and adaptation. *Applied Psychology* 46 (1): 5–34.

Berry, JW. (January 2003). 'Conceptual approaches to acculturation'. In Chun, Kevin M.; Organista, Pamela Balls; Marín, Gerardo. *Acculturation: Advances in Theory, Measurement, and Applied Research*. American Psychological Association. 17–37.

Berry LL. (1993) Our roles as educators: present and future. *Journal of Marketing Education* 15 (Fall): 3–8.

Berthon P, Hulbert JM and Pitt LF. (1999) Brand management prognostications. *Sloan Management Review* 40 (2): 53–65.

Bigné E, Vila-López N and Küster-Voluda. I. (2000) Competitive positioning and market orientation: two interrelated constructs. *European Journal of Innovation Management* 3 (4): 190–8.

Bird B. (1988) Implementing entrepreneurial ideas: the case for intention. *Academy of Management Review* 13 (3): 442–53.

Bird B and Brush C. (2002) A gendered perspective on organizational creation. *Entrepreneurship: Theory & Practice* 26 (3): 41–65.

Birkin M and Clarke G. (1998) GIS, Geodemographics, and spatial modeling in the UK financial service industry. *Journal of Housing Research* 9 (1): 87–98.

Birley S and Westhead P. (1990) Growth and performance contrasts between types of small firms. *Strategic Management Journal* 11: 85–100.

Blackburn R. (2012) Segmenting the SME market and implications for service provision: a literature review. In: ACAS (Advisory, Conciliation and Arbitration Service) (ed) *Research Paper* ref 09/12. London: ACAS.

Bladen and Machin. (2004) Education inequality and the expansion of UK higher education. *Scottish Journal of Political Economy* 51 (2): 230–49.

Bolton JE. (1971) Small Firms. Report of the Committee of Inquiry on Small Firms. (*Bolton Report*). London: HMSO.

Bonney L, Clark, R., Collins, R., and Fearne, A. (2007) From serendipity to sustainable competitive advantage: insights from Houston's farm and their journey of co-innovation. *Supply Chain Management: An International Journal* 12 (6): pp 395–9.

Bonoma T. (1985) *The Marketing Edge: Marketing Strategies Work*, New York, NY: Free Press.

Bonoma T and Clark B. (1992) *Marketing Performance Assessment*, Boston, MA: HBS Press.

Bontis N, Keow WCC and S. Richardson. (2000) Intellectual capital and business performance in Malaysian industries. *Journal of Intellectual Capital* 1 (1): 85–100.

Bracker JS, Keats BW and Pearson JN. (1988) Planning and financial performance among small firms in a growth industry. *Strategic Management Journal* 9 (6): 591–603.

Brigham KH, De Castro JO and Shepherd DA. (2007) A person-organization fit model of owner-managers' cognitive style and organizational demands. *Entrepreneurship Theory and Practice* 31 (1): 29–51.

Broom HN, Longenecker J and Moore CW. (1983) *Small Business Management*, Cincinnati, Ohio: South Western Publishing Co.

Brown G. (1992) *People, Brands and Advertising*, New York, NY: Millward Brown International.

Brush CG. (1992) Marketplace information scanning practices of new manufacturing ventures. *Journal of Small Business Management* 30 (4, October): 41–53.

Brush CG and Peters MP. (1992) Market information scanning practices of new service ventures: the impact of owner/founder experience. Entrepreneurial Management Working Paper 92 3 1. Boston, MA: Boston University.

Bruton GD, Fried VH and Manigart S. (2005) Institutional influences on the worldwide expansion of venture capital. *Entrepreneurship Theory and Practice* 29 (6): 737–60.

Bucklin LP and Sengupta S. (1993) Organizing successful co-marketing alliances. *The Journal of Marketing*, 57 (2): 32–46.

Burden S. (1998) Current trends and issues in the retail sector. *European Venture Capital Journal* 1 (November): 1–5.

Burnes B. (1996) *Managing Change. A Strategic Approach to Organizational Dynamics*, London: Pitman Publishing.

Burns P. (2007) *Entrepreneurship and Small Business*, China: Palgrave MacMillan.

Burrows R and Gane N. (2006) Geodemographics, Software and Class. *Sociology* 40 (5): 793–812.

Busenitz LW and Lau C-M. (2001) Growth intentions of entrepreneurs in a transitional economy: The People's Republic of China. *Entrepreneurship: Theory & Practice* 26 (1): 5–20.

Business Link. (2005a) Here's how I've changed my business for the better – Case studies from businesslink.gov.uk. Department of Trade and Industry.

Business Link. (2005b) Here's how I've started my business – Case studies from businesslink.gov.uk. Department of Trade and Industry.

Business Link. (2005c) Here's how I run my business – Case studies from businesslink.gov.uk. Department of Trade and Industry.

Butler J, Keh H and Chamornmarn W. (2000) Information acquisition, entrepreneurial performance and the evolution of modern Thai retailing. *Journal of Asian Business* 16 (2): 1–23.

Buttle F. (2012) *Customer Relationship Management*, London, Routledge.

Cacciolatti L and Fearne A. (2013) Marketing intelligence in SMEs: implications for the industry and policy makers. *Marketing Intelligence & Planning* 31 (1): 4–26.
Cacciolatti L, Fearne A, Ihua B and Yawson D. (2012) Types, sources and frequency of use of formalised marketing information as a catalyst of SME growth. *Journal of Strategic Management Education* 8 (1): 1–24.
Cacciolatti L, Garcia C and Kalantzakis M. (2015) Traditional food products: the effect of consumers' characteristics, product knowledge and perceived value on actual purchase. *Journal of International Food and Agribusiness Marketing*, 0:1–22.
Cacciolatti L and Molinero CM. (2013) Analysing the demand for supply chain jobs through job advertisements. *KBS Working Paper Series* 264 (January).
Cacciolatti L and Wan T. (2013) A study of small business owners' personal characteristics and the use of marketing information in the food and drink industry: a resource-based perspective. *International Journal on Food System Dynamics* 3 (2): 171–84.
Callahan T and Cassar M. (1995) Small business owners' assessments of their abilities to perform and interpret formal market studies. *Journal of Small Business Management* 33 (4): 1–9.
Callingham M and Baker T. (2002) We know what they think, but do we know what they do? *International Journal of Market Research* 44 (3): 299.
Calof JL. The relationship between firm size and export behavior revisited. *Journal of International Business Studies*. 1994, 25(2): 367–87.
Campbell A. (1997) Mission statements. *Long Range Planning* 30 (6): 931–2.
Cannon T. (1991) *Enterprise: Creation, Developmen and Growth*, Oxford: Butterworth-Heinemann.
Cantillon R. (1755) *Essai sur la nature du commerce en general*, London. Reissued for the Royal Economic Society in 1959, Frank Cass and Company Ltd.
Cantner U, Meder A and Ter Wal ALJ. (2010) Innovator networks and regional knowledge base. *Technovation* 30 (9–10): 496–507.
Capron L and Hulland J. (1999) Redeployment of brands, sales forces, and general marketing management expertise following horizontal acquisitions: a resource-based view. *Journal of Marketing* 63 (2): 41–54.
Carlzon J. (1987) *Moments of Truth*, New York: Ballinger Publishing.
Carson, Cromie S, McGowan P and Hill J. (1995) *Marketing and Entrepreneurship in SME's: An Innovative Approach*, Englewood Cliffs, NJ: Prentice Hall.
Carson D and Cromie S. (1990) Marketing Planning in Small Enterprises: A model and some empirical evidence. *Journal of Consumer Marketing* 7 (3): 5–18.
Carson D and Gilmore A. (2000) Marketing at the interface: not 'what' but 'how'. *Journal of Marketing Theory and Practice* 8 (2): 1–7.
Carson DJ. (1985) The evolution of marketing in small firms. *European Journal of Marketing* 19 (5): 7–16.
Carson SJ, Madhok A, Varman R and John G. (2003) Information processing moderators of the effectiveness of trust-based governance in interfirm R&D collaboration. *Organization Science* 14 (1): 45–56.
Carter S and Jones-Evans D. (2006) *Enterprise and Small Business: Principles, Practice and Policy*.London, Pearson Education.
Casson M. (1982) *The Entrepreneur: An Economic Theory*, Oxford: Martin Robertson.

Chaganti R and Parasuraman S. (1996) A study of the impacts of gender on business performance and management patterns in small businesses. *Entrepreneurship Theory and Practice* 21 (2): 73–5.

Chandler GN and Hanks SH. (1998) An examination of the substitutability of founders human and financial capital in emerging business ventures. *Journal of Business Venturing* 13 (5): 353–69.

Chapman M. (2000) "When the entrepreneur sneezes, the organization catches a cold": A practitioner's perspective on the state of the art in research on the entrepreneurial personality and the entrepreneurial process. *European Journal of Work & Organizational Psychology* 9 (1): 97–101.

Charlton M, Openshaw S and Wymer C. (1985) A poor man's ACORN. *Journal of Economic & Social Measurement* 13 (1): 69–96.

Chaston I. (2009) *Entrepreneurial Management in Small Firms*.London Sage Publications.

Chell E, Haworth J and Brearley S. (1991) *The Entrepreneurial Personality: Cases, Concepts and Categories*, London: Routledge.

Chopra S and Meindl S. (2012) *Supply Chain Management: Strategy, Planning and Operation*, London: Pearson.

Choueke R and Armstrong RK. (1998) The learning organization in small and medium sized enterprises: a destination or a journey? *International Journal of Entrepreneurial Behaviour & Research* 4 (2): 498–505.

Choueke RWE. (1992) Management education in higher education institutions related to the needs of small business management. PhD dissertation, Edge Hill University, UK.

Christopher M. (2005) *Logistics and Supply Chain Management: Creating Value-Added Networks*, Harlow: Prentice Halls Financial Times.

Christopher M. (2011) *Logistics and Supply Chain Management*, Dorchester: Pearson Education Limited.

Cillo P, De Luca LM and Troilo G. (2010) Market information approaches, product innovativeness, and firm performance: An empirical study in the fashion industry. *Research Policy* 39 (9): 1242–52.

Clark J. (2009) Entrepreneurship and diversification on English farms: Identifying business enterprise characteristics and change processes. *Entrepreneurship & Regional Development* 21 (2): 213–36.

Clark KM and Fujimoto T. (1991) *Product Development Performance: Strategy, Organization, and Management in the World Auto Industry*. Boston: Harvard Business School Press.

Cliff JE. (1998) Does one size fit all? Exploring the relationship between attitudes towards growth, gender, and business size. *Journal of Business Venturing* 13 (6): 523–42.

Clow KE and Wachter MK. (1996) Teaching methodologies used in basic marketing: an empirical investigation. *Journal of Marketing Education* 18 (Spring): 48–59.

Cohen WA and Stretch SM. (1989) Problems in small business marketing as perceived by owners. *Proceedings of Research Symposium on the Marketing/Entrepreneurship Interface*. Chicago, IL, 429–32.

Coleman S. (2000) Access to capital and terms of credit: a comparison of men- and women-owned small businesses. *Journal of Small Business Management* 38 (3): 37–52.

Collinson E and Shaw E. (2001) Entrepreneurial marketing–a historical perspective on development and practice. *Management Decision* 39 (9): 761–6.

Colombo MG and Delmastro M. (2001) Techology-based entrepreneurs: does internet make a difference? *Small Business Economics* 16 (1): 177–90.

Conant JS and White C. (1999) Marketing program planning, process benefits and store performance: an initial study among small retail firms. *Journal of Retailing* 75 (4): 525–41.

Cooke P. (1992) Regional innovation systems: competitive regulation in the new Europe. *Geoforum* 23 (3): 365–82.

Cooper AC . (1993) Challenges in predicting new firm performance. *Journal of Business Venturing* 8: 241–53.

Cooper AC, Gimeno-Gascon FJ and CY Woo. (1994) Initial human and financial capital as predictors of new venture performance. *Journal of Business Venturing* 9: 371–95.

Cooper AC, Gimeno-Gascon FJ and CY Woo. (2002) Initial human and financial capital as predictors of new venture performance. *Journal of Business Venturing* 9 (5 [September]): 371–95.

Cooper A, Woo C and Dunkelberg W. (1989) Entrepreneurship and the inital size of firms. *Journal of Business Venturing* 4 (5): 317–32.

Cooper AC. (1982) The entrepreneurship – small business research. In: Kent S, D. Sexton and K. Vesper (eds.) *Encyclopaedia of Entrepreneurship*, Englewood Cliffs, NJ: Prentice-Hall.

Cordes C, Richerson PJ and Schwesinger G. (2010) How corporate cultures coevolve with the business environment: The case of firm growth crises and industry evolution. *Journal of Economic Behavior & Organization* 76 (3): 465–80.

Covin JG and Lumpkin GT. (2011) Entrepreneurial orientation theory and research: reflections on a needed construct. *Entrepreneurship: Theory & Practice* 35 (5): 855–72.

Cromie S and Hayes J. (1988) Towards a typology of female entrepreneurs. *The Sociological Review* 36 (1): 87–113.

Croxton KL, Garcia-Dastugue, S.J., Lambert, D.M.,and Rogers, D.S. (2001) The supply chain management processes. *The International Journal of Logistics Management* 12 (No.2): pp 13–36.

Cunningham AC. (1995) Developing marketing professionals: what can business schools learn? *Journal of Marketing Education* 17 (Summer): 3–9.

Cunningham RM. (1956) Brand loyalty what, where, how much? *Harvard Business Review* 34: 116–28.

Dahlqvist J, Davidsson P and Wiklund J. (2000) Initial conditions as predictors of new venture performance: A replication and extension of the Cooper et al. study. *Enterprise and Innovation Management Studies* 1 (1): 1–17.

Damen L. (1987) *Culture Learning: The Fifth Dimension on the Language Classroom*, Reading, MA: Addison-Wesley.

Das S, Sen PK and Sengupta S. (1998) Impact of strategic alliances on firm valuation. *Academy of Management Journal* 41 (1): 27–41.

David P, Gary P, Paul J, Christopher M and Brychan T. (2011) Graduate entrepreneurs are different: they access more resources? *International Journal of Entrepreneurial Behaviour & Research* 17 (2): 183–202.

Davidsson. (1991) Continued entrepreneurship: ability, need, and opportunity as determinants of small firm growth. *Journal of Business Venturing* 6 (405–29)
Davidsson P. (1989) *Continued Entrepreneurship and Small Firm Growth*, Stockholm: Ekonomiska Forskningsinstitutet.
Davidsson P and Honig B. (2003) The role of social and human capital among nascent entrepreneurs. *Journal of Business Venturing* 18 (1): 301–31.
Davis CD, Hills GE and LaForge RW. (1985) The marketing/small enterprise paradox: a research agenda. *International Small Business Journal* 3 (3): 31–42.
Day GS. (1991) Learning about markets. Cambridge, MA: Marketing Science Institute.
De Bruin A, Brush CG and Welter F. (2006) Introduction to the special issue: towards building cumulative knowledge on women's entrepreneurship. *Entrepreneurship Theory and Practice* 30 (5): 585–93.
de Chernatony L. (1992) *Creating Powerful Brands*, Oxford: Butterworth-Heinemann.
de Chernatony L and McDonald M. (2001) *Creating Powerful Brands in Consumer, Service and Industrial Markets*, Oxford: Butterworth-Heinemann.
Deal TE and Kennedy A. (1983) Culture: a new look through old lenses. *The Journal of Applied Behavioural Science* 19 (4): 498–505.
Debenham JC, G. Stillwell, J. . (2003) Extending geodemographic classification: a new regional prototype *Environment and Planning A* 35 (6): 1025–50
Delbufalo E. (2012) Outcomes of inter-organizational trust in supply chain relationships: a systematic literature review and a meta-analysis of the empirical evidence. *Supply Chain Management: An International Journal* 17 (4): 377–402.
Delmar F and Davidsson P. (2000) Where do they come from? Prevalence and characteristics of nascent entrepreneurs. *Entrepreneurship & Regional Development* 12 (1): 1–23.
Denison T and McDonald M. (1995) The role of marketing past, present, future. *Journal of Marketing Practice: Applied Marketing Science* 1 (1): 54–76.
Deshpande R and Zaltman G. (1982) Factors affecting the use of market research information: a path analysis. *Journal of Marketing Research* 19 (1 [Feburary]): 14–31.
Dess GG, Ireland RD, Zahra SA, Floyd SW, Janney JJ and Lane PJ. (2003) Emerging issues in corporate entrepreneurship. *Journal of Management* 29 (1): 351–78.
DeTienne DR and Chandler GN. (2007) The role of gender in opportunity identification. *Entrepreneurship: Theory & Practice* 31 (3): 365–86.
Dibb S, Sinkin L, Pride WM and Ferrell OC. (1997) *Marketing: Concepts and Strategies*, Boston, MA: Houghton Mifflin.
Dickson PH and Weaver KM. (1997) Environmental determinants and individual-level moderators of alliance use. *Academy of Management Journal* 40 (2): 404–25.
Dickson PH, Weaver KM and Hoy F. (2006) Opportunism in the R&D alliances of SMES: The roles of the institutional environment and SME size. *Journal of Business Venturing* 21 (4): 487–513.
Dickson PR. (1992) Toward a general theory of competitive rationality. *Journal of Marketing* 56 (January): 69–83.
Dierickx I and Cool K. (1989) Asset stock accumulation and sustainability of competitive advantage. *Management Science* 35 (12): 1504–11.
Dollinger M. (1985) Environmental contact and performance of the smaller firm. *Journal of Small Business Management* 23 (January): 24–30.

Dolmans DHJM, De Grave W, Wolfhagen IHAP and van der Vleuten CPM. (2005) Problem-based learning: future challenges for educational practice and research. *Medical Education* 39 (7): 732–41.
Doutriaux J and Simyar F. (1987) Duration of comparative advantage accruing from some start-up factors in high-tech entrepreneurial firms. *Frontiers of Entrepreneurship Research*
Doyle P. (1995) Marketing in the new millennium. *European Journal of Marketing* 29 (13): 23–41.
Doyle P. (2000) Value-based marketing. *Journal of Strategic Marketing* 8 (4): 299–311.
Drucker P. (1974) *Management Tasks, Responsibilities, Practices*, New York: Harper & Row.
Duchesneau DA and Gartner WB. (1990) A profile of new venture success and failure in an emerging industry. *Journal of Business Venturing* 5: 297–312.
Dudley SC and Dudley LW. (1995) New directions for the business curriculum. *Journal of Education for Business* 70 (May/June): 305–10.
Dunn E. (2006) *It's Marketing Jim, But Not As We Know It*, London: dunnhumby.
Dunning JH. The eclectic paradigm of international production: a restatement and some possible extensions. Journal of International Business Studies. 1988 19(1); 1–31.
Durkheim E. (2008) *The Elementary Forms of the Religious Life*, Dover, Dover Publications.
Dwyer FR, Schurr PH, Oh S. Developing buyer-seller relationships. The Journal of Marketing. 1987: 51 (2)11–27..
Dyer JH and Singhe H. (1998) The relational view: cooperative strategy and sources of interorganizational competitive advantage. *Academy of Management Review* 23 (4): 660–79.
Dyke LS, Fisher EM and Reuber AR. (1992) An inter-industry examination of the impact of owner experience on firm performance. *Journal of Small Business Management* (October): 73–86.
The Economist (2007) Snarling all the way to the bank. *Issue*, 25 August 2007
Ecorys (2012) EU SMEs in 2012: t the crossroads: Annual report on small and medium-sized enterprises in the EU, 2011/12. Rotterdam.
Edens KM. (2000) Preparing problem solvers for the 21st century through problem-based learning. *College Teaching* 48 (Spring): 55–69.
Ely RT and Hess RH. (1893) *Outline of Economics*, New York: MacMillan.
Ennis S. (1999) Growth and the small firm: using causal mapping to assess the decision-making process – a case study. *Qualitative Market Research: An International Journal* 2 (2): 147–60.
Ertmer PA and Newby TJ. (1993) Behaviorism, cognitivism, constructivism: comparing critical feartures from an instructional design perspective. *Perform Improve Q* 6 (4): 50–72.
European Commission. (2003) Observatory of European SMEs: Highlights from the 2003 Observatory. In: Jacqueline Snijders, Micha van Lin, Rob van der Horst eds SMEs Highlights from the 2003 Observatory 2003: Observatory of European SMEs. 2003. No. 8.
European Commission. (2005a) 2003/361/EC. In: Union E (ed) *L 124. Official Journal of the European Union:* 36–41.
European Commission. (2005b) *The New SME Definition: User Guide and Model Declaration*. Enterprise and Industry Publications: Brussels.

European Commission. (2008) *The New SME Definition*. Enterprise and Industry Publications: Brussels.
Evans A. (1993) Market orientation versus marketing orientation: the case for a new terminological set. *Discussion Paper Series in Economics*, No 93.40. Sheffield: Sheffield University Management School, 1–17.
Fahey L and King WR. (1977) Environmental Scanning for Corporate Planning. *Business Horizons* 20 (August): 61–71.
Fearne A. (2009) *Sustainable Food and Wine Value Chains*. Adelaide: Government of South Australia, 1–42.
Feige E. Underground activity and institutional change: productive, protective, and predatory behavior in transition economies. In E Feige, editors. Transforming post-communist political economies. Washington, DC: National Academy Press; 1997
Felton A. (1959) Making the marketing concept work. *Harvard Business Review* 37 (4): 55–65.
Finkelstein S and Hambrick DC. (1990) Top management team tenure and organizational outcomes: the moderating role of managerial discretion. *Administrative Science Quarterly* 35 (3): 484–503.
Fisher E. (1992) Sex differences and small-business performance among Canadian retailers and service providers. *Journal of Small Business and Entrepreneurship* 9 (4): 2–13.
Fisher E, Reuber R and Dyke L. (1993) A theoretical overview and extension of research on sex, gender, and entrepreneurship. *Journal of Business Venturing* 8: 151–68.
Fornell C. (1992) A national customer satisfaction barometer: the Swedish experience. *The Journal of Marketing* 56 (1): 6–21.
Fornell C. Rust RT and Dekimpe MG. (2010) The effect of customer satisfaction on consumer spending growth. *Journal of Marketing Research* 47 (1): 28–35.
Frank BG and Krake JM. (2005) Successful brand management in SMEs: a new theory and practical hints. *Journal of Product & Brand Management* 14 (4): 228–38.
Fukuyama F. (1995) *Trust: The Social Virtues and the Creation of Prosperity*, New York, NY: The Free Press.
Fuller PB. (1994) Assessing marketing in small and medium-sized enterprises. *European Journal of Marketing* 28 (12): 34–49.
Gaskill LR, Van Auken HE and Manning RA. (1993) A factor analytic study of the perceived causes of small business failure. *Journal of Small Business Management* 31 (4): 18–31.
Germain R and Cooper MB. (1990) How a customer mission statement affects company performance. *Industrial Marketing Management* 19 (1): 47–54.
Geroski PA. (1995) What do we know about entry? *International Journal of Industrial Organization* 13 421–40.
Gillinsky AJ, Stanny E, McCline RL and Eyler R. (2001) Does size matter? An empirical investigation into the competitive strategies of the small firm. *Journal of Small Business Strategy* 12 (2): 1–13.
Gilmore A, Carson D and Grant K. (2001a) SME marketing in practice. *Marketing Intelligence & Planning* 19 (1): 6–11.
Glazer R, Steckel J and Winer R. (1992) Locally rational decision making: the distracting effect of information on managerial performance. *Management Science* 38 (February): 212–26.

Göbel S. (2000) Klaus B: The success story of an entrepreneur – a case study. *European Journal of Work & Organizational Psychology* 9 (1): 89–92.
Goffee R and Scase R. (1983) Class, entrepreneurship and the service sector: towards a conceptual classification. *Service Industries Journal* 3: 14–22.
Goss J. (1995) "We know who you are and we know where you live": The instrumental rationality of geodemographic. *Economic Geography* 71 (2): 171.
Granovetter MM. (1978) The strength of weak ties. *American Journal of Sociology* 78 (6): 1360–80.
Granovetter MM. (2001) *The Sociology of Economic Life*, Oxford: Westview Press.
Grant RM. (1995) *Contemporary Strategy Analysis: Concepts, Techniques, Applications*, Cambridge: Blackwell.
Gray C. (1990) Business independence – impediment or enhancement to growth in the 1990s?, 13th National Small Firms' Policy and Research Conference, Harrogate, UK,
Gray C. (1998) *Enterprise and Culture*, London: Routledge.
Greenaway D and Haynes M. (2003) Funding higher education in the UK: the role of fees and loans. *Economic Journal* 113 (485): 150–66.
Greenley GE. (1995) Market orientation and company performance: empirical evidence from UK companies. *British Journal of Management* 6 (1): 1.
Gregory J and Sellers LJ. (2002) Building corporate brands. *Pharmaceutical Executive* (January): 38–44.
Gremler DD and Brown SW. (1996) Service loyalty: its nature, importance and implications. New York: International Quality Association, 171–80.
Grönroos C. (1994) From marketing mix to relationship marketing: towards a paradigm shift in marketing. *Management Decision* 32 (2): 4–20.
Grönroos C and Ravald A. (1996) The value concept and relationship marketing. *European Journal of Marketing* 30 (2): 19–30.
Groves K, Vance C and Choi D. (2011) Examining entrepreneurial cognition: an occupational analysis of balanced linear and nonlinear thinking and entrepreneurship success. *Journal of Small Business Management* 49 (3): 438–66.
Gustafsson V. (2009) Entrepreneurial Decision-Making: Thinking Under Uncertainty. In: Carsrud AL and Brännback M (eds). *Understanding the Entrepreneurial Mind*. New York: Springer, 285–304.
H. Gatignon and Xuereb JM. (1997) Strategic orientation of the firm and new product performance. *Journal of Marketing Research* 34 (1): 77–90.
Hakala H. (2011) Strategic orientations in management literature: three approaches to understanding the interaction between market, technology, entrepreneurial and learning orientations. *International Journal of Management Reviews* 13 (2): 199–217.
Hambrick DC and Mason PA. (1984) Upper echelons: the organization as a reflection of its top managers. *Academy of Management Review* 9 (2): 193–206.
Hamel G and Prahalad CK. (1989) Strategic intent. *Harvard Business Review* 67 (3): 63–78.
Hamel G and Prahalad CK. (1994) *Competing for the Future*, Boston: Harvard Business School Press.
Handfeld RB and Bechtel C. (2002) The role of trust and relationship structure in improving supply chain responsiveness. *Industrial Marketing Management* 31 (4): 367–82.

Hanks SH, Watson CJ, Jansen E and Chandler GN. (1993) Tightening the life-cycle construct: a taxonomic study of growth stage configurations in high-technology organizations. *Entrepreneurship: Theory & Practice* 18 (2): 5–30.

Hansen B and Hamilton R. (2011) Factors distinguishing small firm growers and non-growers. *International Small Business Journal* 29 (3): 278–94.

Harker K. (2001) Immigrant generation, assimilation, and adolescent psychological well-being. *Social Forces* 79 (3): 969–1004.

Harris R, Sleight, P and Webber, R. . (2005) *Geodemographics: Neighbourhood Targeting and GIS*, Chichester: Wiley .

Hauge E and Havnes P-A. (2001) *The Dynamics of SME Development – Two Case Studies of the Internationalisation Process*, RENT XV Conference 22–3 November 2001, Turku – Finland,

Havnes PA and Senneseth K. (2001) A panel study of firm growth among SMEs in networks. *Small Business Economics* 16: 293–302.

Hay RK and Ross DL. (1989) An assessment of success factors of non-urban start-up firms based upon financial characteristics of successful versus failed ventures. *Frontiers of Entrepreneurship Research*, 148–58.

Hayek FA. (1948) The Use of Knowledge in Society. *Studies in Philosophy, Politics and Economics*. Chicago: University of Chicago Press.

Hayek FA. (1952) *The Sensory Order*, Chicago: University of Chicago Press.

Hayek FA. (1967) Competition as a Discovery Procedure. *New Studies in Philosophy, Politics, Economics and History of Ideas*. Chicago: University of Chicago Press.

Hayward M. (2005) *Customers Are for Life, Not Just Your Next Bonus*, London: dunnhumby.

Heide JB and John G. (1988) The role of dependence balancing in safeguarding transaction-specific assets in conventional channels. *The Journal of Marketing*, 52:1, 20–35.

Heide JB and John G. (1990) Alliances in industrial purchasing: the determinants of joint action in buyer–supplier relationships. *Journal of Marketing Research*, 27(February),24–36.

Heide JB and Miner AS. (1992) The shadow of the future: Effects of anticipated interaction and frequency of contact on buyer-seller cooperation. *Academy of Management Journal* 35 (2): 265–91.

Henderson BD. (1979) *Henderson on Corporate Strategy*, New York: Mentor.

Herron L and Robinson R. (1993) A structure model of the effects of entrepreneurial characteristics on venture performance. *Journal of Business Venturing* 8: 281–94)

Hill J. (2001) A multidimensional study of the key determinants of effective SME marketing activity: part 1. *International Journal of Entrepreneurial Behaviours & Research* 7 (5): 171–204.

Hills GE and Narayana CL. (1989) *Profile Characteristics, Success Factors, and Marketing in Highly Successful Firms*. Wellesley, MA: Babson College Conference on Entrepreneurship, 69–80.

Hisrich RD and Peters MP. (1992) The need for marketing in entrepreneurship. *Journal of Consumer Marketing* 9 (September): 43–7.

Hisrich RD, Peters MP and Shepherd DA. (2005) *Entrepreneurship*, New York: McGraw-Hill Irwin.

Hoek J, Gendall P and Esslemont D. (1996) Market segmentation: a search for the Holy Grail? *Journal of Marketing Practice: Applied Marketing Science* 2 (1): 25–34.

Hofstede G. (1984) National Cultures and Corporate Cultures. In: RE Samovar and G Porter (ed) *Communication between Cultures*. Belmont, CA: Wadsworth.

Hogarth-Scott S, Watson K and Wilson N. (1996) Do small businesses have to practise marketing to survive and grow? *Marketing Intelligence & Planning* 14 (1): 6–18.

Holbrook MB. (2004) Customer value and autoethnography: subjective personal introspection and the meanings of a photograph collection. *Journal of Business Research* 58 (1): 45–61.

Hollensen S. (2010) *Global Marketing: A Decision-Oriented Approach*, Madrid, Spain: FT Prentice Hall.

Holmen M, Magnusson M and McKelvey M. (2007) What are innovative opportunities? *Industry and Innovation* 14 (1): 27–46.

Howard JA and Sheth JN. (1969) *The Theory of Buyer Behavior*, New York, NY: John Wiley and Sons.

Huang X and Brown A. (1999) An analhysis and classification of problems in small business. *International Small Business Journal* 18 (1): 73–85.

Hughes D. (2009) European food marketing: understanding consumer wants – the starting point in adding value to basic food products. *Eurochoices* 8 (3): 6–13.

Humby C. (2005) *Brand Is Dead, Long Live the Customer*, London: dunnhumby.

Humby CR. (1989) New developments in demographic targeting – the implications of 1991. *Journal of the Market Research Society* 31 (1): 53–73.

Hutt MD, Reingen PH and Ronchetto JR. (1988) Tracing emergent processes in marketing strategy formation. *Journal of Marketing* 52 (1 January): 4–19.

IFC (International Finance Corporation). (2005) *Enabling SMEs to Enter the International Supply Chain*.New York: The United Nations Trade Faciliation Network.

IFC. (2006) Access to Finance for Small and Medium Enterprises (SMEs). *Monitor* 3 (June).

IFC. (2007) *Creating Opportunities for Small Business*. New York: World Bank Group.

IFC. (2008) Linkage Programs to Develop Small and Medium Enterprises. *Monitor*.

Jackson WE and Mishra CS. (2007) Small enterprise finance, governance, and imperfect capital markets: an introduction to the inaugural office depot forum special issue. *Journal of Small Business Management* 45 (1): 1–4.

Javalgi RG and Moberg CR. (1997) Service loyalty: implications for service providers. *The Journal of Services Marketing* 11 (3): 165–79.

Jaworski BJ and Kohli AK. (1993) Market orientation: antecedents and consequences. *Journal of Marketing* 57 (July): 53–71.

Jobber D. (2004) *Principles and Practice of Marketing*, London:McGraw Hill Ed.

Johanson J, Vahlne J-E. The internationalization process of the firm-a model of knowledge development and increasing foreign market commitments. Journal of International Business Studies. 1977; 8(1): 23–32.

Johnson JL and Kuehn R. (1987) The small business owner/manager's search for external information. *Journal of Small Business Management* 25 (3 [June]): 53–60.

Johnston K and Gregory C. (2007) *Food and Drink Industry Evidence Based Paper*, rev. HAJ1. Edinburgh:Scottish Government – Rural and Environment Research and Analysis Directorate.

Bibliography

Joquico JP. (2008) SMEs face constraints in adopting CSR. *Business Weekly* 22 June 08.
Justis RT. (1981) *Marketing Your Small Business*, Englewood Cliffs, NJ: Prentice-Hall.
Kalleberg A and Leicht K. (1991) Gender and organizational performance: Determinants of small business survival and success. *Academy of Management Journal* 34 (1): 136–61.
Kania D. (2001) *Branding.com,New York* US: McGraw-Hill.
Kannana VR and Tanb KC. (2005) Just in time, total quality management, and supply chain management: understanding their linkages and impact on business performance. *Omega* 33: 153–62.
Kaplan JM and Warren AC. (2007) *Patterns of Entrepreneurship*, Hoboken, NJ: John Wiley & Sons, Inc.
Kaplan RS. (2004) *Strategy Maps: Converting Intangible Assets into Tangible Outcomes*. Boston, MA:Harvard Business Press.
Kaplan RS and Norton DP. (2000) Having trouble with your strategy? Then map it. *Harvard Business Review* (September-October), 3–11.
Keh HT, Nguyen TTM and Ng HP. (2007) The effects of entrepreneurial orientation and marketing information on the performance of SMEs. *Journal of Business Venturing* 22 (4): 592–611.
Keller KL. (1993) Conceptualizing, measuring, managing customer-based brand equity. *Journal of Marketing* 57 (1): 1–22.
Keller KL. (2003) *Strategic Brand Management: Building, Measuring and Managing Brand Equity*, Englewood Cliffs, NJ: Prentice-Hall.
Kennedy E, Lawton L and Walker E. (2001) The case for using live cases: shifting the paradigm in marketing education. *Journal of Marketing Education* 23 (August): 136–44.
Kenny B and Dyson K. (1989) *Marketing in Small Business*, London: Routledge.
Ketchen Jr DJ and Hult GTM. (2007) Bridging organization theory and supply chain management: the case of best value supply chains. *Journal of Operations Management* 25 (2): 573–80.
Kets de Vries MFR. (1977) The entrepreneurial personality: a person at the crossroads. *Journal of Management Studies* 14 (1): 34–57.
Kim SK, Hsieh P-H. Interdependence and its consequences in distributor-supplier relationships: a distributor perspective through response surface approach. *Journal of Marketing Research.* 2003: 40(1)101–12.
Kirca AH, Jayachandran S and Bearden WO. (2005) Market Orientation: A meta-analytic review and assessment of its antecedents and impact on performance. *The Journal of Marketing* 69 (2): 24–41.
Kirzner I. (1973) *Competition and Entrepreneurship*, Chicago: University of Chicago Press.
Kirzner I. (1979) *Perception, Opportunity and Profit: Studies in the Theory of Entrepreneurship*, Chicago: University of Chicago Press.
Kirzner I. (1997) Entrepreneurial discovery and competitive market processes: an Austrian approach. *Journal of Economic Literature* 35(1): 60–85
Kirzner I. (1999) Creativity and/or alertness: a reconsideration of the Schumpeterian entrepreneur. *Review of Austrian Economics* 11(1–2): 5–17.
Kleindl B. (2000) Competitive dynamics and new business models for SMEs in the virtual marketplace. *Journal of Developmental Entrepreneurship* 5 (1): 73–86.

Knight F. (1921) *Risk, Uncertainty and Profit*, Chicago: University of Chicago Press.

Knight JG, Holdsworth, DK and Mather, DW (2007) Country-of-origin and choice of food imports: an in-depth study of European distribution channel gatekeepers. *Journal of International Business Studies* 38 (1): 107–25.

Koellinger P. (2008) Why are some entrepreneurs more innovative than others? *Small Business Economics* 31 (1): 21–37.

Kohli AK and Jaworski BJ. (1990) Marketing orientation: the construct, research propositions, and managerial implications. *Journal of Marketing* 54 (April): 1–18.

Kolvereid L. (1992) Growth aspirations among Norwegian entrepreneurs. *Journal of Business Venturing* 7: 209–22.

Korhonen H, Luostarinen R, Welch, L. Internationalization of SMEs: Inward-outward patterns and government policy. MIR: Management International Review, 1996; 36(4): 315–29.

Kotey B and Meredith GG. (1997) Relationships among owner/ manager personal values, business strategies, and enterprise performance. *Journal of Small Business Management* 35 (2): 37–64.

Kotler P. (2000) *Marketing Management*, Upper Saddle River, NJ: Prentice-Hall.

Kotler P, Armstrong, G., Saunders, J., and Wong, V. (2005) *Principles of Marketing*, Harlow: Financial Times Prentice Hall.

Kotler P and Keller K. (1991) *Marketing Management*, Englewood Cliffs, NJ: Prentice Hall.

Kotler PH. (1991) *Marketing Management: Analysis, Planning, and Control*, Englewood Cliffs, NJ: Prentice-Hall.

Kotler PH and Levy SJ. (1969) Broadening the concept of marketing. *Journal of Marketing* 33 (February): 10–15.

Kraft FB and Goodell PW. (1989) *Identifying the Health Conscious Consumer*, Newbury Park, CA: Sage.

Kumar N, Scheer LK, Steenkamp J-BE. The effects of perceived interdependence on dealer attitudes. Journal of Marketing Research. 1995: 32(3) 348–56.Kumar N, Scheer LK, Steenkamp J-BE. The effects of supplier fairness on vulnerable resellers. Journal of Marketing Research. 1995: 32(1) 54–65..

Kuratko D. (2008) *Entrepreneurship: Theory, Process and Practice*, Mason, OH: South Western Educational Publishing.

Lambsdorff, J. G., Taube, M., & Schramm, M. (2004). *The new institutional economics of corruption*. London: Routledge

Lamprinopoulou C, Tregear A and Ness M. (2006) Agrifood SMEs in Greece: the role of collective action. *British Food Journal* 108 (8): 663–76.

Lancaster KJ. (1966) A new approach to consumer theory. *The Journal of Political Economy* 74 (2): 132–57.

Le and Miller. (2004) High school graduation in Australia: Do schools matter? *Scottish Journal of Political Economy* 51 (2): 194–208.

Lee T-S and Tsai H-J. (2005) The effects of business operation mode on market orientation, learning orientation and innovativeness. *Industrial Management & Data Systems* 105 (3): 325–48.

Levitt T. (1960) Marketing myopia. *Harvard Business Review* 38 (4): 45–56.

Levitt T. (1980) Marketing success through differentiation of anything. *Harvard Business Review* 58 (1): 83–91.

Levy M and Powell P. (2005) *Strategies for Growth in SMEs*, Oxford: Elsevier Butterworth-Heinemann.

Li S, Ragu-Nathan B, Ragu-Nathan TS and Rao SS. (2006) The impact of supply chain management practices on competitive advantage and organizational performance. *Omega* 34 (2): 107–24.

Lin CF. (2002) Segmenting customer brand preference: demographic or psychographic. *Journal of Product & Brand Management* 11 (5): 249.

Lindridge A. (2010) Are we fooling ourselves when we talk about ethnic homogeneity? The case of religion and ethnic subdivisions amongst Indians living in Britain. *Journal of Marketing Management* 26 (5–6): 441–72.

Linton R. (1945) *The Cultural Background of Personality*, New York.

Longley P. (2005) Geographical information systems: a renaissance of geodemographics for public service delivery. *Progress in Human Geography* 29 (1): 57–63.

Low MB and MacMillan IC. (1988) Entrepreneurship: past research and future challenges. *Journal of Management* 14 (2): 139–61.

Lumpkin GT and Dess GG. (1996) Clarifying the entrepreneurial orientation construct and linking it to performance. *Academy of Management Review* 21 (1): 135–72.

Lumpkin GT and Dess GG. (2001) Linking two dimensions of entrepreneurial orientation to firm performance: The moderating role of environment and industry life cycle. *Journal of Business Venturing* 16 (5): 429–51.

Mahajan J. (1992) The overconfidence effect in marketing management predictions. *Journal of Marketing Research* 24 (August): 329–42.

Mankelow G and Merrilees B. (2001) Towards a model of entrepreneurial marketing for rural women: a case study approach. *Journal of Development Entrepreneurship* 6 (3): 221–35.

Manolova TS, Brush CG, Edelman LF and Shaver KG. (2011) One size does not fit all: entrepreneurial expectancies and growth intentions of US women and men nascent entrepreneurs. *Entrepreneurship & Regional Development* 24 (1–2): 7–27.

Martin RL and Osberg S. (2007) Social entrepreneurship: the case for definition. *Stanford Social Innovation Review* 5 (2): 27–39.

Matsuno K, Mentzer JT and Aysegul O. (2002) The effects of entrepreneurial proclivity and market orientation on business performance. *Journal of Marketing* 66 (3): 18–32.

Mayes DG and Moir C. (1990) The growth of small firms in the UK. *Competition and Markets*. Basingstoke: Macmillan, 41–62.

McCartan-Quinn D and Carson D. (2003) Issues which impact upon marketing in the small firms. *Small Business Economics* 21 (2): 201–13.

McCullough ME, Tsang JA and Brion S. (2003) Personality traits in adolescence as predictors of religiousness in early adulthood: findings from the Terman Longitudinal Study. *Personality and Social Psychology Bulletin* 29 (8): 980–91.

McDougall PP, Covin JG, Robinson Jr RB and Herron L. (1994) The effects of industry growth and strategic breadth on new venture performance and strategy content. *Strategic Management Journal* 15 (7): 537–54.

McGuire TW and Staelin R. (1983) An industry equilibrium analysis of downstream vertical integration. *INFORMS: Institute for Operations Research* 2 (2): 161–91.

Mead M. (1953) *Cultural Patterns and Technical Change (A Manual Prepared by the World Federation for Mental Health)*, Paris: UNESCO.
Menon A and Varadarajan PR. (1992) A model of marketing knowledge use within firms. *Journal of Marketing* 56 (4 October): 53–71.
Mentzer JT. (2004) *Fundamentals of Supply Chain Management: Twelve Drivers Of Competitive Advantage*, LondonSage.
Meziou F. (1991) Areas of strength and weakness in the adoption of the marketing concept by small manufacturing firms. *Journal of Small Business Management* 29 (August): 72–8.
Miles MP and Darroch J. (2006) Large firms, entrepreneurial marketing processes, and the cycle of competitive advantage. *European Journal of Marketing* 40 (5/6): 485–501.
Milne M. (1999) The promise of problem-based learning. *Chartered Accountants Journal of New Zealand* 78 (March): 37–40.
Miner JB. (1997) *A Psychological Typology of Successsful Entrepreneurs*, London: Quorum Books.
Mitchell RK, Busenitz L, Lant T, McDougall PP, Morse EA and Smith JB. (2002) Toward a theory of entrepreneurial cognition: rethinking the people side of entrepreneurship research. *Entrepreneurship: Theory & Practice* 27 (2): 93–104.
Mitchell V-W and McGoldrick PJ. (1994) The role of geodemographics in segmenting and targeting consumer markets: A Delphi study. *European Journal of Marketing* 28 (5): 54–72.
Mohr J and Nevin JR. (1990) Communication strategies in marketing channels. *Journal of Marketing* 54 (4 October): 36–51.
Monroe KB. (1991) *Pricing – Making Profitable Decisions*, New York, NY: McGraw-Hill.
Moorman C. (1995) Organizational market information processes: cultural antecedents and new product outcomes. *Journal of Marketing Research* 32 (3): 318–35.
Moorman C. Deshpande R and Zaltman G. (1993) Factors affecting trust in market research relationships. *Journal of Marketing* 57 (1 [January]): 81–101.
Moorman C, Zaltman G and Deshpande R. (1992) Relationships between providers and users of market research: the dynamics of trust within and between organizations. *Journal of Marketing Research* 29 (3 [August]): 314–39.
Morgan G. (1997) *Images of Organizations*, London: Sage.
Morgan NA, Vorhies DW and Mason CH. (2009) Market orientation, marketing capabilities, and firm performance. *Strategic Management Journal* 30 (8): 909–20.
Moriarty J, Jones R, Rowley J and Kupiec-Teahan B. (2008) Marketing in small hotels: a qualitative study. *Marketing Intelligence & Planning* 26 (3): 293–315.
Morris E. (2001) Key Challenges of the Next Decade, DfES, 22 October Department for Education and Skills (2003) 'Student loans and the question of debt' http://www.dfes.gov.uk/hegatew at London Guildhall University, 22 October 2001.
Morris MH, Schindehutte M and LaForge RW. (2002) Entrepreneurial marketing: a construct for integrating emerging entrepreneurship and marketing perspectives. *Journal of Marketing Theory and Practice*: 1–19.
Nagarajan M and Sošić G. (2008) Game-theoretic analysis of cooperation among supply chain agents: review and extensions. *European Journal of Operational Research* 187 (3): 719–45.

Narasimhan R, Nair A, Griffith DA, Arlbjørn JS and Bendoly E. (2009) Lock-in situations in supply chains: a social exchange theoretic study of sourcing arrangements in buyer-supplier relationships. *Journal of Operations Management* 27 (5): 374–89.

Narver JC and Slater SF. (1990) The effect of market orientation on profitability. *Journal of Marketing* 54 (4): 20–35.

Nevins JL and Money RB. (2008) Performance implications of distributor effectiveness, trust, and culture in import channels of distribution. *Industrial Marketing Management* 37 (1): 46–58.

Oakey R. (1991) Innovation and the management of marketing in high technology small firms. *Journal of Marketing Management* 7 (4): 343–56.

O'Farrell PN and Hitchens DMWN . (1988) Alternative theories of small firm growth: a critical review. *Environment and Planning* 20: 365–82.

O'Farrell PN and Hitchens DMWN. (1990) Producer services and regional development: key conceptual issues of taxonomy and quality measurement. *Regional Studies* 24 (2): 163–71.

Olavarrieta S and Friedmann R. (2008) Market orientation, knowledge-related resources and firm performance. *Journal of Business Research* 61 (6): 623–30.

Olins W. (2007) *Olins on Br@nd*, London: Thames and Hudson.

Oliva R and Watson N. (2011) Cross-functional alignment in supply chain planning: A case study of sales and operations planning. *Journal of Operations Management* 29 (5): 434–48.

O'Malley L and Patterson M. (1997) Retailer use of geodemographic and other data sources: An empirical investigation. *International Journal of Retail & Distribution Management* 25 (6/7): 188.

Openshaw S. (1989) Making geodemographics more sophisticated. *Journal of the Market Research Society* 31 (1): 111–31.

O'Rourke MPA. (2008) *SME's Biggest Barriers and Risks Identified in 'Think Big'*. Available at: www.eyeswideopen.com.au.

Orser BJ, Hogarth-Scott S and Riding AL. (2000) Performance, firm size, and management problem solving. *Journal of Small Business Management* 38 (4): 42–58.

Ozuah PO, Curtis J and Stein REK. (2001) Impact of problem-based learning on residents' self-directed learning. *Archives of Pediatric and Adolescent Medicine* 155 (June): 669–85.

Pallister J and Law J. (2006) *A Dictionary of Business and Management*. 4th ed. Oxford: Oxford University Press, p. 576.

Pasan M and Shugan SM. (1996) The value of marketing expertise. *Management Science* 42 (3 [March]): 370–88.

Payne A and Frow P. (2006) Customer relationship management: from strategy to implementation. *Journal of Marketing Management* 22 (1–2): 135–68.

Pearce JA. (1999) Who could most effectively influence collegiate business education reform? *Journal of Education for Business* 74 (March/April): 215–19.

Pearce JA. Fritz P and Davis PS. (2010) Entrepreneurial orientation and the performance of religious congregations as predicted by rational choice theory. *Entrepreneurship Theory and Practice* 34 (1): 219–48.

Pelham AM and Wilson DT. (1996) A longitudinal study of the impact of market structure, firm structure, strategy, and market orientation culture on dimensions of small-firm performance. *Journal of the Academy of Marketing Science* 24 (1): 27.

Peña I. (2002) Intellectual capital and business start-up success. *Journal of Intellectual Capital* 3 (2): 180–98.

Pérez-Cabañero C, González-Cruz T and Cruz-Ros S. (2012) Do family SME managers value marketing capabilities' contribution to firm performance? *Marketing Intelligence & Planning* 30 (2): 116–42.

Perry C. (2000) The relationship between written business plans and the failure of small businesses in the US. *International Journal of Retail and Distribution Management* 39 (3): 201–8.

Perry C, Meredith G and Cunnington H. (1988) Relationship between small business growth and personal characteristics of owner-managers in Australia. *Journal of Small Business Management* 26 (2): 76–9.

Perry ML, Sengupta S and Krapfel R. (2004) Effectiveness of horizontal strategic alliances in technologically uncertain environments: are trust and commitment enough? *Journal of Business Research* 57 (9): 951–6.

Peters MP and Brush CG. (1996) Market information scanning activities and growth in new ventures: A comparison of service and manufacturing businesses. *Journal of Business Research* 36 (1): 81–9.

Pitta DA, Franzak FJ and Little MW. (2004) Maintaining positive returns in the value and supply chain: applying tomorrow's marketing skills. *Journal of Consumer Marketing* 21 (July 7): 510–19.

Porter M. (1985) *Competitive Advantage, Creating and Sustaining Superior Performance*, New York: Free Press.

Radaev, V. (2004). How trust is established in economic relationships when institutions and individuals are not trustworthy: The case of Russia, in J Kornai, B Rothstein and S Rose-Ackerman eds, *Creating social trust in post-socialist transition*, London: Palgrave Macmillan.

Ram P. (1999) Problem-based learning in undergraduate education. *Journal of Chemical Education* 76 (August): 1122–7.

Reijnders W and Verstappen P. (2003) *SME en Marketing*, Amsterdam: Kluwer.

Ries A and Trout J. (2001) *Positioning, the Battle for Your Mind*, New York: McGraw-Hill.

Robinson J. (1938) *The Economics of Imperfect Competition*, London: McMillan.

Robinson RB and Pearce JA. (1984) Research thrusts in small firm strategic planning. *Academy of Management Review* 9: 128–37.

Rodríguez C, Carrillat F and Jaramillo F. (2004) A meta-analysis of the relationship between market orientation and business performance: evidence from five continents. *International Journal of Research in Marketing* 21 (2): 179–200.

Romer PM. (1988) *Capital Accumulation In The Theory Of Long Run Growth*. Working Paper: University of Rochester – Center for Economic Research (RCER).

Roos J, Roos G, Edvinsson L and Nicola C. Dragonetti (1997) *Intellectual Capital. Navigating in the New Business Landscape*, London: Macmillan Press.

Rosa P. (1998) Entrepreneurial processes of business cluster formation and growth by 'habitual' entrepreneurs. *Entrepreneurship Theory and Practice* 22 (4): 53–88.

Rose, R. (2000). Uses of social capital in Russia: Modern, pre-modern, and anti-modern. *Post-Soviet Affairs*, 16(1), 33–57.

Rositer J and Percy L. (1996) *Advertising Communications and Promotion Management*, New York, NY: McGraw-Hill.

Ross WT, Anderson E and Weitz B. (1997) Performance in principal-agent dyads: the causes and consequences of perceived asymmetry of commitment to the relationship. *Management Science* 43 (5): 680–704.

Rudelius W, Hartley SW and Gobeli DH. (1989) Managerial Activities in Independent and Corporate Sponsored New Ventures. In: Parker LA (ed) *Research at the Marketing/Entrepreneurship Interface.* Chicago, IL: University of Illinois at Chicago Press, 63–74.

Rumelt RP and Wensley R. (1981) In search of the market share effect. *Proccedings of the Academy of Management, ACAD MANAGE PROC* August 1981 (Meeting Abstract Supplement) 2–6.

Ryan C. (1999) Trends in business curricula: the view from AACSB. *Business Communication Quarterly* 62 (March): 91–6.

Sánchez P, Chaminade C, and Olea M. (2000) Management of intangibles. An attempt to build a theory. *Journal of Intellectual Capital* 1 (4): 312–27.

Sandberg WR and Hofer CW. (1987) Improving new venture performance: the role of strategy, industry structure and the entrepreneur. *Journal of Business Venturing* 2 (1): 5–28.

Sappington DEM and Wernerfelt B. (1985) To brand or not to brand? A theoretical and empirical question. *The Journal of Business* 58 (3 [July]): 279–93.

Saren M. (2000) *Marketing Theory: A Student Text,* London: Cengage Learning.

Savoie JM and Hughes AS. (1994) Problem-based learning as a classroom solution. *Educational Leadership* 52 (November): 54–8.

Say JB. (1880) *A Treatise on Political Economy; or the Production, Distribution, and Consumption of Wealth,* Philadelphia: Claxton, Remsen & Haffelfinger.

Schiffman L, Bednall, D., O'cass, A., Paladino, A., Ward, S., and Kanuk, L. (2008) Consumer Behaviour. In: Lewis S (ed.) *Consumer Behaviour.* French Forest NWS, Australia: Pearson Education, 29–7.

Scholhammer H and Kuriloff A. (1979) *Entrepreneurship and Small Business Management,* New York: John Wiley.

Schroeder JE and Salzer-Möling M. (2006) *Brand Culture*: Routledge Taylor and Francis Group.

Schumpeter JA. (1911) *Theorie der Wirtschaftlichen Entwicklung,* Leipzig: Dunker und Humblat.

Schumpeter JA. (1928) The instability of capitalism. *Economic Journal* 38 (151): 361–86

Schurr PH and Ozanne JL. (1985) Influences on exchange processes: buyers' preconceptions of a seller's trustworthiness and bargaining toughness. *Journal of Consumer Research* 1(13)939–53.

SCOTENT (Scottish Enterprise). (2006a) Farm Administration Courses – SE/1769/Apr06. Scottish Enterprise.

SCOTENT. (2006b) Food Chain Industry Exchange – SE/1770/Apr06. Scottish Enterprise.

Scott JT. (2005) *'Know your product'. Concise Handbook of Management: A Practitioner's Approach,* London:Routledge.

Scott M and Bruce R. (1987) Five stages of growth in small business. *Long Range Planning* 20 (3): 45–52.

Scott WR. (2002) *Institutions and Organizations,* Thousand Oaks, CA: Sage.

Segal MN and Giacobbe RW. (1994) Market segmentation and competitive analysis for supermarket retailing. *International Journal of Retail & Distribution Management* 22 (1): 38–48.

Senauer B, Asp, E, and Kinsey, J. (1992) Food Trends and the Changing Consumer. *Food Trends and the Changing Consumer.* 2006 ed. St. Paul: Eagan Press, 320–1.

Sexton DL. (1989) Growth decisions and growth patterns of women-owned enterprises. *Women-Owned Businesses.* New York: Praeger, 135–50.

Sexton DL and Bowman-Upton NB. (1991) *Entrepreneurship: Creativity and Growth*, New York: MacMillan.

Shane S. (2003) *A General Theory of Entrepreneurship: The Individual-Opportunity Nexus*, Northampton, MA: Edward Elgar.

Shane S and Venkataraman S. (2000) The promise of entrepreneurship as a field of research. *Academy of Management Review* 25 (1): 217–26.

Shapiro BP. (1988) What the hell is 'market oriented'?. *Harvard Business Review* 66 (6): 119–25.

Shaw E. (2004) Marketing in the social enterprise context: is it entrepreneurial? *Qualitative Market Research: An International Journal* 7 (3): 194–205.

Sherer SA. (2005) From supply-chain management to value network advocacy: implications for e-supply chains. *Supply Chain Management: An International Journal* 10 (2): 77–83.

Shocker AD and Weitz B. (1998) *A Perspective on Brand Equity Principles and Issues*, Cambridge: Marketing Science Institute.

Shultz M, Hatch MJ and Larsen MH. (2000) *The Expressive Organisation: Linking Identity, Reputation and the Corporate Brand*, Oxford: Oxford University Press.

Simchi-Levi D, Kaminsky P and E Simchi-Levi. (2009) *Designing and Managing the Supply Chain: Concepts, Strategies and Case Studies*, New York: McGraw Hill.

Simeon R. (2006) A conceptual model linking brand building strategies and Japanese popular culture. *Marketing Intelligence & Planning* 24 (5): 463–76.

Simpson M, Padmore J, Taylor N and Frecknall-Hughes J. (2006) Marketing in small and medium sized enterprises. *International Journal of Entrepreneurial Behaviour & Research* 12 (6): 361–87.

Singh SP, Reynolds RG and Muhammad S. (2001) A gender-based performance analysis of micro and small enterprises in Java, Indonesia. *Journal of Small Business Management* 39 (2): 174–82.

Slater SF and Narver JC. (1994) Does competitive environment moderate the market orientation- performance relationship? *Journal of Marketing* 58 (1): 46–55.

Slater SF and Narver JC. (1995) Marketing orientation and the learning organization. *Journal of Marketing* 59 (July): 63–74.

Slater SF and Narver JC. (2000) The positive effect of a market orientation on business profitability: a balanced replication. *Journal of Business Research* 48 (1): 69–73.

Sleight P. (1997) *Targeting Customers: How to Use Geodemographic and Lifestyle Data in Your Business*, Henley-on-Thames: WARC (World Advertising Research Centre)

Smallbone D. (1991) Success and failure in new business start-ups. *International Small Business Journal* 8 (2): 34–45.

Smart DT, Kelley CA and Conant JS. (1999) Marketing education in the year 2000: changes observed and challenges anticipated. *Journal of Marketing Education* 21 (December): 206–16.

Smeltzer LR, Fann GL and Nikoliasen VN. (1988) Environmental scanning practices in small business. *Journal of Small Business Management* 2–6 (3 [July]): 55–62.

Smith NR. (1967) *The Entrepreneur and His Firm: The Relationship between Type of Man and Type of Company*, East Lansing: Michigan State University.

Solomon MR, Marshall GW, Stuart EW, Barnes B and Mitchell V-W. (2009) *Marketing: Real People, Real Decisions*, London: FT Prentice Hall.

Sparkes A and Brychan T. (2001) The use of the Internet as a critical success factor for the marketing of Welsh agri-food SMEs in the twenty-first century. *British Food Journal* 103 (5): 331–47.

Spender JC and Kessler EH. (1995) Managing the uncertainties of innovation: extending Thompson. *Human Relations* 48 (1): 35–56.

Spillan J and Parnell J. (2006) Marketing resources and firm performance among SMEs. *European Management Journal* 24 (2): 236–45.

Steinhoff D. (1978) *Small Business Management Fundamentals*, Maidenhead: McGraw-Hill.

Stevenson H, Roberts M and Grousbeck HI. (1989a) *New Business Ventures and the Entrepreneur*, Homewook, IL: Richard D. Irwin Inc.

Stewart WH, May RC and Kalia A. (2008) Environmental perceptions and scanning in the United States and India: convergence in entrepreneurial information seeking? *Entrepreneurship: Theory & Practice* 32 (1): 83–106.

Stewart WJ and Roth P. (2001) Risk propensity differences between entrepreneurs and managers: a meta-analytic review. *Journal of Applied Psychology* 86 (1): 145–53.

Stokes D. (2000) Entrepreneurial marketing: a conceptualisation from qualitative research. *Qualitative Market Research: An International Journal* 3 (1): 47–54.

Stoner CR. (1983) Planning in small manufacturing firms: a survey. *Journal of Small Business Management* 21 (1 January): 34–41.

Storey DJ. (1994) *Understanding the Small Business Sector*, London: Routledge.

Stuart RW and Abetti PA. (1990) Impact of entrepreneurial and management experience on early performance. *Journal of Business Venturing* 5 (151–62).

Sweeney JC and Soutar GN. (2001) Consumer perceived value: the development of a multiple item scale. *Journal of Retailing* 77 (2): 203–20.

Tajfel H and Turner JC. (1979) An integrative theory of intergroup conflict. *The Social Psychology of Intergroup Relations* 33: 47.

Tate CE, Megginson LC, Scott CR and Trueblood LR. (1975) *Successful Small Business Management*, Dallas: Business Publications.

Thomas AR and Wilkinson TJ. (2004) It's the distribution, stupid! *Business Horizons* 48 (2): 125–34.

Thompson JD. (1967) *Organizations in Action: Social Science Bases of Administrative Theory*, New York: McGraw-Hill.

Thong JYL. (2001) Resource constraints and information systems implementation in Singaporean small businesses. *Omega* 29 (2): 143–56.

Timmons JA. (1985) *New Venture Creation*, Homewood, IL: Richard D. Irwin Inc.

Tocher N and Rutherford MW. (2009) perceived acute human resource management problems in small and medium firms: an empirical examination. *Entrepreneurship: Theory & Practice* 33 (2): 455–79.

Tonks D. (1990) Pinning down geodemographics. *Marketing Intelligence & Planning* 8 (2): 4–10.
Tuominen M, Möller K and Anttila M. (1999) Marketing capability of marketing oriented organizations, 28th EMAC Conference Proccedings, Berlin, Germany.
Tuominen M, Möller K and Rajala A. (1997) Marketing capability: a nexus of learning-based resources and a prerequisite for market orientation, 26th EMAC Conference Proceedings, Warwick UK.,
Tyebjee TT, Bruno AV and McIntyre SH. (1983) Growing ventures can anticipate marketing stages. *Harvard Business Review* 61 ([Jan-Feb] 1): 62–6.
The UK Parliament. (1985) *UK Companies Act.*
Ulaga W and Reinartz WJ. (2011) Hybrid offerings: how manufacturing firms combine goods and services successfully. *Journal of Marketing* 75 (6): 5–23.
University of Oxford, 2006,; A Dictionary of Business and Management, J Law eds, 4th ed, Oxford: Oxford University Press.
Urde M. (1999) Brand orientation: a mindset for building brands into strategic resources. *Journal of Marketing Management* 15 (1–3): 117–33.
Vallaster C and De Chernatony L. (2006) Internal brand building and structuration: the role of leadership. *European Journal of Marketing* 40 (7/8): 761–84.
Van Trijp H and Meulenberg M. (1996) Marketing and Consumer Behaviour with Respect to Foods. In: Meiselman HL and MacFie HJH (eds) *Food Choice, Acceptance, and Consumption.* London, UK: Blackie, 264–92.
Ven AH, Hudson R and Schroeder DR. (1984) Designing new business start-ups: entrepreneurial, organizational and ecological considerations. *Journal of Management* 10 (1): 89–107.
Venkatraman N and Ramanujam V. (1986) Measurement of business performance in strategy research: a comparison of approaches. *Academy of Management Journal* 11 (4): 801–14.
Vesper K. (1990) *New Venture Strategies,* Englewood Cliffs, NJ: Prentice Hall Inc.
Vickers D. (2005) *Creating the National Classification of Census Output Areas: Data, Methods, and Results.* Leeds: School of Geography, University of Leeds.
Voas D and Williamson P. (2001) The diversity of diversity: a critique of geodemographic classification. *Area* 33 (1): 63–76.
Voss ZG, Voss GB and Moorman C. (2005) An empirical examination of the complex relationships between entrepreneurial orientation and stakeholder support. *European Journal of Marketing* 39 (9/10): 1132–50.
Vozikis GS and Mescon TS. (1987) Marketing and Management Problems over Stages of Organizational and Exporting Development. In: Hills G (ed) *Research at the Marketing/Entrepreneurship Interface.* Chicago, IL: University of Illinois at Chicago Press, 214–31.
Wagner SM, Grosse-Ruyken PT and Erhun F. (2012) The link between supply chain fit and financial performance of the firm. *Journal of Operations Management* 30 (4): 340–53.
Wai-sum S and Kirby DA. (1998) Approaches to small firm marketing. *European Journal of Marketing* 32 (1/2): 40–60.
Watkins BD. (2007) On government programs that increase small firms' access to capital. *Journal of Small Business Management* 45 (1): 133–6.
Weaver KM and Dickson PH. (1998) Outcome quality of small-to medium-sized enterprise–based alliances: the role of perceived partner behaviors. *Journal of Business Venturing* 13 (6): 505–22.

Wee LKN, Kek MAYC and Kelley CA. (2003) Transforming the marketing curriculum using problem-based learning: a case study. *Journal of Marketing Education* 25 (2): 150–62.

Weiler S and Bernasek A. (2001) Dodging the glass ceiling? Networks and the new wave of women entrepreneurs. *The Social Science Journal* 38 (1): 85–103.

Weinrauch DJ, Mann OK, Robinson PA and Pharr J. (1991) Dealing with limited financial resources: a marketing challenge for small business. *Journal of Small Business Management* (October): 44–54.

Wells WD. (1975) Psychographics: a critical review. *Journal of Marketing Research* 12 (2): 196–213.

Westhead P, Ucbasran D and Wright M. (2009) Information search and opportunity identification: the importance of prior business ownership experience. *International Small Business Journal* 27 (6): 659–79.

Wiklund J. (1998) *Small Firm Growth and Performance*, Jönköping: Jönköping International Business School.

Wilson DT. (1995) An integrated model of buyer-seller relationships. *Journal of the Academy of Marketing Science* 23 (4): 335–45.

Wilson N, Hogarth-Scott S and Watson K. (1994) *Winners and Losers: A Study of the Performance and Survival of TEC Supported New Start Businesses in West Yorkshire*, Entrepreneurship Research Conference, Babson College, Boston, MA.,

Wilton PC and Meyers JG. (1986) Task, expectancy, and information assessment effects in information utilization processes. *Journal of Consumer Research* 12 (March): 469–86.

Wind Y. (1978) Issues and advances in segmentation research. *Journal of Marketing Research* 15 (3): 317–37.

Winter M and M Fitzgerald. (1993) Continuing the family-owned home-based business: evidence from a panel study. *Family Business Review* 6 (417–26)

Winter M, Danes SM, Koh S-K, Fredericks K and Paul JJ. (2004) Tracking family businesses and their owners over time: panel attrition, manager departure and business demise. *Journal of Business Venturing* 19 (4): 535–59.

Wong HY and Merrilees B. (2005) A brand orientation typology for SMEs: a case research approach. *Journal of Product & Brand Management* 14 (3): 155–62.

Wonglimpiyarat J. (2010) Innovation index and the innovative capacity of nations. *Futures* 42 (3): 247–53.

Wood L. (2000) Brands and brand equity: definition and management. *Management Decision* 38 (9): 662–9.

Wu D, Baron O and Berman O. (2009) Bargaining in competing supply chains with uncertainty. *European Journal of Operational Research* 197 (2): 548–56.

Wu Y, Loch C and Ahmad G. (2011) Status and relationships in social dilemmas of teams. *Journal of Operations Management* 29 (7–8): 650–62.

Wynarczyk P, Watson R, Storey DJ, Short H and Keasey K. (1993) *The Managerial Labour Market in Small and Medium Sized Enterprises*, London: Routledge.

Yeoh P-L. (2005) A conceptual framework of antecedents of information search in exporting: Importance of ability and motivation. *International Marketing Review* 22 (2): 165–98.

Young S, Ott L and Feigin B. (1978) Some practical considerations in market segmentation. *Journal of Marketing Research*: 405–12.

Zaheer A, McEvily B and Perrone V. (1998) Does trust matter? Exploring the effects of interorganizational and interpersonal trust on performance. *Organization Science* 9 (2): 141–59.

Zahra SA, Neubaum DO and El-Hagrassey GM. (2002) Competitive analysis and new venture performance: understanding the impact of strategic uncertainty and venture origin*. *Entrepreneurship: Theory & Practice* 27 (1): 1–28.

Zeithaml VA. (1988) Consumer perceptions of price, quality, and value: a means-end model and synthesis of evidence. *Journal of Marketing* 52 (3): 2–22.

Zhou KZ, Gao GY, Yang Z and Zhou N. (2005) Developing strategic orientation in China: antecedents and consequences of market and innovation orientations. *Journal of Business Research* 58 (8): 1049–58.

Index

aspirations, 54
available resources, 55

barriers to market entry, 24
barriers to marketing, 23
behavioural segmentation, 104
Bolton report, 17
brand building, 132
   commitment, 133
   communication, 135
   creativity, 135
   cultural factors, 132
   identity creation, 133
   positioning, 133
   statement of intent, 132
branding, 127
branding competitiveness
   cost leadership, 130
   value added, 130
branding importance, 131
   differentiation, 131
   promise of performance, 132
   recognition, 132
   relationship creation, 131
   trust generation, 132
   value creation, 132
brands functions, 127
   communication, 128
   differentiation, 127
   relationships creation, 129
business owner's role, 19

Chain members' coordination, 47
cognitive style, 36, 39
collaboration, 145
   on core competencies, 145
   on non-core competencies, 145
consumer insight, 25
consumers' characteristics, 60
consumers' ratings, 68
cooperation, 147
core competencies, 145

culture, 37
culture, vision and values, 37
cultures and sub-cultures, 54
distribution capacity, 120

effectiveness, 145
efficiency, 145
entrepreneur, 34
entrepreneurial marketing, 11
entrepreneurial orientation, 39
external environment, 45

female business-owners, 56
female entrepreneurs, 59
firm size, 20
functional silos, 47

geodemographic methods
   ACORN, 99
   CAMEO, 100
   MOSAIC, 99
geodemographics, 94
   ACORN, 95
   clustering, 96
   neighbourhoods, 96
   segmenting methodology, 96
   strengths, of, 101
   weaknesses, of, 101
growth, 53
   constraints, 58
   external factors, 57
   firm life cycle, 57
   geographical factors, 57
   size and maturity, 56
   type of market, 58

human capital, 55

innovation capability, 46
institutions, 45
intellectual property, 46
intentions, 54

Index

limited resources, 22

market orientation, 25
market segmentation, 94
  definition, of, 95
marketing expertise, 55
marketing information, 25, 78
  acquisition, of, 80
  asymmetry, 78
  definition, of, 78
  role, of, 78
  sources, of, 81
  types, of, 81
marketing intelligence, 25, 80
marketing opportunities, 64
marketing orientation, 26, 27
marketing planning, 78
mission statements, 131
motivations, 10, 35, 54, 58, 131

non-core competencies, 145

organisational culture, 53
owner's personal characteristics, 56, 83
  age, 84
  education, 84
  entrepreneurial orientation, 85
  gender, 84
  marketing expertise, 84
  previous experience, 84

perceptual maps, 69
performance measures
  customer penetration, 65
  frequency of purchase, 66
  growth, 61
  growth rate, 65
  repeat purchase, 67
  sales per customer, 67
political forces, 46
positioning, 110
  definition, of, 110
previous experience, 56
pricing strategies, 120
product concept, 111
product differentiation, 26
product manipulation, 112
  actual level, 113
  augmented level, 113

  core level, 112
product types, 113
  convenience products, 113
  emergency products, 114
  heterogeneous products, 115
  homogeneous products, 114
  impulse products, 114
  industrial products, 115
  shopping products, 114
  specialty products, 115
  staple products, 114
  unsought products, 115
psychographics, 94, 102
  life style, 103
  strengths, of, 104
  weaknesses, of, 103

regulative system, 46
religion, 54
risk taking, 58

small business owner, 37
SME flexibility, 58
SME organisational characteristics, 82
SMEs, 16
SMEs organisational chatacteristics
  business size, 82
  business strategy, 83
  customer orientation, 83
  scale of operations, 83
social capital, 47
socioeconomic change, 45
stages of business life cycle, 21
stages of marketing orientation, 28
stakeholders, 144
strategies of growth, 59
  commoditisation, 59
  consumers' value provision, 59
  differentiation, 59
  me-too strategies, 60
supply chain, 140
  definition, of, 140
  downstream, 141
  flows, 140
  processes integration, 140
  upstream, 141
supply chain flows, 142
  demand, 142
  finance, 142

supply chain flows – *continued*
   information, 142
   materials, 142
supply chain management, 140
supply chain stakeholders, 47

targeting, 107
   buyers, 108
   non-buyers, 108
technological factors, 46
typologies of small business, 34

UK Companies Act (1985), 17
unique features, 21

value, 60
value concept, 93
   benefits, 93
   cost and risk, 94
value continuum, 123
value creation, 93, 145
   cooperative norms, 146
   environmental uncertainty, 147
   interdependence, 146
   relationship extendedness, 147
   trust and commitment, 146
value proposition, 91
   definition, of, 91
value propositions' features, 91
   clear communication, 92
   clear target, 91
   consistency in deliverance, 92
values, 37
vision, 38